TOM
BRADY
★ ★ ★ ★ ★ **VS.** ★ ★ ★ ★ ★
THE NFL

THE CASE FOR **FOOTBALL'S GREATEST QUARTERBACK**

SEAN GLENNON

TRIUMPH
B O O K S

The Library of Congress has cataloged the previous edition as follows:

Glennon, Sean, 1966–
    Tom Brady vs. the NFL : the case for football's greatest quarterback / Sean Glennon.
        p. cm.
    Includes bibliographical references.
    ISBN-13: 978-1-60078-636-5 (pbk.)
    ISBN-10: 1-60078-636-7 ()
    1. Brady, Tom, 1977– 2. Football players—United States—Biography. 3.
Quarterbacks (Football)—United States—Biography. 4. Quarterbacks (Football)—
Rating of—United States. 5. Quarterbacks (Football)—Statistics. I. Title.
    GV939.B685G58 2012
    796.332092—dc23
    [B]
                                        2012023410

This book is available in quantity at special discounts for your group or organization. For further information, contact:
    Triumph Books LLC
    814 North Franklin Street
    Chicago, Illinois 60610
    (312) 337-0747
    www.triumphbooks.com

Printed in U.S.A.
ISBN: 978-1-62937-324-9
Design by Patricia Frey
Photos courtesy of AP Images unless otherwise indicated

To Mo and Seamus, the all-time greatest wife and son;
and to the best parents ever, Tom and Pat Glennon.

Contents

★ ★ ★

Foreword

I knew Sean Glennon was on to something the first time I talked to him.

I don't mean that I absolutely agree with all of Sean's conclusions in this book. Like I told him, I can say for sure that Tom Brady is *one of* the greatest quarterbacks of all time, and if you put my feet to the fire, I *might* have to say he is *the* greatest of all time. But I also happen to have a lot of respect for Peyton Manning. And, of course, you can't even have the conversation without talking about Joe Montana and Bart Starr.

That's fine. I don't need to agree with Sean a hundred percent, and I don't think he needs me to. What I liked about Sean when I met him wasn't where he was going, it was how he was getting there.

Sean contacted me looking for a quote he could use in his book. He introduced himself as someone who had written some books about the Patriots and said he was writing one about Brady being the greatest quarterback ever. He told me he was a fan of my SiriusXM NFL radio show, *Movin' the Chains*, and a fan of my book, *Take Your Eye Off the Ball: How to Watch Football by Knowing Where to Look*. He was looking for some kind of comment about Tom that he could share with readers. That seemed easy enough.

But then we started talking, and I asked Sean how he was going about this thing, which led to a conversation about football history. We talked about guys like Montana and Starr. We also talked about Dan Marino and Otto Graham. Sean told me he was comparing Tom to those guys and a bunch of others—and he told me that the way he was doing things wasn't about tearing down any of those other great quarterbacks. He was putting everyone's accomplishments out there and leaving most of the decisions to the reader. He was making a case for Brady but doing it in a way that was respectful to those other guys, who had all made huge contributions to the league and the game.

I knew right then that Sean was writing a book that I would want to read and endorse, and I told him so.

But that isn't really what you're interested in. You're here to read about Tom Brady. So let's talk about Tom.

I think if we're going to talk about the guy, we should start by talking about the position he plays. Quarterback is the most important position in all of sports. It's also the toughest to play. A quarterback's job during the week is as intense as the job of head coach. He knows the game plan before the rest of his teammates show up for their first practice. When he's not practicing, he's watching film, because before he takes his first snap in a game, he has to be prepared for everything that can possibly affect his offense.

Once the game starts, a quarterback has to be able to make smart decisions in fractions of a second, usually with defensive players coming at him at blinding speeds. Between plays, he has to process what he's just seen from the defense. When he gets to the line, he has to read a defense that's doing everything it can to disguise its plans, and then he has to make decisions about changing the play… all with the play clock ticking. After the snap, if it's a pass play, he has to read the coverage and know where his open man is going to be. And then he's got to get the ball out of his hands and make sure it's his guy, not a defensive back, who ends up with it. If it's a run, he has to buy that running back the time he needs to hit the hole and pick up yards. And then the whole thing starts again. And again. And again.

If you think any part of that is ever easy, you're fooling yourself.

What it takes to be a great quarterback is to do all of those things *and* be a leader on the field and in the locker room.

Brady does all of it. His accuracy as a passer is incredible. He has an ability like I've never seen to put the ball in a place where his receiver is the only guy who can get to it. That's why he doesn't throw a lot of interceptions.

His recognition of defenses is uncanny. He walks to the line of scrimmage, looks at the defense, and knows at that instant who the ball will go to. He's smart. He keeps calm under enormous pressure. And he is the natural leader that you need a quarterback to be—on the field and off.

The Patriots have a great system, and they can win games in a lot of different ways. But when they've won championships, it's been because of Tom Brady. Bill Belichick certainly knows it.

Belichick can say that every player on the field is as important as the next—actually, Bill *has* to talk that way, because that's the philosophy he needs to sell to his guys in the locker room—but he's not kidding anyone. Bill knows that an offense is only as good as its quarterback and the decisions he makes on the field. Belichick isn't going to give the media anything more than, "Tom's a great player, and we're lucky to have him." But make no mistake, he knows he has one of the best of all time and that Brady is the reason his team has a shot at the Super Bowl every year.

—Pat Kirwan, senior analyst for NFL.com,
cohost of *Movin' the Chains* on SiriusXM NFL Radio,
and editorial consultant to *The NFL Today* on CBS

★ ★ ★

Acknowledgments

I'll start, as always, with my wife, Mo, and my son, Seamus, without whose support and encouragement I'd have collapsed somewhere in the middle of my 14th month working on this book (which was roughly two months after the book morphed from geeky, fun adventure to intense, bruising project that wouldn't stop kicking my butt).

Thanks, too, to everyone at Triumph, particularly Adam Motin and Don Gulbrandsen. This project has been exhausting for me, and far more trouble than Triumph bargained for. All they wanted was a book about Tom Brady. I created a monster that turned around to bite the lot of us. And this book would still be a mess without Laine Morreau's editing. Thank you, Laine.

A special thanks to Pat Kirwan for agreeing to write the foreword and for providing observations for the book. Pat is one of a handful of people whose opinions on all things football I view as approaching gospel. It was an honor just to get to talk to him. Hearing him express excitement about this project and having him agree to lend his voice to the front of this book are, to me, signs that I must have gotten something right.

Bob Hyldburg, whose amazing book *Total Patriots* once again served as a vital resource, was there any time I needed to double-check a Patriots stat or record. He also came through with a great comment about Brady. Thanks, Bob. I owe you. Again.

Thanks to all whose input and observations appear within and/or helped shape this book, and to those who helped connect me with them. They include Jim Kelly, John Elway, Steve Grogan, Gino Cappelletti, Kerry Byrne, Aaron Schatz, Gil Santos, Bill Maier, Tricia Cavalier, and Erich Schubert.

My folks, Tom and Pat Glennon, my sister, Kim Shulman, and my brother, Chris Glennon, are always generous with their support and encouragement. Thank you all.

A warm thank you to everyone in university relations at UMass Amherst who offered words of encouragement and support, and particularly to Michael Grabscheid and Anne Marie Morse.

And, of course, thanks so much to the many friends who are always generous with their input and encouragement. They include Ned Cully, Andy Curto, Don Fluckinger, Shaun Hickson, and George Lenker.

★ ★ ★

A Note on Deflategate

Let's get this out of the way right up front: This is not a book about Deflategate.

The title may have led you to think otherwise. That's understandable. But you need to know that it's not intentional

The thing about the title of this this book—the concept of this book; the *foundation* of this book—is that it's considerably older than Deflategate. The volume you hold in your hand is the second edition of *Tom Brady vs. the NFL*. It's been revised and updated through the end of the 2015 NFL season. But it's a revision of a book originally published in 2012.

And, of course, in 2012, there was no Deflategate.

Then again, there shouldn't have been a Deflategate in 2015, either. And that brings us to another reason that this is not a book about Deflategate. It's a big one. This book is a work of nonfiction. Deflategate, on the other hand, was almost wholly a product of the imagination. *Almost*. Except, that is, for how it cost the New England Patriots $1 million and a pair of draft picks. Those penalties were entirely too real. *Almost*. Except for how it forced Tom Brady to spend more than a year—including an absurd chunk of the critical two weeks leading up to Super Bowl XLIX—addressing demonstrably false accusations that he "participated in a scheme to deflate game balls" (to use the language of the NFL's crack legal team). *Almost*. Except for how Brady likely will always be haunted by the aftereffects of the witch hunt conducted by the NFL and the smear campaign carried out by the league and its lawyers as they fought to uphold a disciplinary suspension that never should have been handed down to begin with.

Brady haters will always choose to suspend disbelief in the matter of Deflategate, because it allows them to argue against the otherwise irrefutable fact of Brady's greatness as a quarterback. But in the real world, Deflategate has been exposed as a jealous fantasy at best, a malicious slander at worst.

★ ★ ★

I have no interest in allowing this book to become mired in Deflategate nonsense. Nor in inflicting any additional Deflategate nonsense upon you.

I can't avoid any mention of the fake scandal, of course. Not as I write about the Patriots' victory over the Indianapolis Colts in the 2014 AFC Championship Game or the buildup to their subsequent victory in Super Bowl XLIX. Nor as I write about New England's 2015 season. Those mentions, though I promise that I've kept them short, provide necessarily context. But my desire, and my approach, has been to reference Deflategate only inasmuch as it affected Brady and his teammates, particularly in their preparations for Super Bowl XLIX. I've chosen not, in those chapters, to rehash the specific events of Deflategate. I've chosen in particular not to address in depth the penalties assessed the team or the federal court battle waged by Brady and the NFL Players Association against the league (the potential source of confusion about the title of this book).

Still, I can hardly pretend it's possible to write a book asserting that Brady is the greatest quarterback in the history of the pro game without somehow address-ing Deflategate. So, while I'm entirely annoyed by the need of it, let's take a few moments to review.

(This, by the way, is where those of you who have had enough of this topic, or who are fully aware of its every development, should skip ahead to the meat of the book. You're not going to learn anything in the paragraphs that follow. You already know my general take on this subject. The only thing you can possibly accomplish by finishing this note is to get angry about the whole thing all over again. You don't need that. Let me take one for the team here.)

★ ★ ★

This is the way Deflategate began. Not with a bang, but a whimper.

January 18, 2015, Foxborough, Massachusetts. The Patriots walloped the visiting Colts in the AFC Championship. The Pats scored a pair of touchdowns in the first quarter, taking advantage of a muffed punt that gave them the ball deep in Indianapolis territory, and a missed field goal that set them up them to start a drive at their own 41-yard-line. And although the second quarter saw Brady throw an interception at the Indy 1-yard-line and the Colts respond with a long TD drive, New England still went into halftime with a 17–7 lead. Then, in the third quarter, Brady threw two more TD passes and LeGarrette Blount added one on the ground, all while the Colts accomplished nothing. With one more Blount score in the fourth, the Pats put their rivals away 45–7. It was the second biggest blowout in AFC Championship history.

Not a good game if you were looking at things objectively, though certainly a fun game for Patriots fans to watch. And surely not the way anyone in or around the Colts organization hoped to go into the offseason. It had to sting.

The fans in New England commenced celebrating. The team commenced preparation for yet another trip to the Super Bowl. And the Colts, and their supporters, commenced wallowing. Or fuming.

Then, as the evening wore on, Indianapolis sports columnist Bob Kravitz got a tip: The NFL was looking into whether the Patriots had taken some air out of footballs before the game. Balls that had been checked before the game had been checked again at halftime in response to concerns voiced by the Colts. The Patriots had been caught. They were in trouble. Kravitz turned immediately to Twitter with that information, and the story quickly began to snowball.

Tom Brady was asked about the allegations the next morning during his regular paid interview on Boston sports radio station WEEI. He laughed it off, clearly surprised to hear about the charge and amused by the latest ridiculous attempt to undercut his team's success. "I think I've heard it all at this point," Brady said, chuckling. "That's the least of my worries, I don't even respond to stuff like this."

And then Brady spent more than a year being forced to respond to stuff like that.

In the days and weeks that followed the win over Indianapolis, the story continued to build. On January 20, ESPN's Chris Mortensen tweeted that sources had told him 11 of the 12 Patriots footballs checked by the NFL at halftime were underinflated by two pounds per square inch each. The information was incorrect. Significantly incorrect. But the NFL failed to make any attempt to contest Mortensen's report even as the false claim catapulted Deflategate to the top of the national news.

The implication was that the Patriots had found a way to take air out of balls after they'd been checked by game officials while inflated to the required minimum of 12.5 pounds per square inch. And the implied reason for the alleged tampering was to make the balls easier for Brady to grip and throw. Had this been true, it would have constituted an equipment violation, albeit not an uncommon one in a league in which other quarterbacks had cavalierly admitted to both underinflating and overinflating balls (beyond the maximum of 13.5 PSI) and in which equipment personnel from two teams (the Carolina Panthers and Minnesota Vikings) during a November 2014 game had been shown on television tampering with balls on the sideline (an offense that had generated nothing more than a low-key warning from the NFL). Somehow, though, the mere suggestion that the Patriots may have taken air out of game balls translated to a major scandal, more important in the eyes of the TV networks than anything taking place on the national or international political stage.

The following 12 days, while the Patriots attempted to prepare for the biggest football game of the year (that is, to do their jobs), were even more of a circus than usual. Press conferences were held in which Bill Belichick detailed the Patriots' attempts to determine the cause of something that didn't happen—that is, to figure out how 11 of 12 footballs could have become significantly underinflated, which at that point everyone (except those in the NFL front office) believed had happened—and Brady failed to convince the media that he wasn't involved in the alleged deflation by offering a plausible explanation for Mortensen's fictional air pressure measurements. "I didn't alter the ball in any way," Brady asserted. The media, also operating in the belief that Mortensen's information was factual, was skeptical to say the least. "How are we supposed to believe that 11 of 12 Patriots balls were so significantly underinflated but the quarterback didn't know anything about it?" members of the media challenged. It would have been a question worth raising, too, if it hadn't been based on a false premise.

Media attention seekers in Indianapolis, Patriots haters nationwide, and even a few respected commentators questioned the legitimacy of the Patriots' AFC Championship victory and Super Bowl bid. The NFL announced that it had hired attorney Ted Wells to conduct an "independent" investigation of what had by then been labeled Deflategate. Wells previously had conducted an investigation into alleged bullying in the Miami Dolphins locker room (and, if you believe those who lost their jobs as a result of that probe, Wells executed an outright frame job).

The Patriots' 28–24 win over the Seattle Seahawks—the team with the best defense in football—in Super Bowl XLIX did nothing to quiet the cries of "Cheaters!" And the Patriots went through their victory parade and into what should have been a glorious offseason with Deflategate and the Wells investigation hanging over their heads.

★ ★ ★

Three months later, on May 6, 2015, the NFL announced the results of the Wells investigation.

Wells and his team, with scientific analysis from Exponent (a California consulting lab known for delivering the results its clients want—for example, conclusions that neither secondhand smoke nor asbestos could be linked to cancer), concluded that the Patriots had conspired to deflate footballs. Exponent looked at the below-regulation air pressure in the Patriots footballs when they were checked at halftime in the AFC Championship Game and concluded those levels were not consistent with what could be anticipated through application of the ideal gas law. The same could not be true, they claimed, of the limited number of Colts balls that were checked at halftime, though those balls, too, had experienced a drop in pressure. And while interviews with Patriots players, coaches and equipment staff had failed to produce a single confession to participation in a scheme to deflate balls, Wells concluded it was "more probable than not" both that such a scheme existed and that Brady was "generally aware" of it. Wells based his conclusions in part on a text from May 2014 in which Patriots locker-room attendant Jim McNally referred to himself as "the deflator," and on the fact that

McNally, on his way to the field with the bag of Patriots game balls for the AFC Championship Game, had ducked into the men's room with the balls for roughly a minute and 40 seconds.

And that was that. Wells concluded that the Patriots, and Brady, were probably guilty of deflating balls. The NFL accepted that conclusion. And so did the media and football fans around the country.

Five days later, the NFL announced sanctions against team and player: The Patriots were fined $1 million and stripped of their first round draft pick in 2016 and fourth round pick in 2017. Brady was suspended for the first four games of the 2015 season. Patriots owner Robert Kraft, though he contested the Wells investigation's conclusions and questioned the fairness of the sanctions, announced that he would not appeal. Reasons for that decision are still unclear, particularly as Kraft has continued to deny any wrongdoing on the part of his team. It seems reasonable, though, to assume that Kraft decided that peace with the league and with the owners of the other 31 NFL teams was more valuable to him than a protracted fight against Commissioner Roger Goodell's unjust penalties.

Brady chose to fight.

The player and his union got no satisfaction from his appeal hearing before Goodell, who not only upheld Brady's suspension but upped the league's rhetoric against the quarterback, claiming Brady had refused to turn over cell phone data as requested by Wells and asserting that Brady had destroyed an old cell phone specifically to keep it out of Wells' hands. (In fact, Brady had agreed to turn over data, but would not release the phone itself into the hands of Wells and the demonstrably leaky NFL front office.) Goodell also changed the league's position on Brady's part in the alleged deflation scheme, moving beyond "more probable than not" and "generally aware" to asserting that Brady "knew about, approved of, consented to, and provided inducements and rewards in support of" ball deflation. The commissioner didn't see fit to explain how he had progressed from one position to the next.

Brady and the NFLPA initially fared better when they took their argument to the federal courts. After court appearances in which Judge Richard Berman repeatedly directed skeptical questions at the league's lawyers regarding multiple aspects of the Wells investigation and the NFL's disciplinary process (questioning, for example, how investigators concluded that texts from May 2014 were related to alleged ball deflation in January 2015), Berman issued a ruling vacating Brady's suspension.

But Berman didn't rule on the matter of whether or how balls were deflated. Nor did he rule on whether Brady was involved in a scheme to deflate balls. He may have been curious about those topics, but it wasn't his role to rule on them. Berman ruled that the NFL hadn't acted properly in applying the suspension and that Brady and the NFLPA hadn't been accorded their contractual rights to mount a thorough challenge of the discipline during the league's appeal process. The United States Court of Appeals for the Second Circuit similarly did not rule on whether ball deflation took place when it reversed Berman's decision in April 2016. In its 2–1 decision, the appeals court ruled simply that Goodell was entitled to impose a suspension regardless of whether any rules had been broken.

Independent scientists, independent legal analysts, and independent thinkers in the media, on the other hand, were not so limited.

By the time Deflategate reached Judge Berman's courtroom, the Exponent "science" that had been cited to support Wells' conclusions had long since been exposed as either unpardonably sloppy or unconscionably fraudulent. Criticisms of Exponent's work were voiced first by Nobel Prize–winning chemist Robert MacKinnon. And while MacKinnon's take was dismissed by the media because of a financial connection between a biotech firm he founded and Robert Kraft's investment firm, no such easy out was available when the American Enterprise Institute echoed those criticisms in a report based on their independent analysis of Exponent's data.

Scientists looking at Exponent's work were struck by the fact that it consistently made assumptions that supported a finding of guilt. It accepted officials' recollections of pregame ball inflation levels, but rejected recollections about which of two pressure gauges had been used to check those levels. Conveniently, that gave Exponent license to ignore halftime pressure measurements consistent with what the ideal gas law would predict. AEI also noted that Exponent failed, in assessing pressure loss in Colts balls, to consider that those balls had been allowed to warm up at halftime before being tested, leading to a faulty conclusion that they'd lost less pressure than the Patriots balls, which were tested cold. Those among numerous other flaws.

M.I.T. professor John Leonard, who identifies as a Philadelphia Eagles fan, conducted his own research, replicating the conditions under which balls were tested, and reached the same conclusions as AEI. Leonard gave lectures based on his research. And in January 2016, Joe Nocera of *The New York Times* reported, "Leonard told me that if an M.I.T. undergraduate made the kinds of mistakes that Exponent made, 'I would force them to repeat the experiment and correct the analysis.' Based on his study of the data, Leonard now says: 'I am convinced that no deflation occurred and that the Patriots are innocent. It never happened.'"

There has been no shortage of other researchers, from other universities—notably Carnegie Mellon, Rockefeller University, and the University of Chicago—who have reached the same conclusions.

And while scientists were picking apart Exponent's findings, legal experts and media members from across the country were picking apart the Wells Report's conclusions and the NFL's disciplinary decisions.

From the time Wells' findings were announced through the NFL appeal and the federal court process to follow, writers including Michael McCann, a law professor who writes legal analysis pieces for *Sports Illustrated*; sports law attorney Daniel Wallach; Stephanie Stradley, a lawyer and football writer in Houston; *Washington Post* columnist Sally Jenkins; and Dan Wetzel of Yahoo Sports, routinely published pieces critical of the Wells Report and the league's actions. Their perspective varied, but their conclusions were the same: There was no real reason to believe there had been any wrongdoing on the part of Brady or the Patriots—the same could not be said of the NFL's handling of the matter—and Brady's suspension should not stand.

With the exception of ESPN—which had carried water for the NFL from the very start of the Deflategate saga—and the sports media in Indianapolis, the perspective of most media slowly but surely swung to the Patriots' favor in the months between September 3, 2015, when Berman's ruling was handed down, and the end of the 2015 postseason. And in February 2016, one of America's most prominent football writers, *Sports Illustrated*'s Peter King, added his voice to the chorus, though he focused not on Brady's legal case, but the NFL's punishment of the Patriots.

"Based on the weight of the evidence from the past 13 months, and that weight being circumstantial and not convincing, there's one conclusion I've reached entering the 2016 draft season: Roger Goodell needs to give back the picks," King wrote in his online column, *Monday Morning Quarterback.*

King didn't expect the league to do the right thing. No one did. But the fact that he had reached the conclusion that the Patriots had been wronged in Deflategate was no less meaningful.

★ ★ ★

What will Deflategate mean for Tom Brady as a player?

It's hard to say. If the suspension holds and Brady misses a quarter of what will likely prove to be one of his final seasons, it will be a simple thing to look at his career numbers and make an educated guess regarding what was lost. Milestones perhaps not reached. Records not broken or extended. Starts and wins wiped off the books. Perhaps even a postseason missed by virtue of an extra Patriots loss or two—or three.

And while there are those who believe that Brady's stellar performance on the field in 2015 was motivated in part by his anger over Deflategate, it's difficult to look at one standout season from a standout career and say, "This proves that Brady was mad as hell and wasn't going to take it anymore."

On the other hand, the fact that 2015, statistically speaking, turned out to be one of the better seasons of Brady's career certainly helps make the point that the quarterback doesn't have a lot of trouble throwing a fully inflated football.

That point goes a bit deeper than 2015, though. Because the NFL began watching the inflation levels of Patriots balls not at the start of the 2015 season, but after halftime of the 2014 AFC Championship.

With that in mind, consider this: Brady in his career has completed 63.6 percent of his passes. His career touchdown percentage is 5.5. His career interception percentage is 1.9. His career TD/INT ratio is 2.9/1. He has thrown for 7.4 yards per attempt. And his passer rating is 96.4.

In the 19.5 games following the events that launched Deflategate—including the hard-fought Super Bowl XLIX and running through the brutal 2015 AFC Championship game at Denver—Brady completed 64.4 percent of his passes, had a touchdown percentage of 5.7 and an interception percentage of 1.4, and a TD/INT ratio of 4.1/1, threw for his standard 7.4 yards per attempt, and earned a passer rating of 99.9. Isolate his 2015 regular season stats against his career numbers (which, of course, are based solely on the regular season) and you get an even more pronounced contrast: 64.4 percent completions; 5.8 percent TDs; 1.1 percent INTs; 5.1 TDs per INT; 7.6 YPA; passer rating, 102.2.

If Brady had actually schemed to deflate balls, he'd inadvertently done the rest of the NFL a favor.

Tell that to the people who assert that Brady must have been part of a ball deflation scheme because he's taken such great care to understand precisely how every factor, no matter how small, affects his performance.

★ ★ ★

The fundamental truth about Deflategate is this: Nothing happened. Or nothing untoward happened with the Patriots balls in the 2014 AFC Championship Game. No one conspired to take air out of footballs. No air was taken out of footballs.

What did happen was that the air pressure in the footballs was altered by way of a fundamental principle of thermodynamics. And the Patriots beat the Colts fair and square.

What also happened is that a scandal was manufactured from whole cloth.

Why that took place, we still don't know for sure.

We know that the Colts raised questions in the week before the game about air pressure in Patriots' game balls. We don't know if those questions were raised as a matter of standard NFL gamesmanship, if they were related to some desire by the Baltimore Ravens to get back at the Patriots for laughing at their unfamiliarity with NFL rules in their divisional round playoff game at New England, or if they were part of an attempt by Colts general manager Ryan Grigson to create a distraction for the Patriots.

We know that the league officials who checked the Patriots' balls (and some of the Colts' balls) at halftime were led by NFL Vice President of Game Operations Mike Kensil. We know that Kensil's 20-year tenure in the New York Jets front office included the offseason in which Belichick spurned New Jersey in favor of New England, a move that enraged Jets brass. We know that Kensil responded to the Colts questions about ball inflation not by informing the Patriots about the concerns and reminding them of NFL equipment regulations (per standard practice) but by initiating an in-game sting operation. We know that Kensil is reported to have told Patriots staffers they were in "big fucking trouble" after the balls were checked. Whether it was Kensil who provided the false information tweeted by Mortensen is a matter of speculation, and probably will remain so as Mortensen has refused to ID his source. That Kensil played a meaningful role in creating Deflategate, however, is without question.

How Deflategate moved from a focused attempt to distract or embarrass the Patriots to the subject of a multi-million dollar investigation, a protracted court case, and a smear campaign against one of game's greatest players remains unclear. One might speculate that the matter had spiraled out of control before Goodell had a chance to rein it in, and that the rest was a matter of ass covering. Or that the league office found that targeting the Patriots helped its relationship with the 31 other teams. Or that the league office's distaste for Belichick drove it to seek ways to pull the rug out from under the Patriots coach at any cost. But that's all speculative.

And it's probably best to leave speculation and innuendo to those who continue to reference Deflategate in an attempt to besmirch Brady's legacy and the Patriots' reputation. They need it more than we do. Because it's all they've got.

The truth is that those lined up against the Patriots and Brady can rant all they want about "the Deflator" and the bathroom. Those things are meaningless. They don't establish guilt, because there was no crime for anyone to be guilty of.

"Why would the guy call himself 'the Deflator?' Do you *really* believe he was talking about losing weight?"

I don't know what he was talking about. I don't care. I know he wasn't talking about deflating footballs, because no footballs were deflated. A guy can walk around calling himself "the Killer," but if you don't have a body, you still don't have a murder

"Why did he spend all that time in the bathroom?"

Really? This is a discussion you want to have?

"Why did Brady destroy his cell phone?"

Because if he hadn't, you'd have learned about far more than his color preferences for pool covers and his wisecracks about Peyton Manning. Remember when those were leaked? From the cell data Brady had provided even while refusing to turn over his phone?

You can argue all day, but it comes back to this: Balls weren't deflated. That's the end of the story. It should have been the beginning of the story—the whole of the story.

So let's move on already.

★ ★ ★

Introduction

I thought Drew Bledsoe should have gotten his job back.

There, I said it. And if you'd been sitting at Thanksgiving dinner with me back in 2001, you'd have heard me say it forcefully.

Bledsoe was the New England Patriots' starting quarterback. Tom Brady had done a terrific job filling in while Bledsoe was injured, but enough was enough with the talk about sticking with the kid.

NFL starters weren't supposed to lose their jobs as a result of an injury. A starter who had been a first overall draft pick—and who was earning $10 million a year—surely didn't sit behind some second-year, sixth-round pick no one had ever heard of three months earlier.

Bledsoe wasn't a perfect quarterback. Far from it. He was frustrating to no end, especially on those plays where you could see a sack coming before the ball was even snapped and you couldn't understand how he didn't see the same thing. Or the ones where you'd cringe knowing he was about to force a pass and throw a pick. But he was the quarterback who had led the Patriots to Super Bowl XXXI just five years earlier. He was an authentic NFL QB, and if the Pats were going to build on their 5–5 record, their best chance would come with Bledsoe taking the snaps.

It wasn't about not believing in Brady. Because there was really not a lot there to believe in. Eight NFL starts. A 5–3 record. Nice enough. But it didn't mean anything. Or at least it didn't seem to mean anything—unless you were Bill Belichick.

There were a lot of us (*a lot*) who thought that with Bledsoe healthy, the job should have been his again. Still, walk around New England today, and you'll encounter more than your fair share of longtime Patriots fans who'll swear to you they always saw something special in Brady. Fans who'll insist they knew Brady was the guy who could lead the Patriots to new heights. They're mostly lying.

Many of the fans who wanted the Pats to stick with Brady in 2001 weren't truly pulling for Brady; they were on the side of *not-Bledsoe*. The ones who now say that they knew Brady was a superstar in the making are the same people who say they always knew the 2007 Giants were going to be trouble. (No one other than Tom Coughlin and Steve Spagnuolo knew the 2007 Giants were going to be trouble.) They're the same people who swear Brady has gone soft since marrying Gisele Bündchen and dismiss the mountains of evidence to the contrary. They're Cliff Clavin at the end of the bar, determined to talk regardless of whether they have anything worth saying.

So yeah, I thought the Patriots should have given Bledsoe his job back. I was wrong. But I can live with that. In football, like just about everything, it works out that most people are wrong about most things most of the time. And the only thing that matters is that the Patriots got it right.

★　★　★

Now comes *my turn* to get it right: Tom Brady is the greatest quarterback in NFL history.

I don't *think* that; I know it. I've spent 18 months looking forward, backward, and sideways at Brady's career and the careers of the best passers ever to take the field, and Brady just keeps coming out on top. Not always by a wide margin (though sometimes it's by a wide margin) but always by enough to make it count.

And that's what's at the heart of this book.

My intent here isn't to argue in favor of my point of view. My intent is to lay out the facts. Because I'm certain that if I do—and if you read as a nonpartisan— you're going to come to the same conclusion.

This book isn't going to convert a Bart Starr loyalist, a Joe Montana loyalist, or even a Peyton Manning loyalist. That's OK. Everyone is allowed to have a favorite football player, and at least in the cases of Starr and Montana, there remains a strong argument to be made. (There hasn't been one for some several years now for Manning, even if his fans can't quite bring themselves to see it.) There are Montana fans and Starr fans who will never be able to look at any other quarterback as better than their guy. Brady could win three straight Super Bowls to round out his career, and they'll still be saying, "Yeah, but, you know, it was really the New England defense."

In writing this book, I discarded the notion that in order to build up one player, you need to tear down another. Including Brady, there are 22 quarterbacks represented in the pages that follow. Seven are active. The other 15 are retired. And of those, all but one—Manning—are in the Pro Football Hall of Fame (and Manning will go in as a member of the class of 2021). There's nothing to be gained by attempting to diminish the careers of great players. What you'll find, for the most part, are celebrations of those players' careers with varying amounts of commentary on what makes Brady better. If Brady is what I believe he is, his achievements will stand on their own in comparison to the greats of the game.

★ ★ ★

In order to truly understand what makes Brady better than anyone else who has ever played the position, you really need to take in his entire career, which is to say that you need to read the whole book. I worked hard (probably harder than I did at anything else during this project) not to get bogged down in stat after mind-numbing stat. But there's no detailing an athlete's accomplishments without citing statistics. There's certainly no comparing athletes who never had an opportunity to compete head-to-head without bringing stats into the mix. A handy side-by-side chart detailing some key statistical areas, achievements, and honors accompanies all but one of the *vs.* chapters. But be warned that those charts aren't meant to provide anything remotely like a complete picture.

Though there are statistics cited throughout the chapters ahead, if I've done my job, I've woven the stats into the narrative of the book effectively enough that they don't slow down the story. But that only works if you, the reader, understand what the numbers represent. Most of what's here is simple stuff: wins and losses, passing yards, touchdowns, pass attempts, completions, and interceptions. Other measures require a bit of explanation up front (you can skip ahead to the end of the bullets if you don't need the help):

- Touchdown percentage: The number of touchdowns thrown (in a game, a season, or a career) divided by the total number of pass attempts. (Note that it's attempts, not completions.) These numbers tend to be fairly low, but higher=better.
- Interception percentage: Total interceptions divided by total attempts. Also usually a fairly low number (and Brady's are lower than most). Lower=better.
- Yards per attempt: Total yards gained divided by total attempts. Higher=better.
- Touchdown-to-interception ratio: Total touchdowns divided by total interceptions. Expressed thus: x.x/1, which is to say x.x touchdowns for every interception. The higher the variable number, the better.
- And then there's the big daddy—the stat that's absolutely critical in any attempt to compare quarterbacks but one that everybody hates: passer rating. It takes more explaining than I can do here. If you want to understand it, turn to the appendix on page 231. If you don't care, then just know this: 80 or better is acceptable, 90 or better is good, 100-plus is really good, and 158.3 is perfect.

You don't have to think a lot about stats for this book to make sense. You just need to get to the point where you know what's good, what's bad, and what's in between. If you don't know football passing statistics already, trust me, you'll pick it up quickly as you go.

★ ★ ★

But this isn't a book for numbers geeks. It's a book about a football player and how and where he fits in the history of the sport. This is a book about Tom Brady, quarterback of the New England Patriots. But it's not a biography (Charlie Pierce wrote that book; it's called *Moving the Chains: Tom Brady and the Pursuit of Everything*, and it's great). It's not a book about Tom Brady the celebrity. It's not a book about Brady's wife, his kids, or his former girlfriends. It's not about Brady's wedding or his car accident. It's not about his diet. And it's absolutely not about his hair.

It's a book about a player who came into the NFL as less than no one—a sixth-round compensatory draft pick, a maybe-but-probably-not—and who has become the winningest QB, by average, not only of his generation but of all time. It's about the only quarterback ever to lead a team to 14 or more wins per season four separate times. It's about a backup QB who was thrust into the starting role because the starter was injured and who went on to win his first 10 playoff games, including three Super Bowls in four seasons.

This is a book about the quarterback who reads and reacts to defenses better than anyone else ever has. It's about a guy who walks to the line of scrimmage with his team's entire playbook in his head, recognizes immediately what the opposing D is going to do, understands exactly what he needs to do to counter that, and does it.

Brady was a sixth-round draft pick for the same reason Montana was a third-round pick, the same reason Starr was selected in the 17th round: because there are qualities that make a great NFL quarterback that aren't measurable by scouts.

Scouts look at arm strength and speed, mechanics and mobility, height and weight. They like Dan Marinos and Peyton Mannings. They like Drew Bledsoes. They like Tim Couches and David Carrs. They like athletic ability, and they don't trust intangibles.

Brady, like Starr and Montana before him, is a quarterback whose success is built on intangibles. He's intelligent, a quick thinker, and a hard worker, someone who never learned to coast on his athletic ability because there was all too often a better athlete somewhere nearby. And as result he is forever prepared. He's calm under pressure because he knows what's going to happen before it takes place.

He's also a natural and instinctual leader and a fierce competitor. He expects to win every contest and he usually finds a way to lead his team to victory. He's tough and he's confident.

And while Brady doesn't have the biggest arm in football, or the best mobility, he has the decided advantage of being one of the most accurate passers in football history. Brady's interception rate is low because he has a knack for putting the ball in a spot where his receiver is the only player who can get to it. Brady also boasts the best quarterback sneak record in NFL history. Through the 2015 season, Brady has carried the ball up the middle on third- or fourth-and-one 104 times in his career. In 95 of those instances, he's produced a first down or a touchdown. He goes under defenses. He dives over defenses. He digs in and gets it done, which is just one way Brady exhibits a toughness he's not credited for nearly often enough.

Perhaps more important than anything, Brady is clutch. He's at his best when the game is on the line. That doesn't mean he always wins—no one does, least of all in the NFL—but it does mean that the Patriots are rarely out of a game. If there's a way to win, Brady will generally find it.

That's what this book is about.

★ ★ ★

A few final notes.

When I discuss fourth-quarter comebacks, and particularly when I cite career totals, I'm not referencing an official statistic. The NFL doesn't track comebacks or game-winning drives. There's no official definition of what constitutes a comeback.

For the purposes of this book, I looked to stats compiled by Scott Kacsmar of Pro-Football-Reference.com. Kacsmar (though he does not agree with me on Brady's place in football history) is an incredible researcher and football historian. His research into this unofficial stat has been exhaustive and the reasoning behind his definition of a comeback is airtight.

When I refer to the NFL MVP, I'm generally referring to the award handed out by the Associated Press, which is the current standard. For players whose careers took place before the AP award was created, I looked to the closest proximate distinction.

The list of quarterbacks singled out for comparison to Brady in this book shouldn't be read as any kind of top 15. Although all of the players likely to appear in most experts' top 10 lists are represented, there are players here who wouldn't make most top 20 lists and players missing who likely would. The passers included here are recognized as greats of the game. Every one of them has made an important contribution to football history. My only intent with this book is to recognize that and to demonstrate that what Brady has accomplished during his career so far is exceptional even as compared to players who were exceptional themselves.

I hope you'll agree that I got it right—or at least figure I came pretty close.

CHAPTER 1

★ ★ ★

By the Numbers

Statistics and records are current through the 2015–16 AFC Championship.

Career Statistics

Regular-Season Win-Loss Record: 172–51 (.771)

Postseason Win-Loss Record: 22–9 (.710)

Overall Win-Loss Record: 194–60 (.764)

Passing Yards: 58,028

Completions: 4,953

Attempts: 7,792

Completion Percentage: 63.6

Touchdowns: 428

Interceptions: 150

Passer Rating: 96.4

Touchdown Percentage: 5.5

Interception Percentage: 1.9

Touchdown-to-Interception Ratio: 2.9/1

Yards Per Attempt: 7.4

Seasons Leading League

Passing Yards: 2

Touchdowns: 4

Completion Percentage: 1
Touchdown Percentage: 2
Interception Percentage: 3
Yards Per Attempt: 1
Passer Rating: 2

Single-Season Bests

Passing Yards: 5,235 (2011)
Touchdowns: 50 (2007)
Interceptions: 4 (2010)
Completion Percentage: 68.9 (2007)
Touchdown Percentage: 8.7 (2007)
Interception Percentage: 0.8 (2010)
Yards Per Attempt: 8.6 (2011)
Touchdown-to-Interception Ratio: 9/1 (2010)
Passer Rating: 117.2 (2007)

Significant NFL Records

Most Consecutive Wins: 21 (2003–04)
Most Consecutive Home Games Won: 31 (2006–11)
Most Wins in a Season: 16 (2007)
Most Wins in a Season and Postseason: 18 (2007)
Most Wins with a Single Team: 172
Most Consecutive Passes Without an Interception: 358 (2010–11)
Most Consecutive 400-Plus-Yard Passing Games: 2 (2011; tied with 7 other players)
Best Touchdown-to-Interception Ratio in a Season: 9/1 (2010)
Most Super Bowls Played: 6 (tied with Mike Lodish)
Most Super Bowls Won by a Starting Quarterback: 4 (tied with Joe Montana and Terry Bradshaw)
Most Career Pass Attempts in the Super Bowl: 247
Most Career Completions in the Super Bowl: 164
Most Pass Attempts by a Winning QB in a Super Bowl: 50 (Super Bowl XLIX)

Most Pass Attempts Without an Interception in a Super Bowl: 48 (Super Bowl XLII)

Most Completions in a Super Bowl: 37 (Super Bowl XLIX)

Most Consecutive Completions in a Super Bowl: 16 (Super Bowl XLVI)

Most Passing Yards in the Super Bowl: 1,605

Most Touchdown Passes in the Super Bowl: 13

Most Career Postseason Wins: 22.

Most Career Postseason Games Played: 31

Most Consecutive Postseason Wins: 10 (2001–05)

Best Postseason Single-Game Completion Percentage: 92.9 (vs. Jacksonville, January 12, 2008)

Most Pass Attempts in the Postseason: 1,183

Most Completions in the Postseason: 738

Most Passing Yards in the Postseason: 7,957

Most Touchdown Passes in the Postseason: 56

Most Completions by a Winning Quarterback in a Postseason Game: 37 (Super Bowl XLIX)

Most Touchdown Passes in a Postseason Game: 6 (January 14, 2002, tied with Daryle Lamonica and Steve Young)

Most 300-Plus-Yard Passing Games in the Postseason: 10

Most Division Titles: 13

Most Conference Championships Played: 10

Most Postseason Game-Winning Drives: 9

Most Postseason Fourth-Quarter Comebacks: 6

Position and Record on All-Time Leader Lists

Wins: Third, 172

Combined Regular Season and Postseason Wins: Third, 194

Career Passing Touchdowns: Third, 428 (tied with Drew Brees)

Single Season Passing Touchdowns: Second, 50 (2007)

Career Completions: Fifth, 4,953

Career Pass Attempts: Fifth, 7,792

Career Completion Percentage: 13th, 63.6

Career Passing Yards: Fifth, 58,028

Career Passer Rating: Sixth, 96.4

Single-Season Passer Rating: Fourth, 117.2 (2007)

Single-Season Passing Yards: Third, 5,235 (2011)

Single-Game Passing Yards: Eighth, 517 (vs. Miami Dolphins, September 12, 2011)

Career Interception Percentage: Second, 1.9

Career TD/INT Ratio: Third, 2.9/1

Single-Season Interception Percentage (full-season starters): First, 0.8 (2010)

Fourth-Quarter Comebacks: Second, 37

Game-Winning Drives: Third, 48

CHAPTER 2

★ ★ ★

Better Than You Realized: College

It can be hard to find Tom Brady in the 1998 Michigan Wolverines team photo. He's there. Second row, not far from the center. Looking maybe a bit serious and certainly more than a bit thin. But more than anything, he looks just part of the crowd.

It's odd, too, because in many ways 1998 was the only uncrowded year of Brady's college career. He was the Wolverines' starting quarterback that season—and no one else was in the mix. It was the first season since he arrived in Ann Arbor three years earlier that Brady was accorded an opportunity to stand out in that way…and, though he delivered on the field, it would also be the last.

Brady wasn't a highly recruited player coming out of Junípero Serra High School in his hometown of San Mateo, California. He was a talented athlete, just not the kind of player—and not at the kind of school—that brings college scouts streaming into town making promises and asking for commitments.

Brady's father, Tom Sr., sent tapes of his son's high school highlights to a handful of schools, and a few of them responded with interest. UCLA was in the picture for a while but backed out after Cade McNown signed a letter of intent. Brady considered the University of Illinois but wasn't bowled over by a visit to Champaign. The University of California–Berkeley offered Brady a guarantee

Tom Brady passes against Penn State on the way to shutting them out 27–0 in Ann Arbor on November 7, 1998.

that he'd start as a sophomore (and a chance to stay close to home), but Brady chose Michigan, a school with a deep football tradition and a place where he'd have a chance to compete against some of the top college teams in the nation. First, though, he'd need to compete simply to get on the field.

Before Brady arrived at Michigan in the fall of 1995, the Wolverines coaching staff turned over. The coaches who had recruited Brady were gone, replaced by Lloyd Carr, a first-time head coach whom Brady had never met. It wasn't what Brady had signed on for.

When he arrived in Ann Arbor, Brady learned that there were seven quarterbacks ahead of him on the depth chart. Playing for Michigan was appealing; the prospect of getting lost in a crowd there wasn't.

But Brady stuck it out, worked hard, and impressed Carr in practice. He wasn't the most athletically gifted of Michigan's quarterbacks, but he was a highly accurate thrower, tough and competitive, and he consistently exhibited keen focus and a cool head under pressure.

By Brady's sophomore season (his third year at Michigan, including a redshirt season), those qualities had paid off. Brady rose to the level of second stringer behind Brian Griese. It was a nice move up the list, but it wasn't what Brady wanted.

Brady thought he should start. He considered himself the better quarterback, and many of his teammates agreed. But Carr saw the quarterbacks as running neck-and-neck. And Griese was a senior; Carr's philosophy was that in a tie, advantage went to the upperclassman. Griese was also the son of Miami Dolphins great–turned–college football analyst Bob Griese. And whether that played a part in Carr's decision-making or not didn't much matter. Griese started, and Brady sat.

★ ★ ★ ★ ★ ★ ★

Joe Montana was "Joe Cool." Brady's very similar, the way he drops back, sits in that pocket, and acts like there's no rush coming. And he's a winner. That's the greatest comparison.

—Charles Woodson

Steamed, Brady considered transferring to Cal but finally resolved that he would stay in Michigan, prove himself to Carr, and ensure himself a place as Griese's successor. Already the hardest-working guy on the Michigan practice field, Brady became the player most serious about game prep. He began spending hours on film study, learning to recognize opponents' defensive alignments and putting himself in position to know in every situation where he'd find an open receiver.

In the meantime, the team's fortunes with Griese behind center made it hard to quibble with Carr's choice. The Wolverines went 12–0, beat Washington State in the Rose Bowl, and took a share of the national title. Then Griese departed for the Denver Broncos, and Brady finally got his team.

Or at least he got it for a season.

★ ★ ★

As a starter in his junior season, Brady led the team to a 10–3 record that included a 45–31 victory over Arkansas in the Florida Citrus Bowl. Michigan split the Big Ten championship with Wisconsin and Ohio State and finished the season as the 12th-ranked team in the nation.

On the way, Brady set a number of school passing records. In a loss to Ohio State on November 21, 1998, Brady established new Michigan single-game records for pass attempts (56), completions (31), and passing yards (375). His 56 attempts remain the record. In a 48–17 win at Hawaii a week later, Brady completed 90 percent of his passes.

That season, Brady set records for attempts (350) and completions (214). His 2,636 total passing yards were the second-most in Michigan history.

Even with all that success, however, in his senior season Brady found himself in competition for the starting job with sophomore Drew Henson. A Michigan native and a gifted athlete, Henson was a fan favorite from the moment he committed to the Wolverines.

Carr was in a difficult position. Brady had earned the right to start. And Brady was the upperclassman. But Henson was the future, the quarterback most likely to lead Michigan to real football glory in the years ahead. Henson was thought to be the player with the better potential as a pro. He was also a kid who had signed a contract to play baseball in the New York Yankees system. Henson

School for Mechanics

Part of what got colleges to pay attention to Tom Brady coming out of high school was the fact that he had worked with throwing coach Tom Martinez. The head coach at the College of San Mateo, Martinez was famed for his ability to improve young quarterbacks' skills. Martinez led his students not only to develop better throwing mechanics, but to understand why proper form led to better play. He was a perfect teacher for Brady, whose abilities were always as much about knowing as they were about doing. And he remained an influence on Brady's game from the time Brady first turned to him for help at age 15 until Martinez's untimely death in February 2012. Even as an NFL superstar, Brady turned to Martinez for help any time he felt his throwing motion was off. Since Martinez's death, Brady has worked with Tom House, a former Major League Baseball pitcher turned pitching coach, to keep his throwing mechanics sharp.

didn't need the Wolverines; the Wolverines needed Henson. And not to start Henson would have been to risk losing him.

Perhaps foolishly, Carr tried to have it both ways. He devised a system in which each week Brady would play the first quarter, Henson would play the second quarter, and Carr would go with the hot hand in the second half.

It worked for a little while. The Wolverines won their first five games. But the platoon system fell down during an early October visit to Michigan State. Neither quarterback put up any points in the first half. And with Henson in after halftime, the Wolverines fell behind 17–0. Carr made the decision to switch to Brady late in the third quarter, and Brady did what he could, throwing for 241 yards and leading a 31-point rally. And though it wasn't quite enough (Michigan lost 34–31), the effort nudged Carr in the direction of making Brady his full-time starter again. A 307-yard effort against Illinois two weeks later cinched it.

★ ★ ★

Brady led the Wolverines to four-straight wins to close the season. In their second-to-last game, against the Penn State Nittany Lions in University Park, Brady led a spectacular comeback from a 27–17 deficit in the closing minutes of the game. He closed the gap with 3:30 remaining with a seven-yard dash up the middle of the field to the Penn State end zone. Then, when a great punt return gave Michigan the ball at the Penn State 35-yard line, Brady capitalized, hitting receiver Marcus Knight with two perfectly placed passes, one that advanced the Wolverines to the Nittany Lions 20 and another for the go-ahead touchdown from 11 yards out.

Brady wasn't done with the spectacular comebacks, though. He rallied the Wolverines again at Ohio State in their final game of the season. And facing fifth-ranked Alabama in the Orange Bowl, Brady twice brought Michigan back from 14-point deficits. Early in the third quarter, with Michigan trailing 14–7, Brady stepped up under pressure from a corner blitz and delivered a 57-yard touchdown pass to receiver David Terrell. And after the Crimson Tide scored back-to-back touchdowns to go ahead 28–14, Brady did it again, finding Terrell for a 20-yard pass to bring the Wolverines within seven and leading a drive that ended with running back Anthony Thomas' three-yard touchdown for the tie. A 25-yard overtime touchdown from Brady to tight end Shawn Thompson sealed the Michigan victory.

Brady finished the game with 34 completions on 46 attempts for 369 yards and three touchdowns in regulation, plus the OT score. The completion total broke Brady's own school record from 1998.

It wasn't the first time Brady had started a season facing significant roadblocks and ended it with a triumph, and it wouldn't be the last. More than anything, though, it was a satisfying end to Brady's college career.

Though he had been forced to fight time and again for the right to start, Brady had made his mark on Michigan football, delivering two bowl victories in two seasons.

Brady had turned out to be a far better quarterback than Carr had given him credit for being. But in fairness to the coach, 31 NFL teams were about to make the same mistake.

CHAPTER 3

★ ★ ★

Ascendance: 2001

Tom Brady didn't win Super Bowl XXXVI.

Sure, Brady was named the game's MVP—and for good reason—but he didn't carry the team that day.

Brady wasn't responsible for shutting down the St. Louis Rams' otherworldly offense. That accomplishment belongs to the Patriots' smart, aggressive defense. And that, no question, was the Patriots' single-greatest achievement in their first Super Bowl win. Had the Rams scored the 31 points they'd put up on average during the regular season—never mind the 37 they averaged in the NFC play-offs—the 2001 Pats would have gone down in the books, alongside the 1985 and 1996 Super Bowl teams, as another plucky squad that fought its hardest but got steamrolled all the same.

Neither, as everybody knows, did Brady put up the points that decided the game. That honor belongs to Adam Vinatieri, who also has the distinction of having posted the winning points in Super Bowl XXXVIII.

Certainly, Brady had a good game, particularly for a kid no one had heard of five months earlier, a second-year backup who'd been thrust into the role of starter in late September after a devastating injury to his team's franchise QB. He threw 27 passes in the game, completing 16 of them (59.3 percent) for 145 yards and a touchdown. He didn't throw a single interception and finished with a passer rating of 86.2.

Those numbers were roughly in line with what Brady accomplished in his 14 regular-season games as a starter. Through the season, Brady threw an average of 29 passes per game, completing 19 of them for 200 yards and a touchdown. He achieved a passer rating of 86.5. Good stuff for a first season as a starter.

But Brady's Super Bowl XXXVI stats wouldn't stack up to what he would achieve in subsequent Super Bowls (wins and losses alike). And they were considerably more similar to what Trent Dilfer, the so-called "game manager," had achieved in Super Bowl XXXV than to Kurt Warner's stats from Super Bowl XXXIV.

They weren't superstar stats, because Brady wasn't a superstar player. He was a 24-year-old kid making his 17th NFL start and doing it on the biggest stage imaginable. And when you consider that (putting out of your head, if you can, all that has come since), you can't help but be astonished by what Brady achieved in the final minute and 21 seconds of the game.

★ ★ ★

You can't start there, though.

Because while the story of *the great Tom Brady* probably begins with the final possession of Super Bowl XXXVI, the story of Tom Brady, starting quarterback for the New England Patriots, opens a good bit earlier than that.

In fact, it starts well before September 23, 2001, the day Brady was yanked up to the top of New England's quarterback depth chart.

The tale of Brady's ascent begins on April 16, 2000, Day 2 of the NFL Draft. It was then that the Patriots selected Brady with the 199th overall pick. The pick was one of three compensatory selections the Pats were awarded as a result of a 1999 off-season in which they lost linebacker Todd Collins, punter Tom Tupa, defensive tackle Mark Wheeler, center Dave Wohlabaugh, and quarterback Scott Zolak to free agency.

Brady was the seventh quarterback taken in what was regarded as a historically thin draft at the position. The top QB prospect that year was Marshall's Chad Pennington, who went 18th overall to the New York Jets. He was the only quarterback taken in the first two rounds.

Hofstra's Giovanni Carmazzi went to the San Francisco 49ers early in the third, followed by Louisville's Chris Redman, who was selected by the Baltimore

Ravens. Late in the fifth round, the Pittsburgh Steelers took Tennessee QB Tee Martin. Marc Bulger from West Virginia went to the New Orleans Saints at the start of the sixth round, and the Cleveland Browns grabbed Spergon Wynn from Southwest Texas State in the middle of the sixth.

When the Patriots got on the board with the first of their two compensatory picks at the end of the round, they had a number of choices, including Todd Husak out of Stanford, JaJuan Seider from Florida A&M, Tim Rattay from Louisiana Tech, Notre Dame's Jarious Jackson, Joe Hamilton from Georgia Tech, Fresno State's Billy Volek, and Michigan's Brady.

In scouting, the Pats had paid particular attention to Brady and Rattay. They liked Brady a bit better.

It wasn't as if they were looking for a starter. Drew Bledsoe, the franchise QB with the huge arm, was in the prime of his career. The Patriots just needed a guy who could potentially move into the roster spot held by John Friesz—a onetime starter in San Diego who'd become a veteran clipboard holder—and perhaps compete with second-year man Michael Bishop for the No. 2 position on the depth chart. That put them in a solid position to take a chance on a kid who'd shown poise and leadership as a college quarterback but who nonetheless had begun his senior year splitting time with sophomore Drew Henson.

Concerns about Brady had nothing to do with his head. Not only had Brady demonstrated good on-field decision-making skills in big games at Michigan, but he'd exhibited an impressive team-first mind-set in the way he handled the situation with Henson. Brady never complained publicly about having the starting job he'd clearly earned taken away in favor of a local hero who consistently failed to live up to his star billing. He simply went out when he was asked to and found ways to win games. Brady also had evinced strong mental capabilities at the annual NFL Scouting Combine, where he profiled well and scored an impressive 33 on the Wonderlic Cognitive Ability Test (a score of 24 on the rapid-fire 50-question test is about the average for quarterbacks).

The concern was Brady's conditioning. Anyone who's seen the photo of Brady in his big, gray gym shorts taken during the combine knows that the young man did not appear to be the prototype of a superstar NFL quarterback. What he looked, more than anything, was soft.

The scouting report said much the same: "Poor build, very skinny and narrow, lacks mobility and the ability to avoid the rush, lacks a really strong arm." An unimpressive physical performance at the combine—his results included a painfully slow 40-yard-dash time of 5.23 seconds and a disappointing 24.5-inch vertical leap—didn't help either.

Brady was a long shot. It's easy now to assert that 30 teams (hell, 31 through most of six rounds) failed to recognize something special. But the truth is, the young man was a late-sixth-round pick because he looked for all the world like a late-sixth-round talent.

Still, if Brady appeared to lack the obvious physical skills to succeed as an NFL quarterback, he certainly didn't want for determination and self-confidence. When Brady arrived in Foxborough, his intent wasn't to compete with Friesz and Bishop; it was to compete with Bledsoe.

That would have drawn a laugh at the time.

Bledsoe wasn't beloved by every Patriots fan, but that was largely because fans have a way of looking most intently at a star quarterback's shortcomings. In Bledsoe's case, those included a lack of mobility and a perceived tendency to make bad decisions (though the latter criticism had more to do with unrealistic fan expectations than with objective reality—Bledsoe made his share of mental mistakes, sure, but so does every quarterback in football). And the mercurial opinions of fans have little to no bearing on NFL teams' decisions.

We know now that the inclination of the Patriots' then-new coach, Bill Belichick, was to judge a player based on how well he executed his duties in the team's system rather than on where he was drafted or what he'd accomplished in the past. We also know that Belichick, who had schemed effectively against Bledsoe as head coach of the Cleveland Browns and defensive coordinator of the New York Jets (and who had observed the quarterback carefully during the season he spent as New England's assistant head coach under Bill Parcells), didn't see Bledsoe as the kind of player who could succeed in his complicated system. But that perspective wouldn't be truly understood for years.

In 2000 these were the established facts: Bledsoe had been the first overall pick in the 1993 draft. He'd been brought in by Parcells, the future Hall of Fame head coach. He was a major factor in Parcells' successful effort to make the Patriots respectable and relevant following what was easily the worst period in a team history that was spotty in reality and downright dismal in public opinion. He had led the Patriots to an AFC Championship Game victory and a Super Bowl berth following the 1996 season. He was the darling of team owner Robert Kraft. He was entrenched.

Brady was none of those things. But he was focused on his goals and confident in his ability to achieve them. And the very first time they met, the young quarterback made an impression on his new team's owner that Kraft was still talking about 12 years later.

Speaking to the media the week before Super Bowl XLVI in February 2012, Kraft recalled: "I still have the image of Tom Brady coming down the old Foxboro Stadium steps with that pizza box under his arm, a skinny beanpole, and when he introduced himself to me and said, 'Hi, Mr. Kraft.' He was about to say who he was, but I said, 'I know who you are. You're Tom Brady. You're our sixth-round draft choice.' And he looked me in the eye and said, 'I'm the best decision this organization has ever made.'"

There's no wisdom in going around making statements like that. But young men have never been celebrated for their humility or their prudence. And no one could argue now that Brady failed to make good on his brash declaration.

★ ★ ★

Brady's self-assuredness certainly didn't translate to a lot of game time during the 2000 season.

With hard work in training camp and the preseason, he won a spot on the roster. But he was inactive for all but two games and saw the field just once, stepping in at the end of a blowout loss at Detroit on Thanksgiving to complete one of three passes for six yards.

Brady's real job was to run the scout team. There, he overachieved. Not content simply to mimic the Patriots' opponent of the week, Brady got his fellow practice players to put in extra hours with him. After they had fulfilled their primary responsibilities, he and the rest of the scout team would work on learning and executing New England's offense. Brady didn't just prepare himself to step in and start if he were called upon; he brought the rest of the scout team along with him.

That got the notice of both Belichick and offensive coordinator Charlie Weis, as did the fact that Brady was consistently the guy working hardest in the weight room and that he always put in extra time with quarterbacks coach Dick Rehbein. Brady may not have been ready to be an NFL starter, or even an active game-day backup, but he was exactly the kind of player Belichick and Weis valued most: a hard worker who was always looking to improve his abilities and a leader who could inspire those around him to elevate their play.

By the time the 2001 preseason rolled around, Friesz was gone. But Bledsoe was arguably more entrenched than ever.

Belichick may not have had a lot of faith in his starting quarterback, but coming off his first season as head coach with a record of 5–11, he didn't have the clout to unseat Bledsoe or to stop the team from making a huge long-term commitment to the QB. In March 2001 the Patriots inked their quarterback to a 10-year $103 million contract, a record-high compensation at the time.

Complicating matters further for Brady and his lofty goals, the Patriots hadn't simply decided to ride with Brady and Bishop as Bledsoe's backups. They brought in Damon Huard, who'd performed well as a backup to Dan Marino in Miami, to join the competition. What's more, they paid Huard a million dollars to be there.

Brady showed up for work and, through training camp and the preseason, showed himself to be the player best suited to back up Bledsoe. Bishop was dismissed in August, and Brady beat out Huard with superior play in preseason games. The press, and some fans, started to take notice of Brady's abilities.

★ ★ ★

It's possible that Brady eventually would have taken the starting job away from even a healthy Bledsoe. (Though not nearly so certain as some Patriots fans are given to believe. It's hard to justify benching the highest-salaried player on your team, no matter what your coach might want.) Bledsoe definitely didn't do much in the little time he had at the start of the 2001 season to justify the team's massive investment in him.

In the season opener at Cincinnati, Bledsoe was sacked all over the field and completed just 22 of 38 passes en route to a 23–17 loss. Two weeks later, when NFL action resumed following a pause brought on by the September 11 terrorist attacks, Bledsoe came out looking even worse at home than he'd been on the road. Facing the New York Jets, he threw a pair of interceptions, took a sack, and committed a killer delay-of-game penalty on a fourth-and-goal that forced the Patriots to settle for a field goal in a tight defensive battle.

Then came the moment that changed Patriots history.

Early in the fourth quarter, with the Pats trailing 10–3 and facing third-and-10 from their own 19-yard line, Bledsoe scrambled to avoid a heavy pass rush and attempted to earn a first down with his legs. But after he had picked up just eight yards, he saw that it wasn't going to happen and stepped toward

By the Numbers	**2001**
Total Yards (14 Starts)	2,843
Yards Per Game	189.5
Attempts	413
Completions	264
Completion Percentage	63.9
Yards Per Attempt	6.9
Touchdowns	18
Interceptions	12
Passer Rating	86.5
Games Rated Higher Than 100	3
Best Single-Game Rating	148.3

the sideline. Jets linebacker Mo Lewis, however, wasn't about to let the play end without dishing out a bit of punishment. Lewis slammed into Bledsoe on the sideline at full speed, knocking the ball out of the quarterback's hands out of bounds. Bledsoe hit the ground and lay there for a while before getting back on his feet.

After a Jets three-and-out, Bledsoe returned to the game and completed one final pass. But it was clear that something was seriously wrong. Brady was sent in to finish the game, and Bledsoe was sent to Massachusetts General Hospital. There, doctors determined that Bledsoe had suffered a sheared blood vessel in his chest, causing severe internal bleeding. Bledsoe was hospitalized for a week, ordered to rest for two, and informed it likely would be several more before he was cleared to go near a football field again.

Brady hadn't won a competition to become the Patriots' starter, but the job was his just the same—at least until Bledsoe was ready to return.

★ ★ ★

Brady was uneven in his initial starts. In a Week 3 home game against the Indianapolis Colts, then an AFC East division rival, Brady played well enough for the Pats to make the most of a spectacular outing by the defense and come out ahead 44–13. Brady completed just 13 passes for 168 yards. He didn't throw a touchdown pass, but neither did he give up an interception. And, for whatever it was worth, he became the first Patriots quarterback to win his first start since Scott Zolak in 1992.

A week later in Miami, Brady completed just 12 of 24 passes for 86 yards, took four sacks, and mishandled a snap, setting up a fumble-return touchdown by Dolphins defensive end Jason Taylor. New England lost 30–10.

The Pats went into Week 5 with a 1–3 record and a season outlook that was dusky—and seemingly headed for pitch black. Then Brady started to play the game at a different level.

Hosting the 3–1 San Diego Chargers, the Patriots opened up a 9–3 lead in the first quarter only to end up in a 26–16 hole late in the fourth as a result of solid play by San Diego quarterback Doug Flutie and blunders by New England's special teams.

Brady led a 69-yard drive—completing five of eight passes for 50 yards—to set up a Vinatieri field goal, making the score 26–19.

The defense did its part, forcing a Chargers three-and-out, and Troy Brown did his, taking San Diego's punt at the 10-yard line and returning it to midfield (the ball was moved back to the New England 40 as the result of a penalty).

Then Brady once again took the reins. With 2:10 remaining, the Patriots were in obvious passing situations on every down, and San Diego went for the throat, loading up in pursuit of the young QB. And still, Brady found a way to complete five of eight passes, including a 16-yard shot to Brown and a 26-yarder to David Patten, to get the Patriots deep into Chargers territory. He finished the drive with a three-yard toss to tight end Jermaine Wiggins for the touchdown that tied the score. The game was headed to overtime.

On New England's first play in overtime, Brady threw what should have been a game-winning pass to Patten. Reading a blitz, Brady changed the play call at the line, freeing Patten, who got behind Chargers cornerback Alex Molden. If Molden hadn't tackled Patten before the ball arrived, the play would have gone 77 yards to the San Diego end zone. As it was, the 37-yard pass-interference call got New England into San Diego territory. Brady threw three more passes to move the offense to the Chargers 26-yard line, and Vinatieri finished the job.

The 29–26 win was anything but perfect, but it was nonetheless meaningful. Brady's leadership had transferred from the practice squad to the starting lineup.

The results spoke for themselves. But that didn't stop Belichick from doing some uncharacteristically praiseful talking of his own about the young quarterback. In his postgame press conference, the famously reserved coach fairly gushed. "I can't say enough about Brady," Belichick offered. "Tom played with a lot of poise. He did a good job, not of avoiding the rush, but of disregarding the rush."

Brady's 54 pass attempts in the game were the most for a Patriots quarterback since Bledsoe's 54 in a 1998 Monday night shootout with Marino's Dolphins. Brady's 33 completions, zero interceptions, and 93.4 passer rating were all better than Bledsoe had achieved in that outing. Brady was named AFC Offensive Player of the Week for the first time in his career as a result of his performance.

A week later, when the Patriots traveled to Indianapolis for their last meeting with the Colts as division rivals (realignment after the season would move Indy to the AFC South after 31 postmerger seasons in the East), Brady played even better.

Brady didn't throw nearly as many passes against the Colts as he had in the game with the Chargers. He made just 20 attempts, completing 16 of them for 202 yards. But his day included three touchdown throws, including a 91-yard hookup with Patten that was at the time the longest play from scrimmage in franchise history (the record would stand for nearly 10 years before being broken by a 99-yard connection from Brady to Wes Welker in the opening game of the 2011 campaign).

Patten got the press at the time, and deservedly so: In addition to the record touchdown play—on which he caught the ball just behind coverage at the Patriots 47-yard line and raced the remaining 53 yards—Patten snagged three other passes, including a six-yard touchdown late in the game, completed a 60-yard touchdown pass to Brown on a flea-flicker, and scored on a 29-yard end-around.

But Brady came out of the game with a 148.3 passer rating and, more

For the Books ★ 2001

League Records
Most Pass Attempts Without an
Interception to Start a Career (162)

Honors and Career Milestones
Super Bowl MVP
Pro Bowl

important, a 3–1 record as a starter. Brady was winning games as the leader of the same offense in which Bledsoe had stalled. Accordingly, Brady was making the team his own.

★ ★ ★

The Patriots lost their next game, falling 31–20 to the Broncos in Denver. The game was notable mainly for the fact that it saw Brady throw his first career interception. Brady's 162 pass attempts without a pick to open a career remains an NFL record.

The Pats went home to face the Atlanta Falcons, and once again Brady lofted three touchdown passes, this time throwing for 250 yards and earning a passer rating of 124.4.

Chatter about the possibility of Brady keeping the starting job even after Bledsoe was cleared to play was growing louder by the week. But, of course, it was just talk. Fan talk. Sports radio talk. It reflected frustration with Bledsoe, nothing more. Everyone knew the unwritten rule: veteran NFL players didn't lose their jobs due to injury. When Bledsoe was cleared to return to the field, he was certain to be back behind center. And Brady would be back on the sideline.

Except it didn't work that way.

The Patriots beat the Bills in Week 9 then lost a close Week 10 contest to the 7–1 Rams, who already were the presumed Super Bowl XXXVI champions.

The Pats were 5–5, two games behind both the Dolphins and the Jets in the AFC East. And the doctors gave Bledsoe the go-ahead to return to the field. Belichick, however, limited that return to the practice field. The coach told his quarterbacks and his team that he was sticking with Brady.

It was official: Brady no longer had the starting job because he was the best *healthy* quarterback on the roster; he had it because his coach believed he was simply the best.

The move reportedly infuriated Bledsoe. Speaking to the media shortly after Belichick's decision was made public, Bledsoe at first tried to say nothing but, in response to repeated questions, eventually offered, "I'll just put it this way: I look forward to the chance to compete for *my* job. And I'll leave it at that." For the most part, though, Bledsoe put the team first, keeping his disagreement with the coach and organization largely to himself through the end of the season.

If being selected as the permanent starter had an effect on Brady, it was only to spur him to reach even greater heights on game days. At home against the New Orleans Saints in Week 11, Brady completed 73 percent of his passes (19 of 26), averaged nearly 10 yards per attempt, and threw for four touchdowns, earning a passer rating of 143.9 and his second AFC Offensive Player of the Week nod. The win was the first of six straight for the Pats to round out the regular season.

New England pulled even with the Jets in the win column with a narrow Week 12 victory in the Meadowlands. And in Week 14, the Patriots held off the Dolphins at home to move into sole possession of first place in the division. A win over the Carolina Panthers in the final game of the regular season secured the division title and a first-round bye in the playoffs.

No one who wasn't a Patriots die-hard really believed the team could accomplish much in the postseason. But the mere fact that the Pats had landed the conference two-seed at least appeared to validate the coach's faith in his new signal caller.

★ ★ ★

Through the first three quarters of Brady's first playoff game, it was hard to say whether Belichick's decision to stick with the young QB made as much sense in the postseason as it had in the regular season.

Playing at night in a blinding snowstorm, both the Patriots and their opponents, the Oakland Raiders, had struggled to move the ball. But the Raiders, behind veteran quarterback Rich Gannon, were having slightly more success than the Pats. A 50-yard drive capped by a 13-yard touchdown pass from Gannon to James Jett early in the second quarter provided the only points of the first half. And in the third quarter, the Raiders added two field goals to the Patriots' one.

When the Pats, trailing 13–3, got the ball with 12 and a half minutes remaining to play, they had little choice but to abandon the ground game and put their postseason hopes in their young quarterback's hands.

Brady rose to the occasion, completing nine straight passes for 61 yards. He got there with more than a little help from outstanding play by his receivers, who managed to catch balls under incredibly difficult circumstances. Patten made one catch after slipping in the snow and jumping back to his feet. On another play, Patten made a spectacular jump to pull in a ball that probably should have been intercepted out of the air. When Brady delivered a ball just off the mark, Brown made an incredible effort to reach out and scoop it up just before it plunged into the snow. Most improbably, on a first down at the Raiders 20-yard line, Brady delivered the ball a bit low to Patten, who juggled it as he fell toward the sideline then tipped it up in the air and into the hands of an oncoming Wiggins. The tight end was just able to pull the ball in to his chest and drag his feet before he too fell out of bounds.

On second-and-goal from the 6-yard line, with no one open and defensive end Reagan Upshaw bearing down on him from behind, Brady charged up the middle and into the end zone. With the play, Brady became the first quarterback in Patriots history to rush for a touchdown in the playoffs. He also brought his team to within three points with eight minutes left to play. There was hope for the Patriots after all.

The teams traded punts back and forth through the next six minutes of game time. A fumble after a nice punt return by Brown might have cost the Pats their last chance to get back in the game, but special teams ace Larry Izzo fell on the ball at the 46, preserving possession for New England. Still, there was just 2:06 to play and 54 yards of glacier between the Patriots and the Raiders' end zone.

On the last play before the two-minute warning, Brady looked at a collapsing pocket and dumped off the ball to tailback Kevin Faulk, who caught it just behind the line of scrimmage and darted seven yards, reaching just into Oakland territory. After the break, Brady barely avoided a sack by linebacker Greg Biekert and scrambled for five yards.

Brady didn't get away from the Raiders on the next play, a first down from the Oakland 42. He was chased down by cornerback Charles Woodson and appeared to fumble near midfield, with Biekert there to recover. But on review, officials ruled that Brady's arm had been moving forward when Woodson delivered the hit, and under the "tuck rule," the result of the play was an incomplete pass.

Brady made the most of his second chance, hitting Patten for 13 yards on the next play. And although the Patriots would gain just one more yard, it was enough to set up Vinatieri to make the greatest kick in NFL history, a 45-yard field goal off the icepack and through the driving snow to tie the game.

The game was anybody's. The Patriots got the ball first in overtime, and Brady didn't let the opportunity go to waste. He connected on seven consecutive pass attempts, moving the Patriots from their own 34-yard line to the Raiders 28. There, the Patriots faced fourth-and-four. And rather than trying his luck with another 45-yard kick, Belichick elected to go for it. Brady responded with the cool head of a veteran, holding the ball for a full three seconds while he went through his reads, finally connecting with Patten on the left side of the field for a six-yard pickup.

Close enough to feel confident in Vinatieri's ability to deliver the game-winning kick, the Pats went to the run. They picked up another 15 yards on the legs of running back Antowain Smith and two more as Brady positioned the ball for the field-goal attempt.

And with Vinatieri's 23-yard game-winning boot on third down, the Patriots advanced to the AFC Championship Game.

★ ★ ★

In Pittsburgh, things got a bit hairy.

The Patriots struck first when Brown returned a punt 55 yards for a touchdown late in the first quarter. But the Steelers' speedy secondary and relentless pass rush made it difficult for the Pats to move the ball on offense. Fortunately, the Patriots *D* was on its game, which allowed the team to maintain a 7–3 lead.

Just inside the two-minute warning of the first half with the Patriots facing third-and-eight from their own 32-yard line, Brady found Brown in the middle of the field at the New England 46, and Brown cut through the secondary for a total pickup of 28 yards. The Pats had the ball in Pittsburgh territory. But they didn't have Brady. The quarterback had taken a hit to the knees from blitzing safety Lee Flowers just after releasing the pass. His left knee was sprained, and his day was over. It fell to Bledsoe to finish the championship.

Bledsoe got the job done. He finished the drive Brady had started, completing three passes, scrambling for four yards, and finally finding Patten in the corner of the end zone to send the Patriots into the locker room ahead 14–3.

With heroics from Brown, stellar defense, and an able performance by Bledsoe in the second half, the Patriots completed a 24–17 win and advanced to Super Bowl XXXVI, where everyone knew that no matter who started at quarterback, they were going to get crushed by the NFC champion Rams.

★ ★ ★

That the Patriots, who went into the Super Bowl as 14-point underdogs, ultimately weren't victimized by the Greatest Show on Turf (as the 2001 Rams were billed) was a tribute to the New England defense. The Patriots harassed the Rams' receivers all day long, knocking the St. Louis offense out of its rhythm and holding it to just three points in the first three quarters. The *D* also put the first Patriots points on the board as cornerback Ty Law picked off a Warner pass near midfield and returned it 47 yards for a touchdown six minutes into the second quarter.

Brady, whose knee had recovered in the week between games, was there to take advantage of the next St. Louis miscue. A fumble by Rams receiver Ricky Proehl that was recovered and returned to the St. Louis 40-yard line by cornerback Terrell Buckley gave New England great field position. With less than two minutes remaining in the first half, Brady quickly marched the offense to the Rams 8, then hit Patten in the corner of the end zone to put New England in front 14–3.

Still, there was no keeping the Rams offense down for a full 60 minutes. And in the fourth quarter, St. Louis came storming back into the game, scoring a pair of touchdowns to tie the score at 17.

When the Patriots got the ball at their own 17-yard line with just 1:21 remaining, the expectation in the stands and in the TV booth was that they'd play it safe, keep the ball on the ground, and try their luck in overtime.

"With no timeouts, I think that the Patriots…with this field position…you have to just run the clock out," offered Fox TV color man John Madden. "You have to play for overtime now. I don't think you want to force anything here. You don't want to do anything stupid. Because you have no timeouts and you're backed up."

But Weis and Belichick took a different view than the old Raiders coach. Going to overtime would have meant risking a coin toss that might have given the Rams first possession. And that would put New England at the mercy of an offense that appeared to have figured out the Patriots' *D.* The Pats had the ball in regulation. That meant they had a chance to win in regulation. No matter how long the odds, they had to go for it.

★ ★ ★ ★ ★ ★ ★

Most guys don't make plays like Tom Brady does. He's pretty special.

—Steve Grogan

On first down, Brady took the snap out of the shotgun, moved toward the line of scrimmage to get away from pass rushers, and dumped the ball to running back J.R. Redmond for a five-yard gain.

"I don't agree with what the Patriots are doing here," Madden opined. "In this field position, I would play for overtime."

Brady brought the offense back to the line of scrimmage with just a minute remaining. He found Redmond in the middle of the field again, this time for eight yards.

As Brady spiked the ball at the New England 30 with 41 seconds left on the clock, Madden noted that the quarterback had been "very, very impressive with his calmness." And the Fox producers began showing video of Vinatieri loosening up on the sideline.

Brady once again hit Redmond, who picked up 11 yards before going out of bounds to stop the clock.

"Now I kind of like what the Patriots are doing," Madden conceded as New England huddled up with the ball at their own 41 with 33 seconds remaining on the clock.

Under heavy pressure from a five-man rush on the next play, Brady rolled out of the pocket and unloaded to nobody on the right sideline. On the next play, Brady hit Brown in the middle of the field at the Rams 45-yard line. Brown cut for the left sideline and picked up another nine yards before stepping out of bounds.

There were still 29 seconds left to play. And Madden came right out and said he'd been wrong. "This is amazing. This is something that I'll admit that, as a coach and as an analyst, I don't think they should have done, but they had the guts, they had the young quarterback, and they did it," he said. "At some point when you're in the Super Bowl you've got to let it all hang out, and I'll say this: Charlie Weis and this Patriots team, they are letting it all hang out."

Brady connected with Wiggins to move the Pats to the St. Louis 30, strutted up to the line of scrimmage as if it were nothing more than any old moment in any old game, and spiked the ball.

"I'll tell you, what Tom Brady just did gives me goose bumps," Madden said as the offense headed for the sideline to make way for the field-goal unit.

Vinatieri's 48-yard field goal as time expired made the Patriots unlikely champions.

"That's the way you should win a Super Bowl," Madden said. "That was a great, great drive."

It was more than that. It was the final exclamation point on a great, great season. It was certainly the greatest moment in New England Patriots history and possibly the greatest moment in Super Bowl history.

Brady was named Super Bowl MVP, and the team was his for keeps. Within a matter of months, Bledsoe was traded to the Buffalo Bills for a first-round draft pick. Brady had accomplished his goal of winning the starting job. He had fulfilled his promise to Kraft; he truly *was* the best decision the Patriots had ever made. And things were only going to get better.

CHAPTER 4

★ ★ ★

Tom Brady vs. Peyton Manning

There will never come a day when Tom Brady's name isn't connected with Peyton Manning's. Not ever.

Brady and Manning are bound together like Bird and Magic, Ali and Frazier, Navratilova and Evert. If you want to discuss the greatness of one, you have to talk about how he stacks up against the other.

That's the way it's been since Brady emerged as an elite quarterback. And that's the way it will continue to be. Even though the rivalry between Brady and Manning is fundamentally dissimilar to other classic sports rivalries.

Ali and Frazier traded punches, Navratilova and Evert traded shots…one athlete against another. And when a bout or a match was over, one competitor had won and the other had lost. Simple.

Bird and Magic had teams around them, but they were still on the court at the same time. They faced each other. Each had an effect on the other's performance.

Really, there's no such thing as a true rivalry between individuals playing the same position in football. The game's just not set up for it. Sure, Brady's Patriots and Manning's Colts and Broncos squared off repeatedly during the two quarterbacks' careers—each team coming away with its share of big wins. But it's not as if Brady and Manning ever actually engaged each other on the field.

At best, a meeting between two teams with star quarterbacks is like an American League pitchers' duel—though in reverse, with the focus on offense rather than defense. Each of the big-name players knows he needs to find a way to put more points on the board than his rival, but neither ultimately has any direct effect on the other's performance.

That makes it tough, if not impossible, to talk about a football rivalry in the context of a single game, or even a series of head-to-head matches.

You can look at stats, of course. You can try to assess leadership, a key component of the position. And if a game is tight, you can potentially look at how each player performs in the clutch. But in the end, each man is facing a different defense with different schemes and abilities. And neither can accomplish a thing without meaningful contributions from the other offensive players around him.

So when you start to talk about Brady and Manning, you can, if you like, look at the results of the 17 meetings between the Pats and Colts/Broncos in which Brady and Manning were calling signals. And if you do, you'll see that Brady and the Patriots went 11–6 overall—9–3 in the regular season and 2–3 in the play-offs. That's a winning average of .647 across the board. Look just a bit closer, and you might also note that Brady's Patriots had a winning record over Manning's Colts both in Foxborough (5–2) and in Indianapolis (3–2). With Manning in Denver, things changed. Brady's Patriots beat Manning's Broncos in all three of their visits to Foxborough, but lost both times the teams met in Denver. (Brady has had a rough time in Denver regardless of who was playing quarterback for the Broncos. He's 2–7 overall in career trips to Mile High.) Talk to Brady fans and you'll hear about the overall numbers. Talk to Manning supporters and you'll hear about the postseason, particularly the AFC Championship, in which Manning's teams hold a 1-3 advantage over Brady's

Slice and dice however you will. The head-to-head numbers get you almost nowhere. Because those 17 games are just that: 17 games. Seventeen of 254 starts in Brady's career (223 regular-season, 31 postseason). Seventeen of 292 starts for Manning (265 regular-season, 27 postseason). That's 6.7 percent of Brady's career starts and 5.8 percent of Manning's, which is an incredibly small sample size.

What's more, even if you were determined to believe you could size up a pair of long careers based on a handful of games, you'd have to consider much more than wins and losses.

Brady and Peyton Manning share a word after the Patriots bested the Colts 27–24 on September 9, 2004.

You'd have to take a hard, detailed look at the quarterbacks' performances, which would involve assessing and adjusting for the defenses each player faced. You'd have to look, for example, at the fact that while Patriots-Colts games in 2001 pitted Brady against the 31st-best defense in the NFL (or, you know, you could say "worst"), Manning was looking across the line at the league's sixth-rated *D*. You'd have to break down what made the Pats' defense work and what made the Colts' *D* fall flat—not just in one game but over the entire season—and assess the success of each QB in that context. And you'd have to make those adjustments for all 17 matchups over 13 different seasons—making your way to the final Brady-Manning showdown, the 2015 AFC Championship Game, in which Brady faced one of the all-time great NFL defenses—just to try to read some meaning into the results.

The exercise would be pointless, mainly because it would be unnecessary. When you look at data from long careers in aggregate, you don't need to make those adjustments. The adjustments make themselves, particularly in the case of players whose teams consistently have finished at the top of their divisions.

When you look across the scope of 254 and 292 games, the level of competition tends to even out. Both Brady and Manning have gone up against great defenses and terrible defenses, strong secondaries and even stronger fronts, every defensive scheme and style, every type of defensive player in football. It's all there. Both QBs have had to try to find ways to win against other teams with standout quarterbacks and high-powered offenses. And both have had opportunities to take advantage of opponents that couldn't hope to survive in a shootout.

★ ★ ★

That leaves you needing only to consider the elements that don't even out.

Playing conditions, for example. The Patriots play their home games outdoors in a region that can produce extremely challenging weather conditions, while the Colts (the team with which Manning made 227 of his 292 career starts) are a dome team. Not only are dome conditions generally friendlier to passers, but weather has been a major factor far more often in Brady's career than in Manning's. And while Manning moved outdoors for the final four seasons of his career, it's worth noting that he landed in Denver, where the advantages offered to the home team by altitude and thin air are well documented.

30

It would be hard to argue, on the other hand, that Manning has benefitted from the same degree of excellence in coaching as Brady. In his Colts career, Manning labored under three different head coaches: Jim Mora, Tony Dungy, and Jim Caldwell. All three coached the Colts to winning records. And both Dungy and Caldwell led the team to the Super Bowl. But it would be absurd to argue that any one of them is on the same level as Bill Belichick, the only head coach under whom Brady has ever played. Neither can one make the case that either John Fox or Gary Kubiak, Manning's coaches in Denver, is on Belichick's level (though Fox has coached two teams to conference championships and Kubiak has a Super Bowl championship on his head-coaching resume).

If you're considering that disparity, though, you also have to consider the fact that Manning played under just one offensive coordinator, Tom Moore, for all but the last of his 13 seasons as the Colts' starter. Even after Moore officially retired following the 2009 season, he was retained by the Colts as senior offensive assistant through the 2010 season. Manning played in two different offenses during his four seasons in Denver. The first was an offense he brought with him from Indy. The second, Kubiak's, was a run-oriented system well suited to the substantially diminished skills Manning brought to the field in 2015.

Brady, in his 14 seasons as the Patriots' starting QB, has been forced to adjust to ongoing changes at offensive coordinator as Belichick's assistants have proven attractive candidates for head coaching jobs elsewhere. Charlie Weis, Josh McDaniels, and Bill O'Brien all have had their turns as New England's offensive coordinator during Brady's tenure. And Brady has performed well under all three.

Brady's Patriots generally had better defenses than Manning's Colts. But the difference wasn't quite as striking as it's sometimes imagined to be. During Brady's 14 seasons as a starter, New England defenses have allowed an average of 18.8 points per game. That's good, but it's hardly suffocating. The Colts, during Manning's 13 seasons behind center, gave up 21.3 points per game. And the Broncos during Manning's tenure allowed 20.9 points per game. The differences may account for some small part of the disparity between the two quarterbacks' winning percentages, but not much. Mostly what the numbers do is reveal the lie in the favorite argument of Manning fans: that Brady has been carried by the Pats' D. (An argument that, in any account, became harder for Manning supporters to make after 2015, a season in which Manning unquestionably was carried all the way to a Super Bowl victory by the Broncos' dominant defense.)

And New England *D*s certainly have benefitted as much from Brady's play as he has from theirs. In fact, on the whole Brady and the Patriots offense have given New England *D*s slightly more to work with than Manning and his offense have accorded the Indy defense. The Patriots have put up an average of 28.2 points per game in Brady's career, while Manning's Colts and Broncos averaged a combined 27.3.

That's a bit surprising, given that the Colts with Manning were designed to be an offensive powerhouse, as were the Broncos for the first three of Manning's four seasons. Manning—who was groomed by his NFL quarterback father from childhood to become a star player and who was the first overall pick in the 1998 NFL draft—has certainly been the center of attention during his career. But he was never the only offensive superstar in the Indianapolis or Denver lineups.

In his rookie season, Manning had the benefit of sharing the Colts' offensive backfield with Hall of Fame tailback Marshall Faulk, who enjoyed one of his best seasons as a pro. Faulk, who had been the second overall pick in the 1994 draft, led the league in 1998 with 2,227 yards from scrimmage. He rushed for 1,319 and caught 86 passes for another 908. Faulk's catches accounted for more than a quarter of Manning's passing production that season.

And when Faulk was traded to the St. Louis Rams following the 1998 season, he was replaced by future Hall of Famer Edgerrin James, whom the Colts selected fourth overall in 1999. James made his mark immediately. He was the NFL's leading rusher in 1999, carrying for 1,553 yards; caught 62 passes for another 586 yards; and was named Offensive Rookie of the Year. In 2000 James rushed for 1,709 yards, again leading the league, and caught 63 passes for an additional 594 yards. His 2,303 yards from scrimmage in 2000 were the most in the NFL. James rushed for more than 1,200 yards in five of his seven seasons in Indianapolis and three times topped 2,000 total yards from scrimmage.

Faulk wasn't the only first-round draft pick waiting for Manning when he joined the Colts. Marvin Harrison, the 19th overall pick in the 1996 draft, was there as well. Harrison had been the Colts' leading receiver in both of his first two years with the team, catching 137 passes for 1,702 yards during his time playing with journeyman quarterback Jim Harbaugh. Harrison's productivity dipped in Manning's first season as the rookie QB focused on the pass-catching tailback Faulk, but it shot back up in 1999, when the receiver accounted for 115 catches and a league-best 1,663 yards. Over his 13 seasons, Harrison proved to be well worth the high draft pick the Colts invested in him. He finished his career with 1,102 catches—second-most in league history (now third-most)—and 128 touchdowns. Harrison, who will become eligible in 2014, is as close as receivers get to being a sure bet for induction in the Pro Football Hall of Fame.

The Colts didn't stop investing first-round picks in offense with Faulk, Harrison, and James either. In 2001 the team invested its first-round pick, 30th overall, in Reggie Wayne, who had set new school records in his four years as a starter at the University of Miami. The pick paid off, as Wayne provided a strong complement to Harrison in his early seasons and later transitioned to become Manning's primary target. In 2007 Wayne led the league with 1,510 receiving yards.

In 2003 the Colts added yet another first-round talent to Manning's offense in tight end Dallas Clark. Even while sharing the field with standout receivers and pass-catching tailbacks, Clark provided a consistent and meaningful target for Manning from his rookie season forward. In 2009, when the Colts won their second Manning-era AFC championship, Clark and Wayne shared the team lead in receptions with 100 each.

The Colts also invested first-round picks in offensive skill players in 2006, 2007, and 2009, drafting running back Joseph Addai, wide receiver Anthony Gonzalez, and running back Donald Brown (who, in fairness, looks like he may turn out to be a swing and a miss).

All told, in the 13 drafts during Manning's tenure, the Colts went with offensive players with their first pick eight times, taking skill players with six of those picks.

The Colts' financial investments during the Manning years reflected their draft priorities, as the team consistently concentrated its spending under the NFL salary cap on Manning and the skill position players around him.

In the post-Manning era, the Colts have continued to emphasize offense with fairly consistent results. Since 2011, the year Manning missed due to injury and in which the Colts may or may not have tanked in order to secure the first overall pick in the 2012 draft, Indianapolis has focused its team-building efforts on surrounding quarterback Andrew Luck with great talent. And in his three healthy seasons, Luck has paid it off, leading Indy to an 11–5 record each year, and leading the league in touchdown passes (40) in 2014.

The Denver Broncos in the Manning era took a more balanced approach. The Broncos used their top draft pick in each year from 2011 through 2015 on a defensive player, a strategy that helped them build a powerhouse unit.

Still, Manning's offenses in Denver have included no shortage of weapons. On his arrival in Denver, Manning joined an offense that included wide receivers Demaryius Thomas and Eric Decker, each of whom had been underutilized but productive in a Tim Tebow–led offense since being selected in the first and third rounds of the 2010 draft. There's no question but that both receivers came on after Manning joined the Broncos (helpful if you're looking to demonstrate that Manning is a better quarterback than Tebow). But it's worth noting that Decker continued to perform at a high level while catching passes from Geno Smith, Michael Vick, and Ryan Fitzpatrick as a member of the New York Jets

You Can't Argue with Figures

	Tom Brady	Peyton Manning
Regular-Season Record	172–51	186–79
Winning Percentage	.771	.702
Postseason Record	22–9	14–13
Winning Percentage	.710	.519
Overall Record	194–60	200–92
Winning Percentage	.773	.685
Passer Rating	96.4	96.5
Touchdown Percentage	5.5	5.7
Interception Percentage	1.9	2.7
TD/INT	2.9/1	2.1/1
Completion Percentage	63.6	65.3
Yards Per Attempt	7.4	7.7
First-Team All-Pro	2	7
League MVP	2	5
Super Bowl MVP	3	1
Super Bowl Record	4–2	2–2

in 2014 and 2015. And that it would be hard to categorize Thomas' production in the 2015 games with Brock Osweiler lining up at QB for Denver as meaningfully diminished from what he achieved during Manning's healthy seasons with the Broncos, particularly if one allows for the fact that Denver had effected a change to a run-oriented offense under Kubiak. Wide receiver Emmanuel Sanders, a much sought-after free agent brought in by the Broncos from Pittsburgh in 2014, similarly showed little dropoff in production while working with Osweiler.

★ ★ ★

Playing for a team that focused on defensive players early in the draft was a change of pace for Manning. It's been the story of Brady's career. Only four times in the Brady era have the Pats chosen offensive players with their first draft pick. Two of those have been linemen, and a third was blocking tight end Daniel Graham. The Pats did invest their second of two first-round picks in the 2004 draft in a pass-catching tight end, making Benjamin Watson the 32nd overall selection in the draft. They also took running back Laurence Maroney with the 21st overall pick in 2006.

The only Patriots first-round receiver with whom Brady has ever shared a field is Terry Glenn, who was in his final season with New England when Brady took over as quarterback in 2001 and who, as a result of a blistering personality clash with Belichick, appeared in only four games that year.

That, of course, is not to say that Brady hasn't at times benefitted from the presence of first-round talent on his offense. Brady's two full seasons with Randy Moss, whom many regard as the most physically gifted receiver in NFL history, were immensely productive. The pairing of Brady and Moss was probably the key factor in the Patriots' phenomenal 2007 season, during which Moss and Brady connected for an NFL single-season-record 23 touchdowns. Moss also led the league in touchdown catches in 2009, when he scored 13 times.

Corey Dillon, with whom Brady shared the offensive backfield for three seasons, didn't come into the league as a first-round pick, but there's no question that he was a first-round talent. Dillon's 1,635 rushing yards in 2004 were a franchise record, and his 144-yard performance against the Colts in the 2004 playoffs was instrumental in the Patriots' run to Super Bowl XXXIX.

Dillon's three seasons with the Patriots were the only ones in which Brady has had the benefit of a marquee running back to take the pressure off the passing game. But Dillon was never a significant target in the passing game. And he never led the league in any statistical category.

And it would be foolish not to acknowledge that tight end Rob Gronkowski, though the Patriots got him in the second round of the 2010 draft, has proven to be better than most if not all of the players taken in the first round that year. Gronk, who surely would have been a first round selection if not for concerns about his health coming out of college, has been more than a force for the Patriots over his first six seasons in the NFL. Despite having been limited to 69 regular season starts in that time, Gronkowski already is in the conversation about all-time greatest tight end. Through 2015, Gronk logged 65 touchdown catches, the third most ever by a tight end, trailing only Tony Gonzalez, who caught 111 TDs over 17 seasons and 254 starts, and Antonio Gates, whose first 13 seasons and 176 starts produced 104 TD catches. Gronk's nine postseason touchdown catches are the most ever by a tight end. He also holds the records for touchdown catches in a single season by a tight end, 17 (tied for fifth most among all players), and receiving yards in a single season by a tight end, 1,327. In setting those marks in 2011, Gronkowski became the first tight end ever to lead the NFL in receiving yards and receiving TDs for a season.

During the 2010, 2011 and 2012 seasons, Brady benefitted not only from Gronk's presence, but from that of Aaron Hernandez. Though he was a fourth-round draft pick, Hernandez certainly wasn't a fourth-round talent. (Hernandez turned out to be a terrible human being, but that doesn't' change the fact that he was an exceptionally good football player.) Hernandez, over three seasons, caught 175 passes for 1,956 yards and 18 TDs. He and Gronk were becoming the most dangerous two-TE combo in football.

With or without Hernandez to complement Gronkowski, Brady unquestionably has performed better with Gronk on the field than without him. But it's still the case that Gronkowski was 12 when Brady won his first Super Bowl. And Brady had been to four championships and won three of them before Gronk and Hernandez got to the NFL.

Brady's top targets in his first four seasons as a starter, during which the Patriots won three Super Bowls, were Troy Brown, an eighth-round pick in 1993 who coasted into the Patriots Hall of Fame but who will go to Canton only to be part of Brady's induction ceremony; David Patten, who went undrafted in 1996 and was in and out of football for five seasons before he joined the Patriots in 2001; Deion Branch, whom the Patriots took with the 65th overall pick in 2002; David Givens, whom the Patriots took in the seventh round in 2007; and tailback Kevin Faulk, a second-round choice for the Pats in 1999. Three of the receivers from that time—Patten, Givens, and Branch—moved on to other teams after enjoying success in New England. Givens accomplished nothing after leaving. Patten had one successful season catching passes from Drew Brees in New Orleans but was otherwise a nonfactor. And Branch enjoyed limited success in Seattle only to reemerge upon rejoining the Patriots in 2010.

Starting in 2007 Brady had success throwing the ball not only to Moss, but to Wes Welker, who was undrafted in 2004 and who came to New England from Miami in exchange for second- and seventh-round draft picks. In Welker's best season before joining the Patriots, he caught 67 passes for 687 yards. In his six seasons in New England, he caught an average of 112 passes per season for 1,243 yards. Welker led the league in catches three times during his stint with the Patriots, In 2011 he gained 1,569 yards and caught nine touchdowns while operating mainly out of the slot.

One might be tempted here to note the degree to which Welker's production dropped in 2013 and 2014 after he left New England to play with Manning's Broncos, but that would be unfair. The Patriots let Welker go for many reasons, not the least of which were mounting concerns related to the punishment he took as a result of his style of play. And his limited production in Denver was a result of those factors, not a reflection on Manning.

Welker's decline in Denver is significantly less meaningful than the corresponding rise of Julian Edelman in New England. Edelman, who played quarterback in college, was drafted by the Patriots in the seventh round, 232nd overall, in 2009. He was a player New England thought it might be able to convert to a kick returner and perhaps a receiver. And working with Brady since Welker's departure, he has more than delivered. Despite time missed as a result of injuries, in 39 games (33 starts) over three years, Edelman has caught 258 passes for 2,720 yards and 17 TDs. He played a critical role in the Patriots' victory in Super Bowl XLIX. And all this, of course, has taken place with Edelman playing alongside Danny Amendola, the undrafted receiver the Patriots signed away from St. Louis as a free agent to replace Welker. Amendola in 42 games (17 starts) with the Patriots has caught 146 passes for 1,481 yards and six touchdowns.

Edelman and Amendola are the most recent examples of receivers who have excelled as a result of being on a team with Brady. There were others in the years between the first run of Super Bowls and 2007, notably Reche Caldwell, a second-round choice of the San Diego Chargers in 2002 whose 61 catches for 760 yards in his lone year in New England, 2006, were more than double his output in any other season in his six-year NFL career.

★ ★ ★

Considering the significant hype that has surrounded Manning since his college years, and given the significant investment the Colts made in surrounding their pedigreed superstar with complementary talent, you'd only expect that Brady's career statistics and accomplishments would pale in comparison to his rival's. And yet, that's been anything but the case.

That's not to say that Manning's career stats aren't incredible. They absolutely are. It's for very good reason that Manning is lauded as one of the best quarterbacks in league history.

Manning accumulated an NFL record 71,940 total passing yards for an average of more than 271 per game. He had a career completion percentage of 65.3. He holds the record for passing touchdowns at 539, which averages out to roughly 32 per season. That said, Manning also threw 251 career interceptions. His touchdown-to-interception ratio is an impressive 2.1/1. Manning's career passer rating is 96.5.

Manning's records are far too numerous to list here, but it's notable that he passed for more than 4,000 yards in 14 different seasons and posted perfect passer ratings in four regular season games and one in the postseason. He holds the record for passing TDs in a season, 55, and passing yards in a season, 5,477 (both from 2013). He is tied with Brett Favre for most wins in the regular season, 186, and in Super Bowl 50 became the first NFL quarterback to reach 200 combined regular season and postseason wins.

Brady, in three fewer seasons than Manning, has thrown for 58,028 yards, an average of 260 per game. His career completion percentage is 63.6. He's thrown 428 touchdowns, for an average of 31 per season, and just 150 interceptions, for an incredible touchdown-to-interception ratio of 2.9/1. Brady's career passer rating through 2015 was 96.4.

Brady has thrown for more than 4,000 yards in a season eight times in his career. Brady has posted perfect passer ratings in only two games, and his career-best season passer rating, 117.2 from 2007, ranks fourth on the all-time list behind Aaron Rodgers (122.5, 2011) Manning (121.4, 2004) and Nick Foles (119.2, 2013). Brady's career postseason passer rating, 88.0 is just ahead of Manning's 87.4. Brady, who has played three fewer seasons than Manning, likely will need just two seasons to pull ahead of Manning in regular season wins. He goes into the 2016 season with 172, 14 shy of the record Manning shares with Favre. But Brady is poised to overtake Manning in combined regular season and postseason wins much sooner. With seven wins in 2016, Brady would become the first NFL quarterback to reach 201 combined victories. Even if he needs an entire season to get there, Brady would hit 201 wins in just 270 starts, whereas Manning needed 292 to reach 200.

And while Manning holds a great number of regular season volume records, Brady holds the vast majority of postseason and Super Bowl volume records. Brady is the NFL's all-time postseason leader in passing touchdowns (56), passing yards (7,957), attempts (1,183), and completions (738). Brady holds the Super Bowl records for passing TDs (13), passing yards (1,605), attempts (247), and completions (164). He also holds the Super Bowl records for completions in a game (37) and consecutive completions (16).

Brady, whose contract runs through the 2019 season, also has a drawn a bead on Manning's regular season records. If he plays out his deal and plays consistently well, Brady has a good chance of overtaking Manning in passing yards and passing touchdowns. (He may have company, too, as Drew Brees is also in the hunt for those volume records.)

So in spite of the much greater portion of his career Manning spent with offensive talent piled up around him, the two quarterbacks' career performance statistics have been significantly comparable, with each coming out better than the other in a handful of key measures.

★ ★ ★

When it comes to winning and losing, however, there's simply no comparison. Brady is hands-down the better of the two in that all-important area.

Brady has a regular-season record of 172–51, for a winning percentage of .771. Manning's regular-season record is 186–79 (.702)—impressive, but not in the same neighborhood as Brady.

And that disparity is nothing compared to the enormous gap between the two quarterbacks' postseason achievements. Brady is 22–9 in the playoffs. That's a winning average of .710. Manning is 14–13—or .519.

More to the point, Manning lost his first three postseason starts (en route to a jaw-dropping nine career postseason one-and-dones). The second-seeded Colts were upset 19–16 by the wild-card Tennessee Titans in the divisional round of the 1999 playoffs, in which Manning completed just 19 of 42 passes. Manning had another unimpressive outing a year later, when the Colts traveled to Miami as a wild-card team and were beaten 23–17 in overtime. Manning finished the day 17-for-32 with a single touchdown. When the Colts next qualified for the playoffs two years later, it was again as a wild-card team. They were blown out by the New York Jets 41–0 in a game in which Manning completed just 14 of 31 passes and threw a pair of interceptions.

It wasn't until the 2003 postseason that Manning's Colts finally logged a victory. And even then they were soundly defeated in the AFC Championship Game—by Brady and the Patriots.

While Manning was flailing, Brady was winning championships. Brady's first 10 postseason starts resulted in Patriots victories, a run that included three Super Bowls. Indeed, though Brady got his first professional start three years after Manning—and though Manning had been to the postseason twice before Brady was elevated to the starting role in New England—by the time Manning logged his first career victory in the playoffs, Brady had won three postseason games and had been named Super Bowl MVP. Brady was a three-time champion and a two-time Super Bowl MVP before Manning made his first appearance in the Super Bowl.

Brady is the only quarterback in NFL history to lead his team to six Super Bowls. Manning has been to four. Brady's Patriots are 4–2 in the Super Bowl and

6–4 in the AFC Championship Game. Manning's teams are 2–2 in the Super Bowl and 4–1 in conference championships.

The contrast between what the two players have accomplished in their Super Bowl appearances is equally telling. Manning's Colts won Super Bowl XLI by a score of 29–17. They traded scores with the Chicago Bears early in the game but went ahead midway through the second quarter and never again lost their lead. In Super Bowl 50, the Broncos won not because of their quarterback, but in spite of him. Manning's stats—13 of 23 for 141 yards, no touchdowns and one interception for a passer rating of 56.6—are the worst by a winning quarterback in Super Bowl history. The Broncos won Super Bowl 50 because of the same crushing defense that got them to the championship game.

Brady's Patriots had to gut out all four of their Super Bowl wins. In their first two, Brady coolly moved his team into position to put the winning points on the board in the final seconds of regulation. In the third, Brady led the Pats on a pair of fourth-quarter scoring drives. The first broke a 14–14 tie, and the second resulted in a game-clinching field goal. And in his fourth Super Bowl win, Brady led the Patriots back from a 10-point fourth quarter deficit against the Seattle Seahawks, a team that boasted the best defense in the NFL Brady was the definition of clutch, orchestrating scoring drives of 62 and 64 yards as the Patriots became the first team in Super Bowl history to win after trailing by more than seven points in the fourth quarter.

And while both quarterbacks have twice been on the losing side in the league championship game, Brady, in both Patriots losses, put his team in a position to win with a touchdown late, only to see the defense that supposedly has carried him through his career give up go-ahead scores.

Manning, by contrast, inarguably cost his team its last chance in Super Bowl XLIV. With the New Orleans Saints leading 24–17 late in the fourth quarter, the Colts advanced deep into Saints territory only to see Manning throw an

★ ★ ★ ★ ★ ★ ★

Tom is the epitome of having that special moxie.

—Charlie Weis

interception at the New Orleans 26-yard line that was returned for a touchdown. The defensive score put the Saints ahead 31–17 and effectively sealed the championship.

And in Super Bowl XLVIII, when the Broncos faced the Seattle Seahawks (the same team that would fall to the Patriots a year later), Manning wilted. The Denver offense in which Manning had set regular season passing records managed just eight points to Seattle's 43. And twice, at crucial moments, Manning put the ball in the hands of the Seahawks' D. His first interception, at the Denver 37-yard line, set up Seattle's first touchdown, which put the Seahawks ahead 15–0. His second was returned 64 yards for a touchdown that put Seattle ahead 22–0 and effectively ended the game before halftime. For the second time in his career, Manning had thrown a pick-six that ended any hope his team had of winning a championship.

The importance of this distinction is open to debate, but it seems worth noting that Brady performed better in both of his Super Bowl losses than Manning did in either of his Super Bowl wins. In Super Bowl XLII, Brady completed 29 of 48 passes for 266 yards, one touchdown and no interceptions, finishing with a passer rating of 82.5. In Super Bowl XLVI, Brady went 27 of 41 for 276 yards, two touchdowns and one interception, earning a passer rating of 91.1. Manning, in Super Bowl XLI, completed 25 of 38 passes for 247 yards, one TD and one INT, and a passer rating of 81.8. And in Super Bowl 50, of course, Manning posted the dismal stats noted above.

Overall, Brady's Super Bowl stats put Manning's to shame. Brady in his six league championship games has completed 164 of 247 passes (66.4%) for 1,605 yards (6.5 yards per attempt), 13 touchdowns and 4 interceptions. His Super Bowl touchdown percentage is 5.3. His Super Bowl interception percentage is 1.6. And his Super Bowl passer rating is 95.3. Manning through four Super Bowls completed 104 of 155 passes (66.5%) for 1,001 yards (6.5 yards per attempt), three touchdowns and five interceptions. That gives him a Super Bowl TD percentage of 1.9, interception percentage of 3.2, and passer rating of 77.4.

On the biggest stage, Brady has consistently exhibited an ability to perform at a high level under ridiculous pressure. Manning showed that he could win when the competition fell away early but wilted when it was crunch time and the pressure was on.

Brady didn't come into the league with Manning's professional football pedigree. He was far from being the first overall draft pick that Manning was. He hasn't been the beneficiary of a pro system that disproportionately values offense over defense. Nor has he been the subject of an NFL hype machine as Manning was. But on the field of play, in every aspect that ultimately counts for something, Brady unquestionably has been the better quarterback.

CHAPTER 5

★ ★ ★

Tom Brady vs. Sid Luckman

Sixty-five years have passed since Sid Luckman played his final game as quarterback for the Chicago Bears—during which time the spirit of Woody Hayes has been progressively nudged aside by the spirit of Sid Gillman. The prevailing offensive philosophy of NFL teams has changed from *run, run, run, think about passing, decide against it and run, then take a moment to recommit to the run* to *air it out, light it up, and look to the running game mainly when you've got a big lead to protect*. And still, Luckman remained the Chicago Bears' all-time leader in both passing yards and passing touchdowns until he was overtaken by Jay Cutler—who took over as passing yards leader at the end of the 2013 season and as passing TDs leader halfway through 2015.

Some of that, of course, has to do with the Bears' failure to draft or develop a great passer—even through years in which the passing game has become evermore critical to success in the NFL. Luckman's stats, after all, include just 14,686 yards and 137 touchdowns. Cutler, who qualifies for no one's list of all-time great NFL quarterbacks, needed just seven years in a Bears uniform to eclipse both of those marks. The Bears fielded good teams and dressed a few capable quarterbacks in the interval. But neither the squad nor its QBs ever were good enough for long enough to knock Luckman off his perch.

At the same time, the fact that Luckman's numbers endured so long also reflects who and what Luckman was as a player and as a figure in NFL history. In short, Luckman was one of the athletes whose talent for throwing a football elevated the forward pass from desperation play to a critical element of the pro football playbook.

Though the pass had been part of American football since it was officially legalized in 1906, it didn't start to become a serious part of the pro game until 1933, when the NFL opened up the entire offensive backfield as the legal zone from which passes could be launched. (Prior to 1933, a passer had to be at least five yards behind the line of scrimmage to throw the ball.) That shift, among other things, made it possible to disguise passing plays, making the pass more difficult to defend.

You Can't Argue with Figures

	Tom Brady	Sid Luckman
Regular-Season Record	172–51	N/A*
Winning Percentage	.771	N/A*
Postseason Record	22–9	5–1
Winning Percentage	.710	.833
Overall Record	194–60	N/A*
Winning Percentage	.764	N/A*
Passer Rating	96.4	75.0
Touchdown Percentage	5.5	7.9
Interception Percentage	1.9	7.6
TD/INT	2.9/1	1/1
Completion Percentage	63.6	51.8
Yards Per Attempt	7.4	8.4
First-Team All-Pro	2	5
League MVP	2	N/A**
League Championship MVP	3	N/A**
League Championship Record	4–2	4–1

* Individual W-L records for quarterbacks were not recorded for seasons prior to 1950.

** Not awarded.

And with the ascent of Sammy Baugh in Washington and Luckman in Chicago at the end of the 1930s, the pass became a major weapon in the battle for NFL championships.

Luckman had been a standout passer while playing tailback at Columbia (in the single-wing offense that was predominant in football at the time, the tailback was the primary passer), completing 180 of 376 attempted passes for 2,413 yards and 20 touchdowns. He was second-runner-up for the 1938 Heisman Trophy.

Luckman's skill drew the attention of Bears coach George Halas, who had seen the future of football (he could hardly have missed it, considering that Baugh was already passing all over the field in Washington) and who was working with visionary University of Chicago coach Clark Shaughnessy to install a version of the T formation that would feature the quarterback, a blocking position in the single-wing, as the focal point of the offense and the emerging passing game.

Halas selected Luckman with the second overall pick in the 1939 draft, and one of the NFL's first great passing quarterbacks was born.

★ ★ ★

In his second year in Chicago, Luckman led the Bears to an 8–3 regular-season record and the most lopsided win in league history, a 73–0 drubbing of Baugh's Washington team in the NFL Championship Game. The 73 points scored in that game remain the most ever posted by one team in any NFL game.

Though the championship was a triumph for Halas and Shaughnessy's offensive system and a defining moment for the Monsters of the Midway, it didn't represent much of a milestone in the emergence of the forward pass. Luckman threw the ball only four times in the game, completing three of his passes for 88 yards, including a 30-yard touchdown strike to end Ken Kavanaugh.

Luckman finished the 1940 season with 48 completions on 105 attempts for 941 yards with four touchdowns and nine interceptions, which calculates to a passer rating of 54.5. Luckman led the Bears to a second-straight league title in 1941, throwing for 1,181 yards and nine touchdowns during a 10–1 regular season and went on to throw for 160 yards in a 37–9 win over the New York Giants in the title game.

The 1942 Bears were very nearly unstoppable. Like the 2007 Patriots, the Bears trampled all over their regular-season opponents. They won all 11 of their regular-season games, shutting out four opponents, holding four more to just a single touchdown, and winning by an average margin of 26.5 points. And like the Patriots 65 years later, the '42 Bears fell in their final game. With a stifling defensive effort, Washington thwarted Chicago's bid for an undefeated season, taking the championship 14–6.

But the Bears bounced back in 1943, largely thanks to Luckman, who turned in one of the all-time great seasons by an NFL passer. Completing 110 of 202 passes, he led the league in yardage (2,194), touchdowns (28, which was unheard of in that era), touchdown percentage (13.9), and yards per attempt (10.9). Luckman's passer rating for the 1943 campaign calculates to 107.5, which would be a great achievement even by modern standards and is absolutely stunning for an era in which sub-50 passer ratings were the standard.

In a Week 8 visit to the New York Giants that season, Luckman became the first passer in NFL history to throw for more than 400 yards in a game. He went 21-for-32 for 433 yards against the Giants. He also completed seven touchdown passes, which remains an NFL single-game record.

The 1943 Bears went 8–1–1, advanced to their fourth-straight championship game, and captured their third NFL title of the still-young decade behind Luckman's effort.

★ ★ ★

Luckman led the Bears to one more championship before his career was over, taking the title with a 24–14 win over the New York Giants that capped an 8–2–1 season in 1946.

In his career, Luckman completed 904 of 1,744 passes. He took the Bears to five NFL Championship Games and came away victorious in four. His 8.4 yards per attempt were an NFL record when he retired and remain second all-time behind Otto Graham's 8.6. And, of course, he held those Bears passing records for more than six decades, however ridiculous that might seem.

Ridiculous not simply because Luckman played at the exact dawn of the age of the NFL passer, but because the league has been tweaking the rules on an ongoing basis since 1978, specifically in order to produce better passing results.

It's impossible to say how a player like Luckman might have fared in the modern NFL, just as it's impossible to say how a player like Tom Brady would have performed in the 1940s. But it's interesting to consider that Luckman and Brady are similar in some important ways. Like Luckman, Brady is a player who trades on his mental abilities as much as his athleticism. He succeeds in part because he's able to execute a complex offense at a high level. That puts Brady a step ahead of the rest of the league, just as Luckman was in Halas' T formation.

Brady's passing stats, by and large, are better than Luckman's were, of course, but that's probably more a function of the evolution of the game than anything else. Still, it would be hard to argue that Luckman was a greater quarterback than Brady. Luckman played against defenses that were neither equipped nor prepared to stop great passers, a luxury Brady certainly has never enjoyed. And still Brady has achieved greater success than Luckman in most key statistical measures.

Luckman probably wasn't the greatest passer in the league, even in his day. That distinction belonged to Baugh. But he was a great champion. And 60-plus years later, it's Luckman's titles, not his team records, that ensure he remains one of the league's greatest players ever.

CHAPTER 6

★ ★ ★

Tom Brady vs. Sammy Baugh

You could call Sammy Baugh the greatest passer of his era, and you'd be right. But you'd also be doing Baugh a major disservice. Because the truth about Slingin' Sammy is that he was a whole lot more than the NFL's top passer over most of his 16-season career. He was also a great defensive back and a great punter too.

What's kind of funny is that Baugh didn't set out to play football at all. Through high school, Baugh had his sights set on professional baseball. He played both baseball and football at Texas Christian University. And after wrapping up his college career in 1937, he signed with both the NFL's Washington franchise and the National League's St. Louis Cardinals.

While Washington made Baugh their starting tailback (the passing position in the single-wing formation that dominated professional football at the time), the Cardinals shipped him off to the minors. And with an $8,000 contract in hand from Washington, a fair sum at the time, Baugh didn't have much difficulty committing to football as his full-time pursuit.

Baugh wasted no time flipping the professional football world on its head. Playing a traditionally run-first game in a solidly run-first league, Baugh passed for 1,127 yards and eight touchdowns in his rookie season. He led Washington to an 8–3 record and the franchise's first NFL championship.

And in the championship game against the Chicago Bears at Wrigley Field, Baugh single-handedly set the NFL on the course it would follow for at least the next 74 years. Baugh completed 18 of 33 passes for 335 yards and three touchdowns en route to a 28–21 victory. Baugh's scoring strikes of 55, 78, and 35 yards—all in the second half—sent the clear message that the NFL was going to become a passing league. The forward pass had previously been viewed as a sometimes-necessary evil. But with the emergence of players like Baugh—guys with big, accurate arms—the passing game was on its way to becoming the stuff champions were made of.

★ ★ ★

Washington got back to the NFL Championship Game in 1940, a season in which Baugh completed an uncanny-for-the-time 62.7 percent of his passes and led the league with 1,367 passing yards and 12 touchdowns. But the final game, in which Washington once again faced Chicago, ended in a 73–0 Bears victory. George Halas' Bears had elevated offense to the next level, operating out of the T formation and bringing presnap motion into the mix.

Baugh had an interesting season in 1943. Still lining up at tailback in the single-wing, he led the league in pass attempts and completions but trailed Chicago's Sid Luckman in total yardage and touchdowns. But while Baugh the passer was caught up in a friendly rivalry with Luckman, Baugh the three-way player was on fire. He led the league in both punting average (45.9 yards) and, as a defensive back, in interceptions (11).

As always, though, individual achievement only went so far in the NFL. The 1943 Bears, behind Luckman, won their third title in four years, and made it clear that the single-wing's day had passed. Washington switched to the T in 1944, and the move began paying major dividends for Baugh in 1945.

★ ★ ★ ★ ★ ★ ★

[Brady's] a hard guy to coach because he's so well prepared. He's seen all the tape, he's studied the film. You can't BS your way through a meeting with Tom Brady, not about football.

—Bill Belichick

You Can't Argue with Figures

	Tom Brady	Sammy Baugh
Regular-Season Record	172–51	N/A*
Winning Percentage	.771	N/A*
Postseason Record	22–9	3–3
Winning Percentage	.710	.500
Overall Record	194–60	N/A*
Winning Percentage	.764	N/A*
Passer Rating	96.4	72.2
Touchdown Percentage	5.5	6.2
Interception Percentage	1.9	6.8
TD/INT	2.9/1	.9/1
Completion Percentage	63.6	56.5
Yards Per Attempt	7.4	7.3
First-Team All-Pro	2	7
League MVP	2	N/A**
League Championship MVP	3	N/A**
League Championship Record	4–2	2–3

* Individual W-L records for quarterbacks were not recorded for seasons prior to 1950.

** Not awarded.

Baugh completed a league-best 128 passes in 182 attempts in '45, throwing 11 touchdowns and just four picks. His 70.3 percent completion rate for the season stood as an NFL record until 1982.

Still, the season wasn't perfect. Washington lost 15–14 to the Cleveland Rams in the league championship game. The deciding points in the game came on a safety that was awarded to the Rams after Baugh hit the goal post (which at the time was positioned on the goal line) while attempting to pass out of his own end zone in the first quarter.

That championship appearance was the last of Baugh's career. Though the quarterback managed a few more standout seasons—he threw for 2,938 yards and 25 touchdowns in 1947 and 2,599 yards and 22 touchdowns in 1948—Washington did not.

★ ★ ★

When Baugh retired at the end of the 1952 season, he walked away with numerous passing records. He led the league in completion percentage for seven seasons and led in pass attempts for four seasons (a mark only exceeded by Dan Marino's five). His five seasons with the league's lowest interception percentage remains a record. And his six seasons as the league's leader in passer rating (a standard that wouldn't be applied until two decades later) has him tied with Steve Young for best all-time. Baugh also remains, and always will, the only player in NFL history to lead the league in completions, punting average, and interceptions in a single season.

The very changes Baugh set in place during his amazing career ensured that he wouldn't remain the league's greatest passer forever. As the passing game continued to evolve, with rule changes designed to create more scoring and the evolution of ever-more-sophisticated schemes, it was inevitable that football would produce players such as Johnny Unitas, Joe Montana, Dan Marino, Peyton Manning, and Tom Brady.

One could spend time wondering what a passer of Baugh's caliber might have accomplished in an era in which every player is a specialist and offenses are structured around the pass. But eventually reality has to creep back in and supplant speculation. And the reality is that—as great as he was—Baugh has been outdone as a passer by Brady and numerous others. Brady has delivered more championships and posted better overall performances in the postseason. Barring outright disaster, Brady will finish his career with significantly better numbers than Baugh in key measurables, including passer rating, completion percentage, yards per attempt, and touchdown-to-interception ratio (an area in which Baugh was very much a product of his age, throwing more picks that TDs).

While many have outpaced Baugh's passing statistics, no one ever has been a more complete football player. And every player who has lined up under center over the last 79 NFL seasons has owed a major part of who he is and what he's accomplished to the groundbreaking play of Slingin' Sammy.

CHAPTER 7

★ ★ ★

The Hangover: 2002

It could have been worse. That's maybe the most honest thing you can say about the Patriots' 2002 season.

The Pats were a team coming off a long 19-game run to Super Bowl XXXVI. They were the defending champions. And they had earned every win in the 2001 campaign, from the time Tom Brady got his first start on September 30 to their final triumph over the heavily favored St. Louis Rams on February 3.

But as the team initiated its title defense seven months after that surprising victory, it would have been hard to argue that the 2001 Patriots hadn't overachieved. The Pats had finished the 2000 season with the sixth-worst record in football. A year later, they not only climbed to the top of the pro football pile, they did it with an untested backup playing the game's most important position.

The Pats were prime candidates for a Super Bowl hangover of massive proportions. They certainly wouldn't have been the first team to collapse outright after winning an NFL championship. Or the last. Sure, the Super Bowl hangover is more common among teams that *lose* on the big stage. But there's also a history of winners falling apart that stretches all the way back to the Super Bowl IV champion Kansas City Chiefs, who labored to a 7–5–2 finish in 1970. And the championship team that immediately followed the Pats, the Tampa Bay Buccaneers, went 7–9 in the season following their victory in Super Bowl XXXVII.

Neither is it uncommon for champions to suffer exactly the kind of season the Patriots had in 2002: one characterized by uneven play and squandered potential. A season of maddening stops and starts, of false hopes and ultimate disappointment. The Pittsburgh Steelers, to name just one example, have done it twice in a decade, hovering around .500 and missing the playoffs after each of their recent championship seasons.

Still, the commonality of the experience is little comfort. Misery may love company, but frustration only finds it annoying. And the 2002 Patriots were nothing if not frustrating.

That's not to say that the season stunk outright. The team finished tied for the best record in the AFC East, after all. And there were plenty of high highs en route. Such as the season-opening Monday night game in which the team officially opened the doors to their new home, Gillette Stadium. Not only did the evening give Patriots Nation a chance to celebrate its champions, it also allowed the Pats to demonstrate that their AFC Championship Game win over the Pittsburgh Steelers the previous season had been anything but a fluke.

The Pats and their Super Bowl MVP quarterback got down to business as soon as the pregame festivities concluded. The New England defense intercepted Pittsburgh quarterback Kordell Stewart on each of the Steelers' first two drives. And Brady made Pittsburgh pay for the second of those picks, completing a four-yard touchdown pass to tight end Christian Fauria to give the Pats a 7–0 lead four minutes into the game. Though the Steelers countered quickly with a touchdown of their own and neither offense accomplished much through the remainder of the first half, the Pats still took a 10–7 lead into halftime.

After the break, it was all New England. Though he took an 11-yard sack on the opening play of the third quarter, Brady proceeded to drive the Patriots 85 yards in three plays all through the air to put the Pats ahead 17–7. The drive turned on two long pass plays: a spectacular 37-yard connection with David Patten on the right sideline on third-and-13 that moved New England into Pittsburgh territory and a 40-yard touchdown strike to Donald Hayes.

The Steelers had the ball for all of two plays before safety Victor Green took it away from running back Jerome Bettis following a 13-yard pickup. And Brady capitalized, completing a 49-yard drive with a 22-yard touchdown pass to rookie wide receiver Deion Branch.

The Pats added a pair of Adam Vinatieri field goals and came away with a decisive 30–14 victory.

Brady, during one stretch, threw the ball on 25 consecutive plays. He came out of the game with 29 completions on 43 attempts (67.4 percent) for 294 yards, with three touchdowns and no interceptions, earning a passer rating of 110.0. He was named AFC Offensive Player of the Week as a result of the effort.

No one could doubt the team's authenticity. And no one could doubt that the Pats had made the right decision in trading their former franchise quarterback, Drew Bledsoe, to the Buffalo Bills.

★ ★ ★

Brady improved his completion percentage in each of the next two games.

In a 44–7 rout of the New York Jets in East Rutherford, he connected on 71.4 percent of his passes, throwing for 269 yards and a pair of touchdowns.

And in a nail-biter of an overtime home win over the Kansas City Chiefs, the best offensive team in the league, Brady completed 39 of 54 (72.2 percent), racking up 410 yards and throwing four touchdowns and just a single interception.

After the Patriots fell behind 17–9 early in the third quarter, Brady led a pair of touchdown drives, scoring on throws of nine yards to Troy Brown and 18 yards to Daniel Graham. Then, early in the fourth, he hit Patten for a 38-yard touchdown that extended the Patriots' lead to 31–17.

The Chiefs were able to charge back and tie the score at 38 on the very last play of regulation. But Brady and Vinatieri combined to ensure that Kansas City didn't get an opportunity to win in OT. On the opening drive of the extra period, Brady moved the Pats from their 30-yard line to the Chiefs 17. And Vinatieri nailed a 35-yard field goal to seal the team's 12th consecutive win. The game was the first in Brady's career in which he threw for more than 400 yards. And Brady finished the afternoon with a passer rating of 110.9.

After that, though, things got tough. The offense wouldn't click. The defense couldn't compensate. And the Pats dropped four straight. Over the course of the first three of those losses—in road games against San Diego and Miami and a home game against Green Bay—Brady threw seven interceptions, half his total for the season, and just five touchdowns.

But Brady and the team regained their swagger in a Week 9 trip to Buffalo. Facing Bledsoe's Bills for the first time, the Patriots dominated. The defense held Buffalo to just seven points. And Brady completed 22 of 26 pass attempts (a season-best 84.6 percent) for 265 yards and three touchdowns. He averaged 10.2 yards per attempt and earned a passer rating of 147.6, his best of the season.

In Chicago a week later, Brady had to dig deep in order to excavate his team from a massive hole. With more than half of the third quarter gone and New England trailing 27–6, Brady went seven-for-seven on an eight-play, 75-yard touchdown drive, which he finished with a 15-yard pass to tailback Kevin Faulk. Even then, the Patriots continued to struggle to finish drives. And following a Chicago field goal with 5:22 remaining in the fourth quarter, the Pats were down 30–19.

Following a nice kickoff return by Branch, Brady and the offense took over at the New England 37. Four completions and 2:20 of game time later, Brady connected with Faulk, who raced down the left sideline to score from 36 yards away. A failed two-point conversion, however, left the Patriots five points behind the Bears with next to no time remaining.

But the defense did its bit, and Brady got the ball back at the New England 44-yard line with 1:50 left to play. Brady hit David Patten for 19 yards on first down, then found Faulk for another seven. He appeared to be intercepted on a third-and-three at the Chicago 30, but defensive tackle Bryan Robinson was unable to hold on to the ball. On a desperation fourth-and-three, Brady picked up the first down with his legs. Two plays later, Brady eluded what appeared to be a certain sack just long enough to get the ball to Faulk seven yards downfield. And on third-and-three from the Chicago 20, with just 28 seconds on the clock, Brady once again eluded an oncoming pass rush and delivered the ball to Patten at the back of the end zone for the go-ahead touchdown.

When the game was over, the Pats had pulled off a thrilling 33–30 comeback victory, and Brady had completed 36 of 55 pass attempts for 328 yards and three touchdowns. Of the 55, 39 of his throws came in the second half.

The wins over Buffalo and Chicago hadn't cured the Patriots' problems, however. A third-straight road game and a date with the revenge-minded Oakland Raiders in Week 11 dropped the Pats to 5–5. And though they seemed to recover over the ensuing three weeks—winning handily in games against

Minnesota, Detroit, and Buffalo—the Pats ran into a tough, physical team on a Week 15 visit to Tennessee. Not only did the Titans batter the Patriots, winning 24–7, but a hit from defensive end Jevon Kearse in the second quarter resulted in Brady suffering a first-degree separation of his throwing shoulder.

The injury took its toll in Week 16. The 8–6 Patriots hosted the 7–7 Jets with a chance to take a big step toward capturing a second-straight AFC East title. But Brady was unable to make anything work. He completed just 19 of 37 pass attempts for 133 yards (a dismal average of 3.6 yards per attempt). And the Pats fell into a second-place tie with New York, a game behind the 9–6 Dolphins in the division race.

2002

By the Numbers

Total Yards	3,764
Yards Per Game	235.3
Attempts	601
Completions	373
Completion Percentage	62.1
Yards Per Attempt	6.3
Touchdowns	28
Interceptions	14
Passer Rating	85.7
Games Rated Higher Than 100	6
Best Single-Game Rating	147.6

★ ★ ★

Still, the Pats would not go gentle into that good off-season. With the Dolphins visiting Foxborough to close the season, the Patriots had one more chance to rage. And so they did.

After falling behind 21–7 with a minute to play in the first half, New England battled back. They moved into field-goal range just before halftime and went into the break trailing 21–10. They added another three points in the third quarter but still found themselves behind 24–13 with five minutes to play in the fourth.

Despite having aggravated his shoulder injury, Brady accounted for all 68 of the Patriots' yards during a two-minute touchdown drive that brought the team to within three points. He connected on six of 10 pass attempts for 67 yards and picked up a first down on a one-yard quarterback sneak at the New England 42-yard line. Brady capped the drive with a three-yard scoring pass to Brown, then found Christian Fauria on a two-point conversion. The defense held Miami to a three-and-out on the ensuing possession. The Pats got great field position after a short punt, and Vinatieri hit a 43-yard field goal to send the game to overtime.

An Olindo Mare kickoff that went out of bounds gave the Patriots excellent field position to start OT. And once again, Brady and Vinatieri conspired to prevent the opposition from ever touching the ball. Brady moved the Pats from their own 40 to the Miami 17, gaining a big chunk with a 20-yard completion to Faulk. And Vinatieri put the winning points on the board from 35 yards away.

The win, in which Brady went 25-of-44 for 221 yards and a touchdown, moved the Patriots into a first-place tie with the Dolphins at 9–7.

A Jets loss to the 12–3 Green Bay Packers later in the day would have put both the Pats and the Dolphins in the playoffs. But the Packers were locked in as the NFC three-seed and were resting starters in preparation for the playoffs. With the gift-wrapped victory, New York also improved its final record to 9–7. And as a result of tiebreakers, the Jets got the division title and the Patriots and Dolphins got tee times.

Brady spent the next several months rehabbing his shoulder. In the end, the injury would require surgery, but not until after the Patriots had won two more Super Bowls. The shoulder would also become a part of Patriots lore, as the team's weekly injury report has listed Brady as "probable: right shoulder" for the bulk of his career.

The 2002 season likewise has maintained its position in Patriots history. Even 13 years later, it remained the only season in which the Patriots with Brady at quarterback failed to reach the postseason.

It was a tough season. For the team and its fans, it's a bad memory. But the reality remains, things could have been a good bit worse.

CHAPTER 8

★ ★ ★

Tom Brady vs. Otto Graham

The Detroit Lions of the mid-1940s were a sorrowfully bad football team. Almost preposterously bad, in fact. They were the kind of bad that makes the Lions of the early 2000s look like a gift from the football gods. Between 1946 and 1949, the Lions won 10 games and lost 37. Their defense gave up an average of nearly 28 points per game. Their offense and defense alike annually ranked worst in the league or very near it. Awful.

It's worth keeping that fact in mind. Because if Otto Graham had elected to play in the NFL after he wrapped up his two-year wartime stint in the coast guard, he'd have wound up with the Lions. Detroit selected Graham, who had been a star of both the football and basketball teams at Northwestern University, with the fourth overall pick in the 1944 draft. And while it's conceivable that Graham would have made the Lions better, it was no less true then than it is now that an awful football team is rarely just a player away from being great.

But when Graham returned, he didn't opt for the NFL in 1946. He was persuaded by Paul Brown to sign with the Cleveland Browns of the upstart All-America Football Conference—at a cost to the new team of $7,500 a year for two years, plus a $1,000 bonus.

The decision worked out OK. Graham spent his entire career, 10 seasons in all, as the Browns' quarterback. And he played in a championship game in every one of his AAFC seasons. Every single one. That's four AAFC championships. And the Browns won them all. And when the new league collapsed and the Browns (along with the San Francisco 49ers and the original Baltimore Colts) were absorbed by the NFL, the Browns simply picked up where they left off. Though the perception had been that AAFC teams didn't have the talent to compete with the established squads of the older league, the Browns won it all in 1950, their first season in the NFL. And then they went on to play in the next five NFL Championship Games, winning two more.

In 1950 the Browns went 10–2 in the regular season. And although Graham, who had been the best passer in the AAFC, did not lead the NFL in any statistical

You Can't Argue with Figures

	Tom Brady	Otto Graham
Regular-Season Record	172–51	57–13–1*
Winning Percentage	.771	.810*
Postseason Record	22–9	4–3**
Winning Percentage	.710	.571*
Overall Record	194–60	61–16–1*
Winning Percentage	.764	.788*
Passer Rating	96.4	78.2*
Touchdown Percentage	5.5	5.6*
Interception Percentage	1.9	6.0*
TD/INT	2.9/1	.9/1*
Completion Percentage	63.6	55.7*
Yards Per Attempt	7.4	8.6*
First-Team All-Pro	2	9 (5 times in NFL)
League MVP	2	3*
League Championship MVP	3	N/A***
League Championship Record	4–2	3–3*

*NFL only

**NFL only; 6–0 AAFC

***Not awarded

★　★　★　★　★　★　★

Tom is truly one of the greatest competitors we've seen in football. The more people say he can't, the more he will. If he puts it in his mind that he's going to do something, he goes out there and does it.

—Trent Dilfer

categories, he proved the decisive factor in the Browns' 30–28 victory over the Los Angeles Rams in the championship game. Graham completed 22 of 33 passes for 298 yards and four touchdowns, throwing just a single interception (for a passer rating of 122.2). And in the final two minutes of regulation, he moved the Browns from their own 32-yard line into position for a game-winning field goal.

★　★　★

Though the Browns lost in each of their next three trips to the NFL Championship Game, Graham's passing numbers improved. He led the league in passing yards, touchdowns, completions, and attempts in 1952. And in 1953 he not only led in yards, but began a three-year run in which he led in completion percentage.

Oddly enough, it was the resurgent Detroit Lions who denied Graham's Browns the 1952 and 1953 championships, winning 17–7 and 17–16 in a pair of games in which Graham struggled. But Graham turned it around in the 1954 championship, throwing for three touchdowns and rushing for another three in a 56–10 blowout victory over Detroit.

At Brown's request, Graham put his retirement plans on hold to lead the team through one final campaign in 1955. And he went out in style, posting a league-leading touchdown percentage of 8.1, the best of his NFL career, and earning a passer rating of 94.0 while leading the Browns to a 9–2–1 regular-season record.

In his final game, another championship meeting with the Rams, Graham threw for 209 yards and two touchdowns and rushed for another pair of scores, lifting the Browns to a 38–14 victory.

Like John Elway 43 years later, Graham went out at the top of his game and on the heels of back-to-back championships. Unlike anyone since, Graham left the game having appeared in six consecutive NFL Championship Games. It's an accomplishment that, let's face it, no one is ever going to match.

During his six NFL seasons, Graham amassed 13,499 passing yards and threw 88 touchdowns. Add in his AAFC numbers, and he gets to 23,584 yards and 174 touchdowns (Graham threw for 25 touchdowns in two of his four AAFC seasons). And his 8.6 yards per attempt remains, after 57 years, the best of all time. (And if you factor in his AAFC stats, Graham gets to an even more impressive 9.0.)

Paul Brown was the engineer of the Cleveland Browns, but Otto Graham was the motor that drove the team.

Graham's accomplishments as a passer seem less impressive in the age of the quarterback. His passing statistics don't measure up to those of a modern player like Tom Brady, may finish his career with triple Graham's 174 career passing TDs and 23,584 career passing yards. Brady and his contemporaries also make Graham's 78.2 career passer rating, amazing for Graham's era, look pedestrian.

But even now, Graham's record as a competitor stands apart from every other player who has ever lined up behind center. Graham's not the greatest of all time. He probably never was. But he wasn't so far-separated from Sammy Baugh in his time. And he's not that far behind Bart Starr, Joe Montana, and Brady even now.

CHAPTER 9

★ ★ ★

Lows and Highs: 2003

The season didn't start well—not for the team and not for the quarterback. To some—or, at the very least, to ESPN's Tom Jackson—it had the look of a season that wouldn't end well either.

The Patriots had lost their season opener. Or, no, that's not quite it. The Patriots had been beaten up and down the field in their season opener. They'd traveled all the way to Orchard Park just to be embarrassed 31–0 by the Buffalo Bills.

Nothing about the game had been even remotely encouraging. But Tom Brady's performance had been just about the worst of it. Brady threw four interceptions. He was sacked twice, losing a total of 20 yards. He connected on just 14 of 28 passes for 123 yards en route to a career-low passer rating of 22.5. He spent the last four minutes of the game on the sideline as backup quarterback Rohan Davey took his turn throwing incompletions.

The Patriots defense did what it could, limiting former New England quarterback Drew Bledsoe to 17 completions for 230 yards and just a single touchdown and forcing a pair of turnovers. But it wasn't nearly enough. Between running back Travis Henry's two touchdowns and defensive tackle Sam Adams' pick six, Buffalo found more than enough ways to tighten the screws.

Making matters worse, the Bills got great production from their newest defensive player, strong safety Lawyer Milloy. The same Lawyer Milloy who'd been released by the Patriots five days earlier after seven seasons in New England. The same Milloy who was one of Brady's closest friends on the team.

Well loved by his teammates, Milloy had been the victim of the Pats' hard-nosed approach to the business of football (some would say of coach Bill Belichick's ruthlessness, and it's possible those things are one and the same). When the team and the player couldn't settle a contract dispute—which is to say, when the player balked at the size of the pay cut the team wanted him to take—the organization made the decision that the two should go their separate ways.

The decision wasn't popular in the Patriots locker room in the week leading up to opening day. "Has it ever been this quiet in here?" linebacker Tedy Bruschi posed while speaking to the media the day after the move was announced. "I don't think it has. I think 'shocked' is the word. You sort of just shake your head and ask yourself, *Why?*"

According to Tom Jackson, the move got even less popular with Patriots players following the embarrassment in Buffalo.

"I want to say this very clearly: they hate their coach," Jackson offered during the Week 2 installment of ESPN's *NFL Sunday Countdown*. "And their season could be over, depending on how quickly they can get over this emotional devastation they suffered because of Lawyer Milloy."

Jackson may have had some insight into the mood in the New England locker room. Or he may have just been talking because it's what he's paid to do. Either way, his dire assessment of the Patriots' season didn't quite play out on the field that Sunday.

Milloy's former unit, in particular, turned in a great day as the Patriots faced the Eagles in Philadelphia. The *D* sacked Eagles quarterback Donovan McNabb eight times, costing Philly 43 yards and forcing a pair of fumbles. They took another fumble away from running back Duce Staley. And they intercepted McNabb twice, including an 18-yard pick six by Bruschi late in the game.

Brady's performance wasn't the stuff legends are made of, but it was exactly as good as the team needed it to be. Brady completed 30 of 44 passes for 255 yards and three touchdowns, had no interceptions, and earned a passer rating of 105.8. Most important, Brady took advantage of the opportunities presented to him—from Philadelphia's turnovers and as a result of solid special teams play by the Patriots.

Brady has the eye of the tiger in Super Bowl XXXVIII against the Carolina Panthers.

In the second quarter, Brady led a 35-yard touchdown drive following a McNabb fumble and turned a muffed punt by Brian Westbrook into a two-play 14-yard touchdown drive. In the third quarter, after Troy Brown returned a punt to the New England 48-yard line, Brady moved the Pats the remaining 52 yards to the Eagles end zone in four plays, going through the air all the way.

In the Patriots' Week 3 home opener, Brady once again collaborated with the defense to secure a win. The quarterback scored on a one-yard run, and cornerback Asante Samuel added a 55-yard pick six as the Patriots defeated the New York Jets 23–16.

But an uneven Week 4 performance by Brady in Washington (25 of 38 for 289 yards with two touchdowns and three interceptions) combined with a mounting list of Patriots injuries to produce a 20–17 loss, dropping New England's record to 2–2.

Things weren't as bad as Jackson had made them out to be, but they weren't good. Not yet, anyhow.

★ ★ ★

Things started to get good in Week 5.

The Patriots returned to Foxborough to face a bruising Tennessee Titans team that had trounced them in their previous meeting late in the frustrating 2002 campaign. The teams battled throughout the afternoon in a game that included seven lead changes and finally broke open on an unforgettable 65-yard pick six by injured Patriots cornerback Ty Law.

While the victory would prove to be meaningful for the Patriots—both as the event that turned the 2003 season around and the starting point for a historic 21-game winning streak—the game was mostly average for Brady.

He put New England's first points of the game on the board with a gorgeous 58-yard touchdown pass to Brown late in the first quarter. Stepping back slightly as the Titans' defensive front pushed New England's offensive linemen toward him, Brady just managed to unload and hit Brown in stride at the Tennessee 10-yard line. The receiver did the rest.

Beyond that, though, Brady's main accomplishment was to get through a difficult game without making the same kind of key mistakes as Titans QB Steve McNair. Brady finished the afternoon 17 for 31 for 219 yards and just the single touchdown. Though he threw no picks, Brady came away with a passer rating of just 88.0.

In the three weeks that followed, Brady played well enough to win but did little to turn heads—except during overtime in Miami, when he and Brown teamed up for the game-winning strike. The play came on New England's first play following corner-back Tyrone Poole's interception of Dolphins QB Jay Fiedler at the Patriots 18-yard line. Brady took the snap from under center; pump-faked to freeze the Miami secondary momentarily, giving Brown a chance to get behind safeties Brock Marion and Sammy Knight; and heaved a pass down the sideline. Brown grabbed the ball in stride at the Dolphins 35 and accelerated beyond the reach of the defensive backs and into the end zone.

By the Numbers   **2003**

Total Yards	3,620
Yards Per Game	226.3
Attempts	527
Completions	317
Completion Percentage	60.2
Yards Per Attempt	6.9
Touchdowns	23
Interceptions	12
Passer Rating	85.9
Games Rated Higher Than 100 *(Includes One Postseason)*	7
Best Single-Game Rating	122.9

It was a pretty play that sealed yet another hard-fought win. It lifted the Pats to a 5–2 record and moved them into first place in the AFC East. There was nothing to apologize for in any of that. But it would still be another two weeks before Brady would have his first truly great moment of the season.

★ ★ ★

The Patriots offense disappointed fans in Foxborough in Week 8, struggling all day to finish drives, or even to convert third downs, against the Cleveland Browns. But the defense stepped up, and the Patriots scratched out a 9–3 win.

Eight days later, the Pats faced the Broncos in a Monday night game in Denver. The Patriots were riding a four-game winning streak, but they knew they were going to have to find a way to put up more points if they wanted to keep winning.

Brady didn't have a great game. But a great game from any Patriots player in Denver, where the Pats had struggled since the earliest days of the AFL, would probably have been too much to ask.

Through much of the game, Brady was uneven but just good enough. By five minutes into the first quarter, he had lost a fumble and thrown an interception. And through the game, he completed just 20 of 35 passes. But the passes on which he connected were both long and effective. He made up for his missteps early in the first quarter by throwing a 66-yard touchdown pass to Deion Branch later in the period. He finished the night with 350 yards, three touchdowns, and a 108.0 passer rating.

The bigger deal, though, was that Brady exhibited his trademark cool head under enormous pressure when it mattered most. Late in the game, with the Patriots trailing 24–23, Belichick opted to take an intentional safety rather than having his team punt out of their own end zone and give the Broncos great field position. The decision proved wise. Though they surrendered two points, the space the Pats gained was well worth the price. New England was able to stop Denver's return of the free kick at the Broncos 15-yard line. Then the defense held firm, forcing a three-and-out.

With the Patriots trailing 26–23, Brady and the offense got the ball at the New England 42-yard line with just 2:15 remaining. And Brady quickly moved the team down the field, hitting running back Kevin Faulk on passes of 5, 19, and 16 yards. Then, from 18 yards out and with 36 seconds left on the clock, he found David Givens at the goal line to put the winning points on the board.

★ ★ ★ ★ ★ ★ ★

One thing that's remarkable about Tom Brady is the way he developed his game from a position as a game-managing, "he just wins" quarterback to one as a statistically dominant quarterback. Based on Football Outsiders' play-by-play breakdown, Brady was the most valuable quarterback in the league in 2007, 2009, and 2010. He also finished in the top five in 2004–2006 as well as 2011. The argument about Brady's wins vs. Peyton Manning's stats ended up moot because, by the end, they both had rings and they both had spectacular numbers. By FO numbers, seven of the 10 most valuable QB seasons of the past 20 years belong to either Brady (4) or Manning (3).

—Aaron Schatz, Football Outsiders

Brady hadn't been perfect, but he'd been perfectly clutch. The effort earned him his first AFC Offensive Player of the Week nod since the 2002 season opener. And the win sent the Pats into their bye week with a 7–2 record and a growing lead in the division title race.

★ ★ ★

The Pats would look to an imperfect Brady to make things right yet again in Week 12, when they traveled to face the Houston Texans. Though he completed 29 of 47 passes for 368 yards and a pair of touchdowns (in a game that lasted almost a full extra period), Brady also threw two interceptions and lost a fumble.

The first interception, thrown midway through the second quarter, proved fairly harmless. Rookie receiver Bethel Johnson was able to strip the ball from safety Eric Brown during the return. And Johnson went on to recover the fumble, which gave the Pats another chance at the Houston 7. Still, the play contributed to a stall in the red zone, and the Patriots had to settle for three points.

The second pick, which came late in the third quarter, was more costly. Snagged by cornerback Marcus Coleman at the Patriots 40-yard line and returned to the 11, it set up a relatively easy two-play touchdown drive and allowed the Texans to pull into a 10–10 tie.

A strip sack at the Houston 36 and a fumble return to the New England 31 six minutes into the fourth quarter allowed the Texans to go ahead 17–13. Then another Patriots error, a blocked punt that was recovered by the Texans at the Patriots' 20, set up a field goal that put Houston ahead 20–13 with just 3:15 remaining in the game.

It appeared the Pats were headed for their first loss since Week 4. But Brady had the opportunity to turn things around once again. And he did. In a drive that started at the New England 20, Brady connected with Deion Branch for 13 yards, tight end Daniel Graham for 33, and Faulk for 21. On fourth-and-one from the Houston 4-yard line, Brady play-faked left, rolled out on a bootleg right, and just managed to get a pass off to Graham, who made a great effort to get into the end zone. The score moved the Pats into a 20–20 tie with 40 seconds remaining in regulation.

Things didn't go smoothly in overtime. The Pats started out strong as linebacker Mike Vrabel intercepted Texans quarterback Tony Banks on the first play of the extra period. But they squandered the opportunity when the normally spot-on Adam Vinatieri, who had doinked a 38-yard field-goal attempt off the right upright at the end of the first half, had a 37-yard try blocked.

The teams punted back and forth, though the Texans appeared to be winning the field-position battle. Finally, with just four minutes remaining in the period, the Patriots got the ball at their own 24-yard line. Brady moved the offense down the field, completing passes of 16, 14, and 13 yards along the way. He appeared to have thrown the game toward an inevitable tie when Texans safety Marlon McCree picked him off at the Houston 5-yard line, but the interception was negated by a holding call on cornerback Marcus Coleman.

Then Vinatieri got his chance to make his earlier errors right, finishing the game with a 28-yard field goal just 41 seconds before overtime was set to expire.

The Patriots advanced to 9–2 for the first time in franchise history. They wouldn't trail an opponent again until midway through the fourth quarter of Super Bowl XXXVIII.

★ ★ ★

That doesn't mean the path to the championship was smooth. In the Patriots' Week 13 showdown with Peyton Manning's Colts in Indianapolis, it took the greatest defensive stand in franchise history—the *D* stopped the Colts on four-straight plays from the New England 1-yard line in the closing seconds of the match—to preserve a 38–34 win.

Brady, though he threw a pair of fourth-quarter interceptions that allowed the Colts to climb back into the game after trailing 31–10, also played a pivotal role in putting New England's 38 points on the board. Brady completed 26 of 35 passes (74.3 percent) for 236 yards and two touchdowns, including a 31-yard strike to fill-in wide receiver Dedric Ward.

Another outstanding defensive effort in snow-blanketed Foxborough a week later accounted for nine of the Patriots' points in a 12–0 win over the visiting Dolphins.

As the season moved toward its end, Brady's performance kept improving. He threw for two touchdowns each in wins over the Jacksonville Jaguars and the Jets, earning passer ratings of 103.6 and 101.7, respectively. Then in Week 17, Brady lofted four touchdown passes, all in the first half, as the Patriots closed their season with a game that was the exact reverse of the opener, a 31–0 rout of the visiting Bills. Brady completed 21 of 32 passes in that game, threw no picks, and posted his best passer rating of the season, 122.9.

At 14–2, the Patriots headed into the playoffs as the AFC's top-seeded team. They had put their difficult 2002 season and the rough start to their 2003 campaign behind them. But there remained a lot of hard work to do.

★ ★ ★

Tough opposition and brutal weather conditions made the Patriots' first postseason game uncomfortable, to say the least.

The Pats caught the Titans, who were a wild-card team but only by virtue of a tiebreaker in the AFC South. Tennessee and Indianapolis both finished the season 12–4. The teams' quarterbacks, McNair and Manning, were named co-MVPs of the league (each got 16 of a potential 50 votes; Brady came in third in the balloting with eight votes). The Colts had swept the Titans in the regular season to earn the division title, but that wasn't terribly important from the Patriots' perspective. The Pats knew Tennessee was as good a team as they were likely to face in January.

Both teams caught some of the most inhospitable game-time temperatures in NFL history. It was bitterly cold in Foxborough during the day on January 10. When the sun went down (which was well before the 8:00 PM kickoff), it got downright ridiculous. At the start of the game, the temperature measured just 4 degrees. With the wind chill, it was minus-10.

And in the frigid nighttime air, both defenses stiffened. The offenses, which had combined for 31 fourth-quarter points in their 38–30 battle back in the first weekend of October, managed just 31 points through the entire game.

The Patriots started with a bang. After the *D* held the Titans to a three-and-out on the game's opening possession, the offense mounted a quick, efficient drive that featured two running plays, netting all of five yards, and four passes, three of which Brady completed. Brady's first pass of the night was a 19-yard strike to Faulk that moved the Pats into Titans territory. On the last, which came after less than three minutes of game time, Brady took the snap out of the shotgun at the Tennessee 45-yard line, dropped back to the 48, and fired down the middle of the field to Johnson, who had a pair of Titans defensive backs beat. The pass connected at the 5, and Johnson cruised into the end zone to put New England ahead 7–0.

Though the Titans tied the score twice during the game, they weren't able to make good on an attempt in the final minutes to send the game into overtime. Brady's numbers for the night, 21-for-41 for 201 yards and a touchdown, weren't spectacular, but they were all the Pats needed them to be. They were better than McNair's. And the Pats advanced to face the other NFL co-MVP in the AFC Championship Game.

Manning proved easier for the Pats to handle than McNair had been. The New England defense's complicated looks and aggressive play had the media darling Indianapolis quarterback confused and frustrated from jump street. The Pats intercepted Manning four times and limited the Indy offense—a unit that had scored 28 points per game in the regular season and put up 41 and 38 against Denver and Kansas City in the playoffs—to just a pair of touchdowns. Patriots running back Antowain Smith helped keep Manning off the field with a clock-devouring 100-yard effort. And Brady and Vinatieri did the rest.

Brady completed 22 of 37 passes for 237 yards and a touchdown. Vinatieri added five field goals. And the Patriots earned the franchise's fourth Lamar Hunt Trophy with a 24–14 victory.

★ ★ ★

The Patriots didn't go into Super Bowl XXXVIII the way they'd gone into Super Bowl XXXVI two years earlier. This time around, no one doubted New England's ability to win the championship.

The Pats were riding a 14-game winning streak. They had the best defense in the NFL and an offense that, while not perfect, was cruelly efficient. The Pats went into the game as seven-point favorites, not because their opponents were weak—the Carolina Panthers had arguably the best pass rush in the league and had limited their NFC postseason opponents to an average of 12 points a game—but because New England had shown an uncanny ability to win no matter what form a game took. From defensive battles to old-fashioned shootouts, the Patriots had solved every puzzle put in front of them from the end of September forward.

They got a little of everything in the Super Bowl.

For most of the first half, the game was dominated by defense. The Patriots offense at times found ways to move the ball, but it amounted to nothing, as drives either sputtered out or ended in frustration. Vinatieri pushed a 31-yard field-goal attempt wide right early in the first quarter and had a 36-yard try blocked nine minutes into the second.

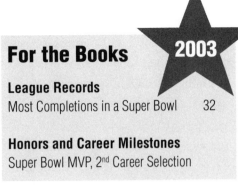

For the Books

2003

League Records
Most Completions in a Super Bowl   32

Honors and Career Milestones
Super Bowl MVP, 2nd Career Selection

Then the scoring opened up. When a strip sack of Panthers quarterback Jake Delhomme gave the Patriots possession at the Carolina 20-yard line, Brady capitalized. He capped a short drive with a five-yard touchdown pass to Branch that put the Patriots on top 7–0 with 3:10 remaining until halftime.

And after the Panthers responded with a scoring drive of their own, leaving 1:07 on the first-half clock, Brady took charge and moved the New England offense from their own 22-yard line to the Carolina end zone in six plays, using just 49 seconds of game time. The drive turned on a 52-yard pass play in which Brady stepped up into the pocket and fired straight down the middle of the field from the Patriots' 34 to hit Branch in stride at the Carolina 24. Branch picked up an additional 10 yards before he was tackled. Three plays later, Brady connected on yet another five-yard touchdown strike, this one to Givens. Even then, the scoring wasn't finished. The Panthers moved into position to allow John Kasay to hit a 50-yard field goal on the final play of the half.

In the third quarter, the game reverted to scorelessness. But the period ended with the Patriots deep in Panthers territory, thanks in large part to a 33-yard pass from Brady to Graham. Then, seven seconds into the fourth quarter, Antowain Smith scored on a two-yard run.

Once again, though, the Panthers countered, moving 81 yards in six plays and scoring on a 33-yard run by DeShaun Foster. A failed two-point try cost Carolina the chance to pull within a field goal of tying the score. But the Panthers capitalized on Brady's lone mistake of the game, an interception near the Carolina end zone, with a tremendous 85-yard pass play from Delhomme to wide receiver

Muhsin Muhammad. And though they once again failed to convert a two-point try, the Panthers took a 22–21 lead.

Brady was having none of it. He moved the offense methodically from the Patriots 32 to the Carolina goal line, connecting with Givens on pass plays of 25 and 18 yards on the way. Then on second-and-goal from the 1, Brady delivered the ball to Vrabel, who had checked in at tight end. The Patriots converted their two-point try and took a 29–22 lead.

The game wasn't over, though. Delhomme found a will of his own and directed a seven-play, 80-yard drive that tied the score with just 1:08 to play.

Once again, it appeared the Patriots would be part of the first Super Bowl ever to be decided in overtime. But once again, Brady had no interest in risking the fate of New England's season on the chance of a coin toss.

The Patriots caught a huge break when Kasay's kickoff sailed out of bounds, allowing the Pats to start at their own 40-yard line.

Brady took it from there, completing a pair of 13-yard passes to Brown (the second of which went mostly toward regaining 10 yards that had been lost on a holding call), a four-yarder to Graham, and finally a 17-yard strike to Branch on the right sideline at the Carolina 23. With just nine seconds left on the clock, the Pats sent in Vinatieri, who once again put the winning points on the board with a clutch kick in the closing seconds of a Super Bowl.

Where Super Bowl XXXVI had been a shocker, Super Bowl XXXVIII was a thriller. What they had in common was a championship team and an MVP—Brady—who completed a Super Bowl–record 32 passes on 48 attempts, amassing 354 total passing yards and throwing three touchdowns for a passer rating of 100.5.

The "dynasty" talk that started in the hours following New England's second championship was still a bit premature. But that wouldn't be the case for terribly long.

CHAPTER 10

★ ★ ★

Tom Brady vs. Johnny Unitas

Johnny Unitas is the reason you love football. It's a fact.

You might not know it. If you're 12, and the only Colts quarterbacks you've ever heard of are Peyton Manning and Andrew Luck, you might think it's a strange thing to say. If you're 65 and a lifelong New York Giants fan, you might consider the suggestion downright asinine. But it's true, just the same. Because Johnny U is the reason *everyone* loves football. He's the reason the NFL is the most successful professional sports league in American history.

Unitas wasn't the greatest quarterback ever—though loyal fans may insist otherwise—but he was the most important. He was the winning quarterback in the 1958 NFL Championship Game, also known as "the Greatest Game Ever Played." He threw for 349 yards and a touchdown in the Baltimore Colts' upset victory over the Giants. He was the architect of the thrilling drive that set up the Colts to tie the score at the end of the fourth quarter and the engine of the drive that put the winning points on the board in overtime.

Most important, Unitas did all of that with the entire country watching. The '58 championship was the first nationally televised NFL game. It's the event credited with setting the league on a course to overtake baseball as America's premier professional sport—and eventually to leave "the national pastime" so far behind

77

in popularity that routine midseason football games now typically draw more TV viewers than the World Series. It turned Unitas into the country's first real celebrity pro football player.

And what makes Unitas' story truly great is that he started his career as a washout.

★ ★ ★

Unitas, who grew up in Pittsburgh, played his college ball off the radar at the University of Louisville. He was a ninth-round selection of his hometown Steelers in the 1955 NFL Draft. But he failed to make the team.

He went to work in construction but kept dreaming about finding a place in the NFL. And he did what he could to stay sharp, playing semipro ball on the weekends.

That course almost never works out for anyone. But Unitas got lucky. In 1956 he got an invitation to try out for the Colts, and head coach Weeb Ewbank saw a guy he thought would make a suitable backup for his second-year QB George Shaw.

Unitas signed with the Colts. And then, four games into the season, Shaw broke his leg and Unitas got his chance. He was shaky in relief of Shaw, but in his first two games as a starter, Unitas led the Colts to wins over Green Bay and Cleveland. In those games, Ewbank saw the qualities that would make Unitas great—an ability to read defenses quickly and make adjustments at the line of scrimmage and a knack for rallying his teammates around him—and with that, Unitas earned the starting job for keeps.

In 1957, his first full year as a starter, Unitas demonstrated that in addition to being a savvy player and an on-field leader, he was also a gifted passer. Unitas led the league with 2,550 passing yards, 24 touchdowns, and 8.5 yards per attempt. His output dipped a bit in 1958, largely because of an injury that cost him two starts, but the results for Baltimore improved. The Colts finished 9–3, earning the first postseason berth in the six-year-old franchise's history.

Baltimore wasn't supposed to be able to compete with New York in the championship, though. The Giants were an established team. They were four-time league champions, most recently in 1956. They had bullied their way to the championship with two-straight victories over the Cleveland Browns, one at the

You Can't Argue with Figures

	Tom Brady	Johnny Unitas
Regular-Season Record	172–51	118–64–4
Winning Percentage	.771	.645
Postseason Record	22–9	6–2
Winning Percentage	.710	.750
Overall Record	194–60	124–66–4
Winning Percentage	.764	.649
Passer Rating	96.4	78.2
Touchdown Percentage	5.5	5.6
Interception Percentage	1.9	4.9
TD/INT	2.9/1	1.1/1
Completion Percentage	63.6	54.6
Yards Per Attempt	7.4	7.8
First-Team All-Pro	2	6
League MVP	2	3
Super Bowl MVP	3	0
League Championship Record	4–2	3–1*

*2 pre–Super Bowl NFL championships, plus Super Bowl V

end of the regular season to tie Cleveland in the standings and another in a one-game playoff that decided the Eastern Conference title. They'd been a winning team for five seasons running.

The Giants had history, they had momentum, and they had home-field advantage. Heading into the final two minutes of the championship game, they also had the lead. New York had taken a 17–14 advantage early in the fourth quarter with a 15-yard touchdown pass from Charlie Conerly to Frank Gifford. And they'd thwarted two attempts by Baltimore to move back in front or tie the score with stout defensive efforts that kept the Colts out of field-goal range.

And when a punt planted Baltimore at their own 20-yard line with 1:56 to play, there was little reason to believe the result would be anything but another stalled drive followed by a celebration by the Yankee Stadium crowd.

But Unitas, the consummate competitor, wasn't of a mind to be witness to that spectacle. Though he started the drive with a pair of incompletions, on third down he found Lenny Moore for 11 yards. Then he turned to his favorite target, Raymond Berry, hitting the receiver with three passes in a row to move the Colts to the Giants 13-yard line. And with the last seconds running off the game clock, place-kicker Steve Myhra put the tying points on the board from 20 yards away.

After the Giants failed to move the ball on the first possession of the league's first-ever overtime period (the OT rule had only just been adopted), Unitas once again moved the Colts from their own 20, this time with a methodical drive that mixed passes to Berry, running back Alan Ameche, and tight end Jim Mutscheller with carries by Ameche. And it was Ameche who finished the drive with a one-yard touchdown run.

The timing of the spectacle had been perfect—for Unitas and the NFL alike. Americans were riveted by the game and energized by the young Baltimore quarterback. Unitas became a household name. And pro football went from niche sport to growing national passion.

★ ★ ★

Johnny U kept those new fans engaged by continuing to play great football throughout the next couple of seasons.

He led the Colts to another 9–3 season and another NFL title in 1959, this time with a convincing 31–16 win over the Giants, in which Unitas completed 18 of 29 passes for 264 yards and two touchdowns and rushed for an additional score. Unitas led the league in passing yards (2,899) and set a new single-season record with 32 passing touchdowns (breaking Sid Luckman's 16-year-old record of 28). He was honored as the NFL MVP for the first time.

Though the Colts were a .500 team in 1960, Unitas once again topped the league in passing yards (3,099) and touchdowns (25).

Unitas played for another 13 seasons. And though his output was up and down (as, not coincidentally, was his health), Unitas usually offered Colts fans hope. He turned in stellar seasons in 1963 and 1964, though he had an uncharacteristically awful outing in the 1964 NFL Championship Game, throwing for just 95 yards and giving up a pair of interceptions in a 27–0 loss to the Browns.

He missed all but five 1968 regular-season games due to a preseason injury to his throwing arm and made an appearance in the fourth quarter of Super Bowl III as the Colts scrambled to stem the tide of a loss to Ewbank's AFL-champion New York Jets. And though he led the Colts to an 11–2–1 record and an AFC championship in 1970, Unitas was knocked out of the game in the second quarter of Baltimore's Super Bowl V victory over the Dallas Cowboys.

Unitas ended his career like a lot of great players before him and since, not with a bang but a whimper. In 1973 he was traded to the San Diego Chargers, where he started four games and spent the balance of the season mentoring rookie QB Dan Fouts.

Most of the records Unitas held at the time of his retirement have been bested over the pass-happy seasons that followed. But he still owns a piece of the marks for most consecutive seasons leading the league in pass attempts (three), along with George Blanda and Drew Bledsoe, and most seasons leading in touchdowns (four), along with Len Dawson, Steve Young, Brett Favre, Drew Brees and Peyton Manning.

Unitas held the record for consecutive games with at least one touchdown pass, 47, for 52 years before it was broken by Brees in the 2012 season. In the years since, Tom Brady and Peyton Manning also have posted longer TD streaks than Unitas.

Unitas' place in pro football history was never contingent upon records, though. Neither did it ever depend on his ability to claim the title of all-time greatest quarterback. Even in his day, Unitas was considered second in that regard to Bart Starr. (He arguably trailed the likes of Sammy Baugh, Sid Luckman, and Otto Graham on the all-time list as well.) And in the years since his retirement,

★ ★ ★ ★ ★ ★ ★

[Brady's] ability to put the ball on the money and do it consistently— he's going to go down as one of the best ever. When you look at the quarterback position and how you play it, Tom Brady is a great example of that.

—John Elway

he's certainly been eclipsed by Joe Montana and Tom Brady and, some would argue, by another former Colts QB.

Unitas loyalists like to insist that statistics don't matter. They argue that Johnny U played in a different era. They claim his leadership and his seeming ability to will his team to victory make him the best no matter what the numbers say. They fall back on intangibles because the tangible evidence shows them something they can't accept: Unitas, though great, doesn't have a strong position in the conversation about the greatest ever. Unitas' ability to will his team to victory resulted in 29 career game-winning drives. That's nice, but it's not Brady's 48 (or the current record holder Manning's 56). He made a big impression by delivering championships relatively early in his career, but his team qualified for postseason play in only five of his 17 seasons. In the 1964 championship, Unitas was completely unable to get out of the way of the Cleveland defense. And in Super Bowl V, Unitas' final trip to the championship game, it was Earl Morrall who ultimately led the Colts to victory.

Brady will go into the 2016 season with the ability to reach more than one and a half times as many regular season wins and four times as many postseason wins as Unitas. He's delivered more championships for the Patriots than Johnny U did for the Colts. And he's outperformed Unitas in every meaningful passing statistic. Brady's a greater QB than Unitas was, and he's not the only player to hold that distinction.

But it doesn't matter that Johnny U wasn't the best. He was the biggest, which is exactly what the NFL needed him to be.

CHAPTER 11

★ ★ ★

Dynasty: 2004

If your standard of measurement involves championships, then 2004 stands along with 2014 as one of Tom Brady's greatest seasons to date. Brady's stats in the '04 season aren't the best he's ever posted: he threw for fewer yards than in all but one of his 10 subsequent full seasons; he attempted, and completed, fewer passes than in any season other than 2001; and his completion percentage was a "mere" 60.8, a number he's topped in all but two seasons. But Brady's performance in '04 was the best of his three early Super Bowl championship seasons.

Brady finished the 2004 campaign with a passer rating of 92.6, the first time in his career that he topped 90. His touchdown-to-interception ratio of 28/14 (2:1) was the best of his career at the time. His yards per attempt jumped to 7.8 from a previous best of 6.9. He went through the entire postseason without throwing a pick, earned an overall playoffs passer rating of 109.4, and in the AFC Championship Game led an offensive effort that piled up 34 points on the league's best defense.

Brady had emerged as New England's leader in his first season under center. In 2003 he firmly established himself as one of the elite quarterbacks of his era. But it was over the course of the 2004 season that he seriously and permanently inserted himself in the discussion of the game's all-time greats—and left his friendly rival Peyton Manning in the dust. Oh, and along the way, he led the Patriots to the status of bona fide NFL dynasty—the first of the salary-cap era.

Brady looks for a receiver against the Seattle Seahawks during a game on October 17, 2004. The Patriots won their 20th consecutive game with a 30–20 victory.

By the time the confetti started flying in Jacksonville, Florida, on February 6, 2005, Brady, at age 27, had won three Super Bowls. He was the youngest quarterback in NFL history to accomplish that feat, beating his boyhood idol Joe Montana by five years, Terry Bradshaw by three, and Troy Aikman by two. (It's worth stopping here to note, by the way, that as of February 2016—which is to say, through Super Bowl 50—the youngest active NFL QB to have won even a single championship, Russell Wilson, was already 27. In other words, there appears to be no risk of Brady's accomplishment being matched any time soon.)

With most of his career still in front of him, Brady already had secured a spot in the Pro Football Hall of Fame.

★ ★ ★

The Patriots opened the 2004 regular season not just as the defending Super Bowl champs but as a team in the midst of an impressive winning streak. How many games that streak included was a matter of perspective. From the standpoint of the NFL's official records keepers, who consider only regular-season games, it was 12. As seen by plain old everyday football fans, who tend to view a winning streak simply as a series of consecutive victories, it was 15. Either way, it was heading in the direction of historic.

The Chicago Bears in 1933 and '34 had won 17 consecutive regular-season games. Adding in the Bears' victory over the New York Giants in the 1933 NFL Championship Game brings the total to 18, which is the same overall number the Miami Dolphins achieved in 1972 and '73.

So New England was six wins away from breaking the Bears' regular-season record and just four out from the unofficial regular-season/postseason combined mark.

But the Pats didn't talk about streaks. They were Bill Belichick's team, and they hewed to their head coach's philosophy, which said the only goal that ever mattered was the immediate one: find a way to beat the team you're scheduled to play next.

In their season opener, that team was the same one the Pats had faced in the AFC Championship Game not quite nine months earlier: the Indianapolis Colts. While New England had relied largely on defense to beat Indianapolis in the playoffs, this time, with the *D* getting off to a shaky start, the team looked to its quarterback to carry the day. And Brady came through.

Though the offense struggled early in the Thursday night game, it came to life midway through the second quarter. With the Pats trailing 10–3, Brady and the team's new running back, Corey Dillon, combined on a long march to a tying touchdown. Dillon got things going with a 38-yard dash from the New England 25-yard line to the Indianapolis 37. And Brady finished the drive with a 16-yard strike to Deion Branch in the middle of the Colts' end zone.

The Colts had a 17–13 lead at halftime, but it didn't survive long after the break. Four minutes into the third quarter, Brady found David Patten in the right corner of the Indianapolis end zone for a 25-yard touchdown. And with just a bit more than a minute remaining in the third, he hit tight end Daniel Graham in almost the exact same spot from eight yards away.

Brady's lone mistake of the game, an interception to Colts cornerback Nick Harper midway through the fourth, hurt the quarterback's stats but not the team, as Indy failed to capitalize. And in the end, the New England defense stepped up and did its part, stopping a final Colts desperation drive and setting up a 48-yard field-goal attempt that Indianapolis place-kicker Mike Vanderjagt pushed wide right with only seconds remaining.

Brady finished the game with 26 completions on 38 attempts for 335 yards, three touchdowns, and a pick, earning a passer rating of 111.2. And the Patriots initiated their title defense with their 16th consecutive victory.

★ ★ ★

Brady and Dillon continued to play at a high level in the weeks that followed. When the Seattle Seahawks visited Foxborough in Week 6, Dillon rushed for 105 yards and a pair of touchdowns while Brady threw for 231 and a score, fueling the Patriots' 20th consecutive overall win and 17th successive victory in the regular season. The Pats had tied Chicago's 70-year-old record.

A week later, with the New York Jets in town, the Patriots made the all-time record their own, winning 13–7 on a day when Brady completed 20 of 29 passes for 230 yards and a touchdown, earning a passer rating of 104.1.

There was a reason the Bears had held their record for so long, though. It was one of the very reasons Belichick has always insisted on his one-game-at-a-time approach: Wins are harder to come by in the NFL than they are in any other professional sport. No matter how hot a team may be, the odds eventually even things out.

The team, and its fans, would have preferred not to have the streak come to its end in such a brutal fashion— in a game known as the Halloween Massacre, a 34–20 loss to the Steelers in Pittsburgh that wasn't nearly as close as the final score—but no one had been under the illusion that it could last forever.

The end of the streak might have

By the Numbers 2004

Total Yards	3,692
Yards Per Game	230.8
Attempts	474
Completions	288
Completion Percentage	60.8
Yards Per Attempt	7.8
Touchdowns	28
Interceptions	14
Passer Rating	92.6
Games Rated Higher Than 100 *(Includes Two Postseason)*	10
Best Single-Game Rating *(Divisional-Round Playoff)*	130.5

proven more difficult to take if not for the fact that Brady and the Patriots got back in the winning business during a visit to St. Louis the very next week. Although their defensive secondary was crumbling—both starting cornerbacks, Ty Law and Tyrone Poole, had been lost to injuries, and Asante Samuel missed much of the game after injuring his shoulder—the Patriots turned in a performance against the Rams in which they clicked in every phase of the game. Adam Vinatieri kicked four field goals and threw a touchdown pass to Troy Brown on a trick play. Dillon rushed for 112 yards and a touchdown. And Brady completed 18 of 31 passes for 234 yards, including two short touchdown throws, one to Bethel Johnson and one to linebacker (and part-time tight end) Mike Vrabel.

With the exception of a miserable Monday night in Miami in Week 15—a game in which Brady threw four interceptions (though he also matched his season high with three touchdown passes) and the Patriots blew an 11-point fourth-quarter lead—New England rolled through the remainder of the season.

And Brady turned in some exceptional performances along the way. In a Monday night game against the Kansas City Chiefs in a louder-than-bombs Arrowhead Stadium, Brady completed 17 of 26 passes for 315 yards (that's 12.1 yards per attempt) and a touchdown. That, along with Dillon's 98 yards and two touchdowns and a great performance by the New England defensive front allowed the Pats to overcome the ongoing struggles of their ever-more-depleted secondary and log a 27–19 win. Brady's night included a 26-yard touchdown pass to Branch, who was in the lineup for the first time since Week 2, when he suffered a knee injury. The quarterback came away with a passer rating of 119.9.

When the Patriots hosted the Cincinnati Bengals in Week 14, Brady and Dillon carried the team. New England's struggling defense allowed Cincinnati to amass 478 yards of total offense and put 28 points on the board. But Dillon ran for 88 yards on 22 carries and scored a touchdown against his former team. And Brady connected on 18 of 26 pass attempts for 260 yards and a pair of touchdowns, including a 48-yard strike to Patten that put the Patriots ahead for good at 14–7 halfway through the second quarter. Brady's 127.1 passer rating was his best of the regular season.

The day of the Bengals game had begun with reports confirming that Charlie Weis—the only offensive coordinator Brady had known to that point in his career—would be leaving at the end of the season to take over as head coach at his alma mater, Notre Dame. The 35–28 win over Cincinnati, which clinched the AFC East title, took some of the edge off the news. But there remained a sense of urgency. Weis was leaving, and it was safe to assume that defensive coordinator Romeo Crennel also would be departing at the end of the season to assume head coaching duties somewhere (ultimately the Browns). The Patriots were headed toward an off-season full of change, and no one knew what that might mean. The team needed to make the most of the postseason opportunity it had earned.

The Pats took a huge step in the right direction with a 23–7 dismantling of the Jets in the Meadowlands. Brady completed 21 of 32 passes for 264 yards and two touchdowns, earning a 112.0 passer rating, and New England clinched a first-round bye in the playoffs. More encouraging in some ways, the Patriots defense held the 10–4 Jets scoreless for most of the game before giving up a touchdown in garbage time.

A 21–7 win over the visiting San Francisco 49ers in Week 17—a game in which Brady went 22-for-30 for 226 yards and two touchdowns despite playing only three full quarters (Rohan Davey was sent in at the start of the fourth)—got New England to 14–2, the best record ever achieved by a defending Super Bowl champion.

* * *

Things only got better for Brady and the Patriots in the playoffs.

The Pats opened the postseason the same way they had started the regular season: hosting the Colts. Indy came to town as the conference three-seed, having finished the season with a record of 12–4 and winning the AFC South title for the second consecutive season. They also came in with the league's most prolific offense, a unit that scored nearly 33 points per game during the regular season and that put up 49 in its wild-card-round matchup with Denver. The Colts' quarterback, Manning had been named NFL MVP, drawing 49 of 50 committee votes.

The Pats D had done a great job during the regular season of keeping opponents off the scoreboard—they allowed just 16.3 points per game, which tied them for second-best in the NFL—but with ongoing injury issues in the secondary, New England was thought to be vulnerable to a vertical passing attack. And there was no team more dangerous in that regard than Manning's Colts.

Indy was certainly confident enough going into the game. Vanderjagt, who had blown the Colts' final chance in the season opener, told the press the Patriots were "ripe for the picking." And the organization seemed to agree. Well before kickoff, the Colts contacted the top-seeded Pittsburgh Steelers looking to secure extra tickets for the AFC Championship Game the following week.

Whether they had forgotten the way their three previous meetings with New England had turned out, bought into their own hype, or simply assumed they would beat the Patriots didn't matter. The Colts believed they were headed for a win.

The Patriots weren't so sure. New England welcomed their rivals back to snowy Foxborough with a bruising physical performance on both sides of the ball.

* * * * * * *

You can see it in his eyes, his preparation and his play. Winning Super Bowls is his destiny.

—Deion Branch

Led by the linebacker corps, the defense smacked the Colts around throughout the late afternoon and evening. They took the ball away three times, twice on fumbles and once via interception. And they limited the Indianapolis offense to three points, by far the unit's lowest total of the season.

The Patriots offense, as it had all season, got its direction from Brady and its power from Dillon. The Pats controlled the ball for nearly 38 minutes of game time, most of it behind three long drives, two of which (both in the second half) resulted in touchdowns.

Dillon pummeled the Colts. He gained 144 yards on 23 carries and made sure Indy defenders took away a new bruise from every tackle. Brady completed 18 of 27 passes for 144 yards and a touchdown. The quarterback added a rushing touchdown at the end of the fourth-quarter drive that effectively sealed the Patriots' 20–3 victory. Brady, whose longest pass play of the day went for 17 yards, came away with an impressive postseason passer rating of 92.2.

★　★　★

The Patriots moved on to Pittsburgh for a conference championship matchup with the 16–1 Steelers and the league's top-rated defense. And they proceeded to show NFL fans everywhere what a team on a mission could accomplish.

New England dominated on both sides of the ball from the very start of the game. The Steelers' first two possessions ended in turnovers, and the Patriots

For the Books　2004

League Records

Most Consecutive Postseason Wins (Tied Bart Starr)　　　　　9

Team Records

Most Career Postseason Touchdowns　　　　　　　　　11

Honors and Career Milestones

Pro Bowl, Second Career Selection

offense made the most of both opportunities. After safety Eugene Wilson intercepted Pittsburgh quarterback Ben Roethlisberger at midfield on the opening drive, the Pats moved into position for a 48-yard field goal by Vinatieri. Then, when linebackers Rosevelt Colvin and Tedy Bruschi combined on a strip-and-recovery at the New England 40 during a Jerome Bettis carry, the offense wasted exactly no time. On the first play of the ensuing drive, New England's fifth offensive snap of the game, Brady launched a bomb down the middle of the field and connected with Branch for a 60-yard touchdown. There were seven minutes left to play in the first quarter, and the game was essentially over.

The Pats added two more scores in the second quarter—a nine-yard strike from Brady to Givens and a backbreaking 87-yard pick six by safety Rodney Harrison—to take a 24–3 lead into halftime.

In the second half, it was more of the same: Dillon scored on a 25-yard rush. Vinatieri added a 31-yard field goal. And Branch capped things off with a 23-yard touchdown dash on an end-around. Meanwhile, Roethlisberger was picked off by Wilson once again.

In the game, Brady completed 14 of 21 passes for 207 yards and two touchdowns. Considering the quality of the defense he had faced, his 130.5 passer rating for the game went way beyond impressive.

The 41–27 win sent the Patriots to the Super Bowl for the second consecutive year and the third time in four seasons. New England was one win away from *dynasty*.

★ ★ ★

That kind of status doesn't come easy, though. Nor do Super Bowl championships. And there was little question as the Patriots headed to Jacksonville, Florida, for Super Bowl XXXIX that the Philadelphia Eagles were going to be at least as tough an opponent as the St. Louis Rams and Carolina Panthers had been.

The Eagles were a lot like the Patriots. On defense, they could give up yards at times, but they refused to surrender points, and they were expert at taking the ball away. Their offense was balanced and capable of exploding, particularly when they could get wide receiver Terrell Owens in sync with quarterback Donovan McNabb. They'd captured the NFC East title and the conference one-seed with a 13–3 record, and they'd handled their postseason opposition fairly easily. They were dangerous.

The game reflected the teams' similarities. Defense prevailed in a scoreless first quarter. And in the second, both offenses started to come to life. Philadelphia struck first with a six-yard touchdown pass from McNabb to tight end L.J. Smith that capped a nine-play, 81-yard drive. But the Pats pulled even before halftime as Brady took advantage of a short field after the Eagles were forced to punt from deep in their own territory. Brady directed a three-minute drive from the Philadelphia 37-yard line, finishing it off with a four-yard touchdown toss to Givens.

The teams again swapped touchdowns in the third quarter, though they did it in reverse order. New England's score came on the opening drive of the second half after Brady moved the Patriots from their own 31-yard line to the Eagles 2, largely with passes to Branch of 27, 15, and 21 yards. On first-and-goal with Vrabel once again checked in at tight end, Brady put the ball where only the big linebacker could get his hands on it. And after batting it in the air once, Vrabel pulled in the pass for the score.

McNabb, though, engineered a nice 76-yard drive of his own to even the score near the end of the period.

But then Brady took over, leading a methodical drive from the New England 34 that bridged into the fourth quarter and ended with a two-yard Dillon run, putting the Patriots back on top 24–17. In the middle of the quarter, after a 19-yard pass from Brady to Branch and a 15-yard roughing-the-passer call on Eagles defensive tackle Corey Simon helped move the Pats to the Philadelphia 4, Vinatieri hit a 22-yard field goal that gave the Patriots a 10-point lead.

The Eagles closed the gap to three, but an interception by Rodney Harrison on Philadelphia's final possession preserved the Patriots' 27–24 triumph.

Brady finished the day 23-for-33 for 236 yards and two touchdowns, with a passer rating of 110.2. His numbers for the postseason: 55 of 81 for 587 yards, five touchdowns, no interceptions, and a passer rating of 109.4.

The Patriots became the first team since the 1997 and 1998 Denver Broncos to win back-to-back Super Bowls and the first since the Dallas Cowboys of 1992–95 to capture the Lombardi Trophy three times in four seasons.

More impressive in many ways is that, over a two-year stretch, Brady's Patriots had won 34 games and lost only four.

The Patriots were an official NFL dynasty. Brady was officially one of the most successful quarterbacks ever to play the game. And while the team would undergo massive changes in the off-season, losing both coordinators and an assortment of players, they had a head coach and a quarterback who were clearly the best in the game.

It was undeniable: any Patriots season that began with Belichick on the sideline and Brady behind center was going to be a season filled with possibility and hope.

CHAPTER 12

★ ★ ★

Tom Brady vs. Roger Staubach

Under a slightly different set of circumstances, Roger Staubach might have turned out to be the uncontested greatest quarterback ever to play the game. Staubach certainly was talented enough to have had that kind of career. It's just that the navy—and the Vietnam War—kind of got in the way.

Staubach was at a disadvantage before the Dallas Cowboys ever selected him in the 10th round of the 1964 draft. (Staubach also was chosen by the Kansas City Chiefs in the 16th round of the AFL Draft, though by the time he actually played his first professional game, the two professional leagues were in the midst of solidifying their merger.) As the 1963 Heisman Trophy winner, he would have gone much earlier in the draft if it hadn't been for the fact that he played his college ball for the U.S. Naval Academy. That came with a commitment to serve in the navy, and it meant Staubach wouldn't be available to play pro ball until the 1969 season, at which point he'd be 27 years old.

Still, Dallas made the pick and retained Staubach's rights. And after he finished his navy hitch, which included a one-year tour of duty in Vietnam, Staubach reported to the Cowboys, where he got a front-row seat for two years while Craig Morton tried to fill Don Meredith's shoes.

By the time Staubach took his first snap as the Cowboys' full-time starter midway through the 1971 season, he'd long since celebrated his 29th birthday. And what he did for Dallas in the 1971 campaign and the eight seasons that followed raised forever the question of what might have been had Staubach spent the preceding seven years playing football.

★ ★ ★

Beginning with his first start against the St. Louis Cardinals in Week 8, Staubach led the Cowboys to 10 victories in a row. That included the remainder of the regular season, during which time Staubach completed 83 of 139 passes for 1,249 yards and 10 touchdowns, all while throwing just a single interception. His passer rating for that run was 110.3. His passer rating for the full 1971 season, including the games in which he shared time with Morton, was 104.8. That's an outstanding single-season passer rating by modern standards. For the early 1970s, when defenses ruled the NFL, it was phenomenal.

But that's not all. Staubach started strong and ended stronger. In three consecutive games in Weeks 11, 12, and 13, Staubach turned in games in which his passer rating was 140 or better, and during that short stretch he threw eight touchdowns without a single pick.

Then, in his first full season as an NFL starter, Staubach led a Cowboys team that had never been able to win big games all the way to a Super Bowl championship.

Staubach's performance against the Miami Dolphins in Super Bowl VI was even more impressive than anything he had accomplished in the regular season. Facing a Miami defense that allowed just 12.4 points per game during the regular season and that shut out the Baltimore Colts in the AFC Championship Game, Staubach completed 63 percent of his passes. He threw for 119 yards and two touchdowns, earned a 115.9 passer rating, and propelled his team to a 24–3 victory. Staubach was named Super Bowl MVP as a result of the effort.

Staubach missed most of the 1972 season with a separated shoulder. But he resumed his career in 1973 and started every Cowboys game, save two, until he retired at the end of 1979.

Dallas was a playoff team in seven of Staubach's eight seasons as the team's principal starter, six times as NFC East champions. They advanced to the NFC Championship Game five times and played in four Super Bowls, winning two.

★ ★ ★

The Cowboys certainly had their chances to win a third championship, but they fell just short in both Super Bowl X and Super Bowl XIII.

In Super Bowl X Dallas jumped out to an early lead over the Pittsburgh Steelers and carried a 10–7 advantage into the fourth quarter, only to surrender 14 points and the championship through a blocked punt that resulted in a safety, a Staubach interception that set up a field goal, and an improbable 64-yard touchdown pass from Terry Bradshaw to Lynn Swann. Staubach threw three picks in the game (though one of them was on a Hail Mary in the final seconds).

The prevailing belief in Dallas is that tight end Jackie Smith cost the Cowboys a victory in Super Bowl XIII by dropping a catchable pass in the end zone late in

You Can't Argue with Figures

	Tom Brady	Roger Staubach
Regular-Season Record	172–51	85–29
Winning Percentage	.771	.746
Postseason Record	22–9	11–6
Winning Percentage	.710	.647
Overall Record	194–60	96–35
Winning Percentage	.764	.733
Passer Rating	96.4	83.4
Touchdown Percentage	5.5	5.2
Interception Percentage	1.9	3.7
TD/INT	2.9/1	1.4/1
Completion Percentage	63.6	57
Yards Per Attempt	7.4	7.7
First-Team All-Pro	2	0
League MVP	2	1
Super Bowl MVP	3	1
Super Bowl Record	4–2	2–2

the third quarter. But the truth is that Dallas had plenty of chances to win and was simply outplayed by the Steelers, if only by a matter of inches. Staubach, for his part, turned in a strong performance in the 35–31 loss, completing 17 of 30 passes for 228 yards with three touchdowns and just a single interception.

Staubach led the league in passer rating in four of his eight seasons as the Cowboys' starting quarterback. He retired with a career passer rating of 83.4, which at the time was a record. He was a great passer during the era in football in which passing was most difficult.

If he'd been able to play longer, or perhaps if he'd played at a different time, Staubach almost certainly would have ended up at or near the top of any conceivable list of all-time greats. But he didn't. And so he sits on that list below the guys who have benefitted from playing in a more pass-friendly league and below the guys who got to play full careers. Guys like Baugh, Starr, Montana, and Brady (and, to Staubach's credit, not too many others).

Of course, it's notable at the same time that Brady has doubled Staubach's win totals in both the regular season and the postseason. Brady also has two more championships to his credit than Staubach, and has been named MVP of three Super Bowls to Staubach's one. Brady also has better passing statistics almost across the board.

Staubach's military service cost him the opportunity to play during most of his twenties. If he'd had those years, Brady might still be scrambling to catch up with him. But one can't judge real careers based on hypotheticals. One has to go by reality, which puts Staubach in the history books as a guy who made a lot of a limited number of chances, who was unquestionably great, but who's not eligible for consideration as the greatest. That might not be fair, but like a lot of things in football, it's just the way the ball bounces.

CHAPTER 13

★ ★ ★

Pretty Good's Not Good Enough: 2005

Maybe the Patriots were adjusting. New England's coaching staff had undergone major changes following the team's second consecutive Super Bowl win. Offensive coordinator Charlie Weis had left to take over as head coach at Notre Dame. And defensive coordinator Romeo Crennel had moved on within the NFL, assuming the top job with the Cleveland Browns and taking a handful of Patriots assistants with him. Bill Belichick elevated defensive backs coach Eric Mangini to the role of defensive coordinator, but left the top offensive job officially open while he gave quarterbacks coach Josh McDaniels a season-long play-calling tryout. That kind of turnover isn't easy to deal with when you're trying to compete at the highest level. And it undoubtedly took its toll.

Maybe the Patriots were tired. They'd played 38 games over the course of their back-to-back championship seasons, 73 games over four years. That was nine more games than most other teams, which wasn't even to mention the fact that winning tends to land you in high-profile TV slots more often. That's more night games. More Mondays. More Thursdays. More Saturdays. More disruptions to the normal flow of a season schedule.

There are many reasons why no team has ever won three consecutive Super Bowls, but the unrelenting wear that comes with playing into February year after long year is certainly one of the big ones.

It might have been injuries. The Patriots couldn't keep running backs or defensive backs healthy all season long. Starting cornerback Tyrone Poole was lost for the season with an ankle injury in Week 1. Star safety Rodney Harrison blew out a knee in Week 3. Left tackle Matt Light also went down for good in Week 3. Richard Seymour, the team's best pass rusher, suffered a weird knee injury in Week 6 and missed the next four weeks. Except for Tedy Bruschi's seemingly miraculous recovery from an off-season stroke, there was no good health news to be had from the start of September through the middle of January.

Or, you know, maybe it was just the single-elimination nature of the NFL playoffs. Participate in enough postseason games, and eventually you're bound to have things break the wrong way—and when they do, there's no bouncing back the following week.

Whatever the reason (or, more likely, reasons), 2005 wasn't happening for the Patriots.

★ ★ ★

Even so, it was more than a respectable season for New England's quarterback.

There's a perception that injuries to running backs Corey Dillon and Kevin Faulk forced the Patriots to go to the air more frequently in 2005 than they had in previous seasons. And there's a certain degree of truth to that. Without question, the Pats were more reliant on Tom Brady's arm in '05 than they had been the previous season, when Dillon carried the ball 345 times for a career-best 1,635 yards and 12 touchdowns. But the run-pass balance in 2005 wasn't all that different from what it had been in 2003.

The major difference for Brady didn't come so much in pass attempts as it did in completions and yardage. For the season, Brady went 334-for-530, racking up an NFL-best 4,110 yards and passing for 26 touchdowns. The total yardage was the best of Brady's career to that point; it was more than 400 yards more than what he'd achieved in 2004 and close to 500 better than his 2003 mark. His completion percentage, 63, was his best since 2001, when he attempted only 413 passes and connected on 264 of them (63.9 percent). His passer rating, 92.3, was second only to the 92.6 he'd achieved en route to Super Bowl XXXIX. Brady finished half a dozen games with a passer rating of more than 100, threw for better than 300 yards in four different games, and led four game-winning drives.

Two of those comebacks were particularly memorable. Brady didn't throw for a touchdown in the Patriots' Week 3 matchup with the Steelers in Pittsburgh, but he was a perfect 12-for-12 for 167 yards in the fourth quarter. With the Pats trailing 13–10 early in the final frame, he moved the team

By the Numbers ★ 2005

Total Yards	4,110
Yards Per Game	256.9
Attempts	530
Completions	334
Completion Percentage	63.0
Yards Per Attempt	7.8
Touchdowns	26
Interceptions	14
Passer Rating	92.3
Games Rated Higher Than 100 (Includes One Postseason)	7
Best Single-Game Rating	140.4

76 yards through the air, completing passes of 19 and 30 yards to Troy Brown and David Givens, respectively, and setting up a seven-yard touchdown run by Dillon. And later, when the Pats got the ball on their own 38 with 1:21 to play, he quickly drove the team into range for a game-winning field goal by Adam Vinatieri. Brady's passer rating for the game was 92.7; his passer rating in that clutch fourth quarter was 118.7.

Brady had an even more impressive outing two weeks later when the Pats visited the Atlanta Falcons. Banged up going into the game, the Patriots suffered even more injuries throughout the afternoon. Brady kept the offense humming, but as the game wore on, it was clear to see that the *D* was wearing down. And when the home team, which had trailed 28–13 at the end of the third quarter, tied the score with a touchdown and a two-point conversion late in the fourth, it appeared New England was headed for a tough loss.

Things got a good bit worse before they got better. The Patriots got the ball back with just under four minutes to play. And thanks to a solid kickoff return by Bethel Johnson, they got to start at their own 36. But after committing penalties on their first two snaps—a false start followed by a holding call that negated a 16-yard pass play—the team ended up facing first-and-25 from the 21. And the

For the Books 2005

League Records
Most Consecutive Playoff Wins   10

Honors and Career Milestones
First 4,000-Yard Season
Second-Team All-Pro
Pro Bowl, 3rd Career Selection
Sports Illustrated Sportsman of the Year

long field felt longer still when Dillon, who had gained 106 yards on 23 carries, headed to the locker room with a foot injury.

It all turned around, though, when veteran Atlanta cornerback Allen Rossum decked Deion Branch before the ball could arrive on a deep out, giving the Pats a fresh start at the Falcons 44-yard line. Brady delivered a pair of bullets, the second of them with two pass rushers a step away, to move New England to the 29. Patrick Pass, stepping in for Dillon, added 15 yards. And Adam Vinatieri made the game-winning field goal with 17 seconds left on the clock.

Brady finished the game with his best stats of the season. He completed 22 of 27 passes (81.5 percent) for 350 yards and three touchdowns, with one interception, earning a passer rating of 140.4. He was named AFC Offensive Player of the Week as a result of the effort.

The quarterback's heroics didn't carry over to the following week, however. The Patriots fell 28–20 to the Broncos in Denver and went into their bye week with a 3–3 record. Nor were Brady's efforts through the balance of the season— much of which he played with a sports hernia—enough to make the Pats anything more than a dangerous but ultimately uneven team.

★ ★ ★

New England finished 10–6, won another AFC East title, and readily dispensed with the 12–4 Jacksonville Jaguars in the wild-card round behind a respectable but wholly unspectacular day for Brady. Though he threw three touchdowns and ended the night with a 116.4 passer rating, Brady completed just 55.6 percent of his passes and took four sacks.

The victory was Brady and Belichick's 10th straight in the postseason, breaking an NFL record that had been held by Bart Starr and Vince Lombardi since their win over the Oakland Raiders in Super Bowl II.

As if to illustrate the impossibility of sustaining such streaks, however, the Patriots fell in the divisional round to the second-seeded Broncos. The game turned on a series of Patriots blunders—including a pair of interceptions thrown by Brady (one of them in the Broncos' end zone on a play that might have put the Patriots ahead 13–10 early in the second half)—a missed field goal by the usually automatic Vinatieri, and a muffed punt by the usually reliable Troy Brown.

It was one of those games in which nothing ever seemed to go the Patriots' way. And it only made sense for 2005 to end that way. It had been one of those seasons. No matter how much went right, all that seemed to matter were the things that kept going wrong. In the NFL, those seasons just happen sometimes. You don't have to like it, but there's not a whole lot you can do about it.

CHAPTER 14

★ ★ ★

Tom Brady vs. Terry Bradshaw

Terry Bradshaw was an average quarterback most of the time. And, contrary to popular perception about his big-game capabilities, Bradshaw was almost never a great quarterback.

He was, however, a quarterback who had a knack for having his biggest moments just when his team needed him most and right when everyone was watching. That worked out well for the Pittsburgh Steelers—if not so much for the Dallas Cowboys and the Los Angeles Rams—and it worked out swimmingly for Bradshaw, who is, without question, the least likely quarterback ever to win four Super Bowls.

OK, to be fair with that last bit, Bradshaw is one of exactly three QBs ever to win four Super Bowls. And the others are Joe Montana and Tom Brady. There's not a lot of measuring up to a standard like that.

And likely or otherwise, Bradshaw owns four rings. He also has the distinction, again along with Montana, of having played in four Super Bowls and never lost. There are only seven QBs in NFL history who have played in four or more Super Bowls. Tom Brady has a record of 4–2. John Elway went 2–3. Roger Staubach was 2–2 (with both losses coming courtesy of Bradshaw's Steelers), a mark matched by Peyton Manning. And Jim Kelly, of course, was a perfect 0–4.

Brady jokes with Terry Bradshaw during an interview after being named Super Bowl MVP on February 3, 2002.

The undefeated distinction offers some meaningful bragging rights for Bradshaw and Montana.

Where the two 4–0 Super Bowl champions part ways, though, is in the rest of their careers. Montana's, of course, was great—the best of all time, according to some, certainly one of the top two or three. Bradshaw's was good enough for a guy whose team was built on crushing defense and a powerhouse running game.

Bradshaw didn't throw the ball all that well, but that was OK, because Steelers coach Chuck Noll didn't ask Bradshaw to throw the ball all that much. Only in a handful of seasons during his 14-year career did Bradshaw crack the top 10 in pass attempts, pass completions, or passing yards. Bradshaw's main responsibility in Noll's offense was to hand the ball to running backs Franco Harris and Rocky Bleier.

Bradshaw's other big responsibility was to not put the Pittsburgh defense in tough situations. Because the reality under Noll was that the Steel Curtain defense was the engine that drove championships. In Pittsburgh's four Super Bowl championship seasons in the Noll era, the *D* never ranked worse than fifth in the league and never allowed more than 16.4 points per game. In 1978, en route to Super Bowl XIII, the Steelers defense gave up a league-best 12.2 points per game in the regular season. It allowed just 15 total points in Pittsburgh's two AFC playoff games. In 1975, when the Steelers won Super Bowl X, the *D* held opponents to just 11.6 points per game.

In that context, and in an era ruled by defense league-wide, Bradshaw's completion ratio—which hovered around 50 percent throughout his career—was serviceable. His penchant for throwing as many picks as he did touchdowns was more of a problem. But it wasn't one the Steelers couldn't overcome. Bradshaw was a risk taker. He consistently threw passes he shouldn't have. He also had a big arm and wasn't afraid to expose himself to punishment in order to use it. Sometimes that came with a cost. Other times it came with a celebration.

★ ★ ★

In Super Bowl X, the Steelers second consecutive appearance in the championship game, Bradshaw put the winning points on the board with one of the most spectacular, daring, and ultimately painful plays of his career. (Bradshaw had been a virtual nonfactor in Super Bowl IX, completing just 9 of 14 passes as

You Can't Argue with Figures

	Tom Brady	Terry Bradshaw
Regular-Season Record	172–51	107–51
Winning Percentage	.771	.677
Postseason Record	22–9	14–5
Winning Percentage	.710	.737
Overall Record	194–60	121–56
Winning Percentage	.764	.684
Passer Rating	96.4	70.9
Touchdown Percentage	5.5	5.4
Interception Percentage	1.9	5.4
TD/INT	2.9/1	1/1
Completion Percentage	63.6	51.9
Yards Per Attempt	7.4	7.2
First-Team All-Pro	2	1
League MVP	2	1
Super Bowl MVP	3	2
Super Bowl Record	4–2	4–0

Harris, Bleier, and the defense carried the team to a 16–6 win over the Minnesota Vikings.)

The Steelers had rallied from a 10–7 halftime deficit to take a 15–10 lead over the Cowboys. Late in the fourth quarter, with the game's outcome still very much in the balance, the Steelers faced third-and-four from their own 36-yard line. Bradshaw read *blitz* and knew that Lynn Swann would end up in single coverage. He took the snap, stepped up into the pocket to avoid linebacker D.D. Lewis, and launched the ball deep down the field just a fraction of a second before he was hammered by safety Cliff Harris and defensive tackle Larry Cole. Swann made the catch at the Dallas 7, shook off cornerback Mark Washington, and stepped into the end zone to extend the Steelers' lead to 21–10.

The play was Bradshaw's last of the game, as he was knocked unconscious by the hit he took from Cole. But with little time remaining, Pittsburgh was able to hold on for a 21–17 victory.

★ ★ ★

Bradshaw's performance in Super Bowl XIII three years later was spectacular all around. He completed 17 of 30 passes for a then-record 318 yards and four touchdowns, while throwing just a single interception. And it was behind that effort that the Steelers once again bested Roger Staubach's Cowboys, this time by a score of 35–31. Bradshaw earned a passer rating of 119.2 and his first nod as Super Bowl MVP for the effort.

His second Super Bowl MVP honor came in spite of an uneven performance in Super Bowl XIV. Bradshaw put up 309 yards and two touchdowns in the 31–19 win over the Los Angeles Rams, but he also threw three interceptions in the course of the game.

But Bradshaw was able to make a huge impression with a single play early in the fourth quarter. With the Rams ahead 19–17 and Swann—who had landed on his head after making an aerial catch earlier in the game—sidelined, Pittsburgh faced a third-and-eight at their own 27. Bradshaw play-faked halfheartedly then rocketed the ball to wide receiver John Stallworth, who was blazing down the middle of the field. Rams cornerback Rod Perry, who was beat by half a step at most, tried to make a play on the ball and missed, which allowed Stallworth to make a grab at the Rams 35 and speed the rest of the way down the field into the end zone untouched to put the Steelers on top.

Super Bowl XIV was the last championship for Bradshaw. The quarterback took a lot of punishment behind a shaky offensive line in 1980. And his play continued to deteriorate thereafter, until a nagging elbow problem finally forced him to retire in 1983.

Bradshaw, who had rarely led the league in any statistical category, left the game with few individual distinctions. But with a league-record four Super Bowl championships to the Steelers' credit (at the time, no other team had won more than two), that didn't really matter. It was as true then as it is now: rings trump records.

There's no point in talking about how Bradshaw measures up to the truly elite quarterbacks statistically. He doesn't. And when you get to the QBs who have great career stats *and* multiple championships, Bradshaw falls way behind. Tom Brady may not have Bradshaw's spotless win-loss record in the Super Bowl, but not only has Brady played in more Super Bowls than Bradshaw, he's won a far higher percentage of his regular-season games, logged considerably more total playoff victories, and exceeded the Steelers great by an enormous margin in virtually every meaningful statistical measurement.

That doesn't mean Bradshaw isn't worth celebrating, of course. Bradshaw wasn't a great quarterback. But he was a great football player. And that's something he can be proud of.

CHAPTER 15

★ ★ ★

You Can't Win 'Em All: 2006

Somewhere there's an alternate universe in which Tom Brady led the Patriots to victory over the Indianapolis Colts in the 2006 AFC Championship Game then on to a win over the Chicago Bears in Super Bowl XLI. And somewhere else there's another, where the Pats fell to the San Diego Chargers in the second round of the AFC playoffs.

Then there's the universe we inhabit: The one in the middle. The one where the Pats got past the Chargers even though they never should have—even though Tom Terrific effectively threw away the game. The one where New England collapsed in Indianapolis a week later, blowing a 21–6 halftime lead to suffer the team's first conference championship loss of the Brady-Belichick era (at the time, the team's sole loss in six trips to the AFC title game).

In our universe, there's really not that much more to tell about the Patriots or the Tom Brady of 2006. Neither team nor quarterback enjoyed a great season (not by their own impossibly high standards, anyway). And both suffered from the same ailment: a patchwork receiving corps that barely managed to get the job done in the regular season and couldn't take advantage of an incredible opportunity in the playoffs.

The ugly truth is that the season was sunk long before the moment on January 21 when cornerback Marlin Jackson slipped in front of Benjamin Watson at the Indianapolis 35-yard line and made the interception that sealed the Colts' comeback win. It was sunk in the off-season, when Deion Branch opted to hold out with a year left on his rookie contract. It became unrecoverable as soon as the Patriots agreed to trade Branch to Seattle for a first-round draft pick.

With Branch's departure, the Patriots had lost three of Brady's top targets from the team's Super Bowl seasons. David Patten, who had averaged close to 800 yards receiving in his three healthy seasons with the Pats, signed a free-agent deal with Washington following Super Bowl XXXIX. David Givens, who had been the team's most productive pass-catcher in 2004, left for the Tennessee Titans after catching a respectable 59 balls for 738 yards as Brady's No. 2 target in 2005. And Branch, who was traded a week into the 2006 season, not only had been the MVP of Super Bowl XXXIX (a game in which he hauled in a record 11 catches for 133 yards), he'd also been Brady's go-to receiver in 2005, catching 78 passes for 998 yards.

Troy Brown was still on board and still ready to give everything he had to the team every Sunday. But at 35 years old and in his 14th season with the Pats, Brown was on the downside of his career. His productivity had dipped from 101 catches for 1,199 yards in 2001 to 39 for 466 yards in 2005. He was an important contributor, a guy with a great football head who knew how to operate in the slot, but he wasn't an outside-the-numbers receiver who could carry a team.

So what the Patriots ended up with—in addition to Brown and the tight end Watson, who certainly had shown a lot of promise but who wasn't likely to become a guy who would stretch the field—was a group of castoffs from other teams.

There was Reche Caldwell, a second-round pick of the San Diego Chargers who'd accomplished most of nothing in his four seasons as a target for Drew Brees. There was Jabar Gaffney, a solid but unspectacular receiver who'd failed to live up to the expectations of the Houston Texans, who took him with the first pick of the second round in 2002, and was signed and released by the Philadelphia Eagles during the preseason. And there was Doug Gabriel, whom the Patriots acquired from Oakland in exchange for a 2007 fifth-round draft pick just before the start of the regular season. Gabriel brought both height and speed to the position, but he hadn't done anything noteworthy in his three seasons with the Raiders.

The Patriots also had a second-round draft choice of their own in Chad Jackson. But the rookie missed the preseason with a hamstring injury and never (ever) managed to find a groove in the Patriots offense.

So it wasn't exactly a shock that neither Brady nor the Patriots had a spectacular season. Of course, *spectacular* (or maybe it's *unspectacular*) is a relative term.

★ ★ ★

The 2006 Patriots finished with a 12–4 record and an AFC East title. And while those accomplishments were attributable in part to the fact that the Pats had the league's second-ranked defense, it would be difficult to argue that their seventh-ranked offense was simply along for the ride.

Brady passed for 3,529 yards, with 24 touchdowns and 12 interceptions, finishing the season with a passer rating of 87.9. Those numbers look like nothing in comparison to what the quarterback has accomplished in subsequent seasons, but they were in line with what he'd put up in all three of the team's Super Bowl–championship years.

Brady finished five games with a passer rating of better than 100. And he had a couple of memorable outings. In a Week 8 visit to Minnesota, he completed 29 of 43 passes for 372 yards and four touchdowns. The Patriots put up 31 points against a Vikings defense that had allowed an average of less than 16 per game and hadn't surrendered more than 19 in any previous match. The game was the first since 2003 in which Brady threw for more than three touchdowns.

The quarterback's next four-TD outing wasn't so long in coming. Brady had another great day in Week 11, when the Pats took on the Packers in Green Bay. His 244 passing yards in the game included a 54-yard catch-and-run touchdown connection with Caldwell.

It was telling, though, that the Patriots sandwiched back-to-back home losses between the Minnesota and Green Bay trips. The first of those losses, which came in a Sunday night game against the Colts, was particularly tough to watch. It would have been one thing if the Pats had come out on the wrong side of a shootout with the high-powered Indianapolis offense, but that wasn't the story of the game. What did happen was that while the New England defense stepped up and made things as difficult as possible on Peyton Manning and the Colts, Brady and his receivers struggled all night against a weak Indianapolis D. Brady threw four interceptions, two of which were tipped by Patriots receivers into the hands of Indy's defensive backs. One of Brady's picks took place in the end zone, taking seven points off the board in a game the Pats would lose by exactly that margin.

The Colts were 7–0 going into that game, but everyone knew they weren't really that good. The Patriots should have been able to win. Brady certainly had his chances to make it happen. And the worst part of that midseason loss was that it was the determining factor in where the two teams, both of which finished 12–4, met in the AFC Championship Game.

The Pats' second home loss came at the hands of the New York Jets. It marked the first time since 2002 that New England had lost two straight.

Then, starting with the win at Green Bay, the Pats went 6–1 down the stretch (during which time the Colts won only three of seven games).

Brady had just one bad game along the way, a murderous affair in Miami in which he completed just 12 of 25 passes, took four sacks, and lost a pair of fumbles en route to a 21–0 shutout.

In the Pats' six wins, Brady completed 68 percent of his passes (128 of 188), throwing for 1,399 yards and nine touchdowns with only three interceptions, for an overall passer rating of 99.1.

★ ★ ★

By the end of the regular season, Brady's stats for the season were seventh-best in the league and third-best in the conference, behind Manning and Carson Palmer. Caldwell had a career year, catching 61 balls for 760 yards and four touchdowns. Watson had his best season as a Patriot, catching 49 passes for 643 yards and three touchdowns. Brown, though he spent part of the season playing defensive back, had a productive season in the slot, logging 43 catches for 384 yards and four touchdowns. Brown also hit a career milestone, passing Stanley Morgan to become the Patriots' all-time leader in receptions.

The Patriots' fourth-most-productive pass catcher for the season was running back Kevin Faulk, who had 43 receptions for 356 yards and a pair of touchdowns. That wasn't unusual, as one of Faulk's greatest attributes was that he provided a rock-solid outlet for Brady on checkdowns. But it pointed to a meaningful fact: three of Brady's most productive targets for the season—not merely in catches but in yards—had been a slot receiver, a tight end, and a tailback. It was no mystery why the quarterback's passing average, 221 yards per game, was his lowest since his first season as a starter.

And that told everybody what they needed to know about New England heading into the playoffs: opposing defenses didn't have to respect the Pats outside the numbers, because there was no one there whom the quarterback trusted.

2006

By the Numbers

Total Yards	3,529
Yards Per Game	220.6
Attempts	516
Completions	319
Completion Percentage	61.8
Yards Per Attempt	6.8
Touchdowns	24
Interceptions	12
Passer Rating	87.9
Games Rated Higher Than 100 *(Includes One Postseason)*	6
Best Single-Game Rating	128.2

Of course, that information proved little help to the Jets, who had to travel to Foxborough in the wild-card round. New York surrendered a touchdown on the Patriots' opening drive, during which Brady completed four of six passes for 50 yards. And though the Jets found a way to keep the game competitive for a while after that, the Patriots scored a second touchdown with 14 seconds left in the first half to push the score to 17–10. Short passes, consistent production on the ground from both Corey Dillon and Laurence Maroney, and outstanding defense in the second half sealed a 37–16 New England victory. Brady finished the day 22-for-34 for 212 yards and two touchdowns (one each to Faulk and tight end Daniel Graham), with a passer rating of 101.6.

★ ★ ★

In the Patriots' divisional-round matchup with the Chargers in San Diego, it took a combination of luck, outstanding defense by New England, mistakes by Chargers players and coaches, and one of the greatest heads-up plays of all time from Brown for the Patriots to overcome an off day for Brady and eke out a narrow victory.

Brady completed just 27 of 51 passes, scoring two touchdowns but throwing three picks to emerge with a passer rating of only 57.6. His final interception of the game, which came as the Pats trailed 21–13 with just more than six minutes remaining, should by all rights have ended New England's postseason. But Brown made a split-second switch from receiver to defensive back and stripped the ball from Chargers safety Marlon McCree. Caldwell fell on the fumble, giving the Patriots another chance. And this time Brady zoned in and got it right. He drove the Pats to the Chargers' end zone. Then, on the two-point conversion that tied the game, he sold a fake high snap, opening up a running lane for Faulk.

On the team's next possession, Brady moved the Patriots into position for the game-winning field goal with a 19-yard pass over the middle to Graham and a perfectly placed 49-yard pass to Caldwell down the right sideline. Stephen Gostkowski nailed a 31-yard kick to put the Pats on top. And when San Diego's kicker, Nate Kaeding, missed a desperation 54-yard attempt in the closing seconds, New England had its improbable victory. With the 24–21 win, the Pats advanced to the AFC Championship Game.

No one could deny that the Patriots had advanced deeper into the postseason than they should have. But that was also the case for the Colts and Peyton Manning, who actually fared worse in their divisional-round win over the Ravens in Baltimore than the Patriots did in San Diego. The Colts topped the Ravens on the strength of five field goals by turncoat place-kicker Adam Vinatieri while Manning went 15-for-30 for 170 yards with no touchdowns and two picks, walking away with a passer rating of 39.6.

Heading into the AFC Championship Game, then, it seemed that for all the flaws in the Patriots' offense, anything could happen. And almost everything did. The Patriots—behind solid play by the offense, a lucky break on a goal-line

★ ★ ★ ★ ★ ★ ★

Brady is one of the guys who got people to say it's not about the big arm, it's about the good decisions. He was doing things that veteran quarterbacks do in his third, fourth, fifth NFL starts. And then to win consistently when your defense is collapsing around you, which is what happened in two of those Super Bowls, that's the sign of a great quarterback.

—Kerry Byrne, Cold Hard Football Facts

fumble by Maroney that fell into guard Logan Mankins' hands in the end zone, and a poor decision by Manning that led to a pick six—opened up a 21–3 lead early in the second quarter. That put New England in an enviable position. The Pats didn't need to shut down Manning for the entire game. All they needed was for Brady to come close to matching his rival's output.

That New England couldn't achieve even that goal after taking a 21–6 lead into halftime was attributable largely to one major blunder by Caldwell.

By midway through the fourth quarter, Manning had brought his team back from the brink, driving the Colts to three touchdowns and successfully executing a two-point conversion—during which time the Pats scored only once—to tie the score at 28.

But then the Pats got an opportunity to turn momentum around. A punt return by Brown, a face-mask call on the Colts, and a pair of passes to Caldwell and Gaffney moved the ball to the Indianapolis 13.

The Pats lost five yards on an illegal shift penalty, but it shouldn't have mattered. Because on first-and-15 from the Indy 18-yard line, Caldwell was left uncovered on the right side of the field. He made sure Brady knew it too, and the quarterback came through. Brady delivered the ball into the hands of his receiver, who had a clear path to the end zone. The play should have put the Pats ahead 35–28. But Caldwell dropped the ball. It was the receiver's second major drop of the second half, and it ultimately left the Pats to settle for three points instead of seven.

The difference proved deadly as the Colts added a touchdown late in the game to go up by four and put New England in a desperate position with a minute to play. The pick by Jackson stopped New England from overcoming the deficit. But it was the absence of reliable receivers that cost Brady and the Patriots an opportunity to win their fourth Super Bowl.

At least, that's how it happened in this universe. You know, the one that counts.

CHAPTER 16

★ ★ ★

Deadly Combination: Brady and Belichick

Tom Brady was still officially a college football player on one of the most important days of his NFL career: January 4, 2000. Brady was just three days removed from his final game as quarterback of the University of Michigan Wolverines, still basking in the glory of his incredible performance against Alabama in the Orange Bowl.

It would be more than a month before Brady would get a chance to participate in the NFL Scouting Combine and three before he'd learn whether a team would take a chance on him in the draft. It was a time of uncertainty for Brady. Not his first as a football player—not even his first since the middle of his senior season—but perhaps the most open-ended since he'd committed to Michigan five years earlier. Brady didn't know where, or whether, he'd be playing football come September.

In New Jersey, on the other hand, there was considerably less uncertainty. At least for a few hours. The New York Jets were preparing that day to introduce their new coach, Bill Belichick. Bill Parcells had announced a day earlier that he was retiring from coaching (again) after three seasons on the Jets sideline. Belichick was Parcells' hand-picked successor. A former head coach of the Cleveland Browns, Belichick had served as assistant head coach under Parcells in

New England and New York. Belichick's contract stipulated that the Jets head coaching job would be his if Parcells left the post. And from January 3 through January 4, it was.

But at the press conference at which he was to be officially introduced by the team, Belichick had a change of heart. Moments before he took the podium, he scribbled perhaps the shortest letter of resignation in football history on a sheet of paper: "I resign as HC of the NYJ." He addressed the media as scheduled, but when he talked, he talked about his misgivings about the job he'd waited three seasons to get.

The Jets ownership was in transition. Leon Hess had died the previous May, and his estate was in the process of selling the team. Belichick, who had been coach of the original Browns in the turbulent season before the organization relocated to Baltimore, wasn't interested in waiting around to see what form new ownership would take. Not when he knew there was a stable team that wanted him as its head coach just up I-95 in Foxborough.

And after a few weeks of wrangling and bickering over Belichick's contract and his obligations to the Jets, the New England Patriots agreed to send a first-round draft pick to New York in exchange for the right to hire Belichick.

One could spend a lifetime pondering what-ifs and never come to a meaningful conclusion. What if Belichick had stayed in New York? How might the coach have fared? What then for Brady in the draft? It's a bit like wondering what might have happened had Jets linebacker Mo Lewis not taken out Drew Bledsoe in 2001. No one knows. And it doesn't matter.

Belichick landed in New England, where he had the full support of his friend, owner Robert Kraft. The coach brought in Jets director of pro personnel Scott Pioli to serve as New England's general manager. And the pair had the wisdom

★　★　★　★　★　★　★

Tom Brady? He'll kill ya. If he catches you half asleep, he'll punch you right in the face with the stretch. You can be as multiple as you want on defense, but when you play Tom Brady, he regulates you. He turns you into trash.

—Jon Gruden

to listen to quarterbacks coach Dick Rehbein when he petitioned them to take Brady in the sixth round of the 2000 draft.

The events of January 4, so far from Ann Arbor, had set momentous wheels in motion for coach and quarterback alike. The coach was looking to use a low-risk pick on a backup quarterback he might be able to groom. The player was looking for a place where he could once again fight his way to the top of the depth chart. And somehow, at least in part because Belichick had resigned as HC of the NYJ, the kid who had battled his way past obstacle after obstacle to land the starting job for the Michigan Wolverines—and then to hold on to it—landed with the NFL coach most likely to give him a chance to battle his way to a starting job in the pros.

★ ★ ★

Belichick demands the same thing from all of his players, and he demands it time and again: "Do your job."

The coach is a master of complex schemes, a designer of defenses that befuddle opposing quarterbacks, a mastermind of an ever-changing offense that is, from game to game and week to week, whatever the defensive coaches on the other sideline least want it to be. To play effectively for him requires mental agility and physical toughness, discipline, dedication, and attention to detail.

When he says "Do your job," what he means is, "Be where you're supposed to be when you're supposed to be there, handle your assignment and expect the guys around you to handle theirs, and be prepared for anything."

Belichick coaches "situational football." Players prepare for anything that can happen in a game. They have a plan for every contingency and internalize that plan to the point where they can execute it instinctually. Every player is expected to know what his role is in every situation. No one is supposed to be taken by surprise...by anything. When Belichick says "Do your job," what he means is, "Know your role."

The coach could not have found a better candidate to run his offense if he'd drafted 100 first-round quarterbacks. He surely didn't have the quarterback he needed on his roster when he arrived in New England.

Drew Bledsoe was a great competitor, he had a monster of an arm, and he was as tough a quarterback as the Patriots had seen since Steve Grogan. He was a good teammate and a strong leader. But Bledsoe wasn't a quarterback who could play the game Belichick's way. The coach knew that. He'd known who Bledsoe was during his time in Cleveland and his years in New York. Bledsoe wasn't a quarterback who would take what a defense gave him. He wasn't the type who could walk to the line of scrimmage, survey the team lined up against him, know what was coming, and know how to take advantage of it. He was a player who believed he could beat his opponents simply because he was more skillful than they were. He was a player who decided what he wanted to do and then tried to make it happen.

Bledsoe wasn't the kind of player who was going to succeed in Belichick's vision of the game. Brady was. He was a player who succeeded with practice and preparation. He knew that if he studied and studied and studied a defense, he could go into any play knowing what was in store for him—and consequently knowing how to counter it. He was an instinctual leader who could inspire the players around him to try harder without having to chase after them to do it. He was exactly the kind of player Belichick needed to turn his ideas about football into reality on the field. Brady started doing just that as soon as he was given an opportunity to line up under center. And he's done it with ever more devastating results in each season since.

★ ★ ★

Belichick and Brady have been the most dangerous combination of coach and quarterback in the history of the NFL—more dangerous than Lombardi and Starr, Shula and Marino, or Walsh and Montana. They are the winningest coach-quarterback pair in NFL history, holding records for both regular-season wins (172) and postseason wins (22).

They are the only coach-quarterback tandem ever to advance to six Super Bowls and the only one to win three Super Bowl championships in four years. Along with Chuck Noll and Terry Bradshaw, they are one of only two coach-QB duos to win four Super Bowls. They produced the only 16-win regular season in league history and have won 14 or more games in each of four seasons. Despite constant changeovers in both on-field personnel and coaching staff, in 14 seasons

Tom Brady and Bill Belichick have paired up to form a powerhouse quarterback-coach combo the likes of which have not been seen before…and probably never will be again.

together, they have never finished with a record that wasn't at least tied for the best in their division. And only once have they fallen short of posting a double-digit win total for a season. Not only that, they've never failed to finish above .500. They are the only coach and quarterback ever to lift a team to seven straight division titles—and to 13 division championships overall. And they are one of just two coach-QB combos ever to reach five straight conference championships, along with John Madden and Ken Stabler.

There have always been the questions, and there may always be, about whether Brady made Belichick or Belichick made Brady. Could the coach have succeeded without the quarterback? Would the quarterback have so much as started a game, let alone 254 of them, if he hadn't wound up playing in the coach's system?

The answer is probably both more and less complicated than the questions imply. Belichick made Brady, and Brady made Belichick. Their success is indivisible. There's little doubt that either has the skills to succeed without the other (Belichick, at least, has shown it, coaching a Matt Cassel–led Patriots team to 11 wins in 2008.) But together, they're more than successful; they're very nearly unstoppable.

CHAPTER 17

★ ★ ★

Nearly Perfect, Seriously Amazing: 2007

If it hadn't been so painful, so agonizing, so brutal...or, OK, if it hadn't been so *final*...it would hardly be worth mentioning. Just one of those singular, awful moments when everything that can possibly go wrong does. A blemish on an otherwise glorious season.

A circus catch—one hand and a helmet, purely spectacular, impossible not to admire except for the circumstances. A 12-yard gain on third-and-11. A defensive play-calling gamble that left a capable 5'9" No. 2 cornerback isolated on an outstanding 6'5" wide receiver. A go-ahead touchdown with 35 seconds on the clock. Then a final, desperate attempt to rescue a season. An incompletion, then a sack for a 10-yard loss. A beautiful 64-yard pass knocked away at the New York Giants 20-yard-line. And another deep pass slightly underthrown into double coverage and knocked away at the Giants 27.

Game over. *Super Bowl* over. Season over.

It was the only way an 18–1 record can ever be a negative: when it could have been—and needed to be—19–0.

If you could set that ending aside—you can't, of course, but let's pretend, because the rest of the story really is worth retelling—you'd be better able to appreciate the amazing journey Tom Brady and the 2007 Patriots took to arrive at that ultimate moment of heartbreak.

It was the greatest regular season in NFL history, a thrilling ride during which the only real questions posed were about whether the Patriots were accomplishing too much.

The quarterback, meanwhile, could hardly have accomplished anything more. Brady's 2007 performance easily outshone any ever turned in by Brady or any other QB. Ever.

★　★　★

It's worth noting that the whole thing had its roots in another disappointing loss: the 2006 AFC Championship Game, in which the Patriots blew a 21–6 halftime lead against the Colts in Indianapolis.

The battle was ultimately decided by the Patriots receivers' inability to get open and by an unforgivable drop by Reche Caldwell of what should have been an easy touchdown completion. The collapse cost the Patriots a chance to reach their fourth Super Bowl in six years.

And while the entire team, including Brady, shared blame for the 38–34 defeat, no one could have failed to conclude that a Patriots team with better receivers would have cruised through the conference championship and, in all likelihood, hoisted another Lombardi Trophy.

It was clear as soon as the game ended that things had to change. And change wasn't long in coming. The first move came in early March, when the Patriots exploited a business error on the part of the Miami Dolphins to back their division rivals into a corner and force a trade for underappreciated slot receiver/kick returner Wes Welker.

It was fairly surprising that the Pats were able to wrest Welker from Miami. Undrafted in 2004, Welker initially was signed as a rookie free agent by the San Diego Chargers. He joined the Dolphins after San Diego cut him one game into the 2004 season. In 2006 Welker was one of Miami's top receivers, catching 67 passes for 687 yards.

Welker entered the 2007 league year as a restricted free agent. Had Miami offered him the high RFA tender of $2.35 million, which would have required any team signing him away to send the Dolphins first- and third-round draft

Leading the Pats to an almost perfect season, Brady celebrates a second-quarter touchdown during their 20–10 win over the New York Jets on December 16, 2007.

picks as compensation, it would have all but guaranteed that he would stay with the Dolphins. Even a middle tender—$1.85 million in salary and compensation of a first-round pick for signing him away—likely would have allowed Miami to retain Welker's rights. But the Dolphins had offered Welker the low tender: $1.35 million and, more important, a cost of only a second-round pick should he sign with another team.

That mistake made the receiver easy pickings for the Pats. In a position to offer Welker a deal the Dolphins couldn't possibly match, the Patriots worked out a trade with Miami. They sent a second- and seventh-round pick south, which allowed them to ink Welker to a cap-friendly contract. And so the Pats secured the player who would become the league's most productive pass catcher over the following five seasons.

The Patriots' second big off-season move came on Day 2 of the 2007 NFL Draft, when New England shipped a fourth-round pick they'd acquired from the San Francisco 49ers a day earlier to the Oakland Raiders in exchange for Randy Moss, one of the most physically gifted wide receivers ever to play the game.

While there were questions at the time about whether Moss had lost a step (the Raiders were convinced that he had, though their motivation to make a deal with the Pats had more to do with the fact that Moss had worn out his welcome in the Oakland locker room), those questions didn't last. By Week 1 of the 2007 season, it was clear that New England had taken Oakland for a major ride. Moss was still the best wide receiver in the NFL. And suddenly he was paired with football's best quarterback.

The results were nothing less than league-shattering.

★ ★ ★

The Patriots opened the season with a blowout win over the New York Jets in the Meadowlands. Brady passed for 297 yards and three touchdowns. He connected with Moss nine times for 183 yards, including a beautiful 51-yard touchdown pass thrown perfectly to his receiver in triple coverage. The 38–14 win, Brady's 146.6 passer rating, and the unstoppable appearance of the Brady-to-Moss combination made it clear that it was going to be a difficult season for New England's remaining 12 opponents.

In Week 2, with the Spygate controversy swirling around the team, Brady and company took the show to prime time. Brady hit Moss and Welker eight times each, for 105 and 91 yards respectively, on his way to 279 yards and three touchdowns. Two of those touchdowns went to Moss, on perfectly executed plays of 23 and 24 yards. Brady's 80.6 percent completion percentage (25–31) was a key factor as the Pats beat the San Diego Chargers 38–14.

Brady and the Patriots continued to take apart their opponents over the following six weeks. Brady threw for 311 yards and four touchdowns in a 38–7 win over the Buffalo Bills. He finished the game with a stellar passer rating of 150.9, and was named AFC Offensive Player of the Week. Brady connected for another three scores in a 34–13 road win over the Cincinnati Bengals and three more when the Pats beat the Cleveland Browns in Foxborough.

In Week 6 the Patriots traveled to Dallas to take on the unbeaten Cowboys in a game that was billed as a potential Super Bowl XLII preview. New England got out to a great start, putting up 14 first-quarter points as Brady hit Moss in the back of the end zone from the Dallas 6-yard line then found Welker, who caught the ball at the Dallas 14 and zipped into the end zone for a 35-yard catch-and-run touchdown.

The Cowboys made it a game, however. They climbed to within four in the second quarter when their two defensive ends combined on a scoring play. Greg Ellis strip-sacked Brady, and Jason Hatcher picked up the ball and charged 29 yards for a touchdown. Then, after applying pressure and forcing the Pats to go three-and-out on the opening possession of the second half, Dallas marched 74 yards and took a 24–21 lead on an eight-yard pass from Tony Romo to Patrick Crayton.

Five minutes of game time and 77 yards later, the Patriots took the lead back with Brady's fourth touchdown pass of the game, a short strike over the middle to tight end Kyle Brady. And when Brady found Donte Stallworth at the Dallas 40 on what Stallworth would turn into a 69-yard touchdown play early in the fourth quarter, the game was effectively over. The touchdown was Brady's fifth of the day, tying what at the time was a career best.

With the victory, Brady tied Dallas legend Roger Staubach for the most wins, 76, by a quarterback in his first 100 starts. Brady finished the game with 31 completions on 46 attempts for 388 yards. With his five touchdowns and no interceptions, he earned a passer rating of 129.6. For the second time in the 2007 season, he was named AFC Offensive Player of the Week.

"The reason Brady is one of the best quarterbacks of all time? Days like Sunday," Peter King wrote in his *Monday Morning Quarterback* column. "Sick. Just sick."

Buzz about Week 9's showdown with the defending Super Bowl champion Colts began to build.

★ ★ ★

The Patriots had Miami and Washington to get through on their way to Indianapolis, but those teams proved to be little trouble. In Miami, Brady threw five touchdown passes in the first half as the Pats built a 42–7 lead. The Brady-and-Moss show was at its most entertaining, with the pair hooking up for touchdowns of 35 and 50 yards, both thrown into double coverage at the goal line.

Bill Belichick took the highly unusual step of replacing Brady with Matt Cassel early in the fourth quarter but put his starter back in the game after Cassel threw a pick six to Dolphins defensive end Jason Taylor. Brady responded by throwing a bullet that connected with Welker on a crossing pattern at the Miami 10. And when Welker finished the play with a dive into the end zone, Brady had thrown six touchdowns in a game for the first time in his career.

That touchdown count set a new franchise record. Moreover, Brady had thrown five or more touchdowns in two consecutive games, tying a league record set by Daunte Culpepper with the Minnesota Vikings in 2004.

On the way to those six touchdowns, Brady completed 21 of 25 passes (84 percent). The game also marked the first of two times in Brady's career in which

★ ★ ★ ★ ★ ★ ★

When you have a guy like Tom leading your team, you are willing to do anything by all means necessary to make things happen. He's not just the best quarterback I've ever played with, but the best quarterback that has ever been put in this league.

—Randy Moss

he has posted a perfect passer rating, 158.3. It wasn't at all surprising when Brady was honored with a second consecutive AFC Offensive Player of the Week award.

At 7–0, the 2007 Patriots had posted the best start in franchise history. The Patriots were clearly on track for a historic season though, outside New England, many were less than delighted to see it. Led by ESPN's Gregg Easterbrook, a chorus of critics charged that the Pats' unstoppable scoring machine amounted to unsportsmanlike conduct. Easterbrook speculated that the Pats were angry about Spygate and the penalties assessed by commissioner Roger Goodell (heavy fines for Belichick and the franchise, plus the loss of a first-round draft pick) and were meting out their wrath on opponents by "running up the score."

"On Sunday, the Patriots led the winless Dolphins 42–7 late in the third quarter, yet Tom Brady was still behind center. And he wasn't just handing off the ball to grind out the clock, either. Rather, he was back in the shotgun, still throwing to run up the score," Easterbrook wrote in *Tuesday Morning Quarterback*.

The Patriots were vindictive and classless, Easterbrook wrote. He went to the absurd extreme of labeling a professional football team "evil" because its players had committed the heinous crime of scoring touchdowns against other professional football players whose job it was to stop them.

★ ★ ★

Complaints about New England running up the score only grew louder after the Pats' 52–7 win over Washington in Week 8.

Washington arrived in Foxborough with a 4–2 record and the fifth-ranked defense in the league. They had given up just 5.6 yards per pass attempt over the first six weeks of the season and had allowed 13 points per game over the three weeks before their matchup with New England. Though Washington's offensive production was thin, there was hope among Washington fans and Patriots haters alike that the defense could hold Brady in check. It couldn't.

The Patriots scored on their first possession of the game and continued to score at will throughout the contest. By the time Brady was pulled in favor of Cassel midway through the fourth quarter, he had thrown for three touchdowns and rushed for two more. He averaged 8.1 yards per pass during the game. The effort gave Brady a career victory over every team in the NFL except his own and put him at 30 passing touchdowns for the season, two ahead of his previous career-high mark.

This time, criticism about the Patriots running up the score came in spite of the fact that Brady had sat out the final eight minutes of the game. It came in part because Cassel added a rushing touchdown, putting the Patriots up 52–0 in a game they would eventually win by a score of 52–7.

Washington coach Joe Gibbs left the field without shaking Belichick's hand, though he later claimed to have "no problem" with the Patriots' aggressive approach to the game.

Gibbs' players weren't so diplomatic. "You've got no choice but to be upset when the other team does that kind of stuff, throwing the ball," defensive end Phillip Daniels said after the game. "Late in the fourth quarter, you're up by 38 points, and they're still throwing the ball and going for it on fourth down. That's, like, a slap in the face."

ESPN's John Clayton opined that the Patriots were clearly out for blood: "Belichick has assembled perhaps the most [dominant] team in NFL history, and he's intent on destroying all opponents in his path."

That may have been so. But there were still teams in the league that could and would stand up to the Patriots. And the 2007 edition of the Pats' annual battle with the Colts would make it clear that things wouldn't always come easy.

★ ★ ★

New England and Indianapolis went into their Week 9 matchup with unde-feated records—the Patriots at 8–0 and the Colts at 7–0. The game, which *Sports Illustrated*'s Paul Zimmerman labeled "Super Bowl XLI½," marked the latest point in a season at which undefeated teams ever had squared off head to head.

For large chunks of the afternoon, it appeared the Colts would emerge still perfect and would be favored to win their second consecutive championship.

For the first time in the 2007 season, the Patriots failed to score on their first possession of a game. Brady was sacked for a 10-yard loss on New England's first offensive play and managed only 12 yards on the following two snaps.

Brady drove the team to a touchdown and a 7–3 lead early in the second quarter, but the Colts added a second field goal. Then, following safety Antoine Bethea's interception of Brady at the Indy goal line, the Colts put up seven as running back Joseph Addai took a three-yard dump-off pass an additional 70 yards to the Patriots' end zone. The Colts went into halftime ahead 13–7.

The Patriots could get nothing going in the third quarter. And the Colts opened the fourth with another pick of Brady, after which Manning led an eight-play, 32-yard touchdown drive to put the home team up 20–10. It looked very much like the Patriots were headed for their first loss since their last trip to Indy. But Brady wasn't ready to call it a night.

By the Numbers 2007

Total Yards	4,806
Yards Per Game	300.4
Attempts	578
Completions	398
Completion Percentage	68.9
Yards Per Attempt	8.3
Touchdowns	50
Interceptions	8
Passer Rating	117.2
Games Rated Higher Than 100 *(Includes One Postseason)*	12
Best Single-Game Rating	158.3*

(*Perfect)

In a drive that featured a classic 55-yard pass to Moss who was matched up against an undersized Bethea, Brady got his team into the Colts' end zone in a minute and a half. A stellar defensive series, followed by a 23-yard punt return by Welker, allowed the Patriots to start their next drive at midfield. Brady again exploited Bethea, this time playing out of position for a 33-yard strike to Stallworth that moved the Patriots into the red zone. On the next play, Brady hit Kevin Faulk at the 10, and Faulk took care of the rest, scrambling into the end zone to put the Patriots ahead 24–20.

That score stuck, and the Patriots left Indianapolis with their most important, and most hard-fought, win of the season. Brady had three touchdowns in the game. It was his ninth consecutive game with three or more touchdown passes, which broke Manning's record of eight. He also finished the game with 33 touchdowns in the season, breaking Babe Parilli's 43-year-old franchise record of 31.

And it was time to start wondering if a perfect season really might be possible.

★ ★ ★

An undefeated season remained highly unlikely. There were good reasons that only one team in post-AFL/NFL merger history, the 1972 Dolphins, had ever progressed through an entire season without suffering a single loss. No matter

133

how good any professional football team may be, it has to square off weekly against an opposing team made up of elite athletes.

Under those circumstances, it's not at all surprising that teams that come out on top three-quarters of the time almost always win their divisions. Teams that prevail in 13 or 14 games more often than not grab one of their conference's top seeds. And in the 34 seasons since the NFL adopted its 16-game season, only five times has any team managed to finish 15–1. Until 2007, no team had made it all the way to 16–0.

The 1972 Dolphins played a 14-game regular-season schedule. Their final record, including Super Bowl VII, was 17–0. To exceed that accomplishment by two wins, particularly in the era of the salary cap and the competitive balance it breeds, would border on impossible.

Still, as the Patriots returned from their Week 10 bye to clinch the AFC East title with a 56–10 romp over the division-rival Buffalo Bills in Orchard Park, it was growing increasingly difficult to dismiss the possibility. The Pats were 10–0, and there was no hint that any team in the league had a realistic chance of coming between them and nine more wins.

Brady, meanwhile, with his five touchdown passes against the Bills, not only grabbed another franchise record—his 185 career touchdowns put him three ahead of Steve Grogan—but extended his NFL record streak of consecutive games with at least three touchdown passes to 10. Four of Brady's touchdown passes were thrown to Moss—and all of those in the first half.

Hosting the 5–5 Philadelphia Eagles in Week 12, the Pats very nearly stumbled, needing a fourth-quarter touchdown drive and an interception in the end zone by Asante Samuel to hold on to a 31–28 victory. Brady completed only one touchdown pass in the game (which he dropped into the hands of 2006 holdover Jabar Gaffney in the left corner of the end zone from 19 yards out on the final play of the second quarter), but he still racked up 380 yards through the air. And the team set a new franchise scoring mark with their 442nd point of the season.

A shot to Gaffney in the left corner of the end zone would turn out to be an even bigger deal the following week, when the Patriots faced the Ravens in Baltimore. Trailing 24–20 late in the fourth quarter, New England needed Brady to overcome a subpar performance and lead his team to victory. He didn't disappoint, driving the Pats 73 yards on 13 plays—including a scramble to convert on fourth-and-six—and capping the effort with an eight-yard strike to Gaffney in the game's final minute.

The win elevated the Patriots to 12–0. And Brady's two touchdowns in the game gave him 41 for the season. Peyton Manning's single-season record of 49 touchdowns was well in sight.

★ ★ ★

Both Brady and the team went back to making it look easy when they returned to Foxborough for the first of three home games, hosting the Pittsburgh Steelers.

After falling behind 3–0 early, New England came alive and ultimately routed Pittsburgh 34–13. Brady put up four passing touchdowns, including a 63-yard strike to Moss, who was left all alone on a post pattern when the Steelers bit on a play fake by an offense that almost never bothered to call running plays.

The game also featured a 56-yard touchdown throw to Gaffney on a flea flicker that, by all rights, ought to have failed. Moss dropped Brady's opening lateral, but the receiver stuck with it, picked up the ball, and got it back to Brady, who promptly aired it out and found Gaffney eight yards behind Pittsburgh's safeties and streaking toward the end zone.

The win ensured the Patriots a first-round bye in the playoffs. The touchdown passes gave Brady his 11th game of the season with three or more, breaking a tie with Dan Marino for the single-season record. And Brady's performance in the game—32-for-46 for 399 yards and a passer rating of 125.2—earned him a fourth AFC Offensive Player of the Week nod.

Brady went without a touchdown for the only time in the 2007 season in a 20–10 win over the Jets in Week 15. But the win at least assured that the Patriots would have home-field advantage throughout the postseason.

And Brady got the touchdown machine cranked back up in time for a Week 16 meeting with the Dolphins. He hit Moss twice and Gaffney once (with a perfectly placed sideline throw that resulted in a 48-yard score) to push his season total to 48. With their 28–7 win, the Patriots became the first team in NFL history to achieve a record of 15–0. They were just one win away from regular-season perfection.

★ ★ ★

Two days before the new year, the Patriots traveled to the Meadowlands to take on the Giants with hopes of completing the league's first 16–0 season.

The Saturday night game was hyped nearly as much as a Super Bowl. The NFL Network, which had the broadcast rights for the game, boasted in a press release of having scheduled "65.5 hours of programming devoted to this historic game." Not surprisingly, most of those hours were devoted to the Patriots and their "Path to Perfection."

To turn on NFL Network, ESPN, Sirius NFL Radio, or any national sports broadcasting outlet—or to read a newspaper or visit a sports website—during the six days leading up to the game, one might have believed it *was* Super Bowl week, or at the very least that only one game of any import was on the schedule for Week 17. (Never mind that Cleveland, Tennessee, Washington, Minnesota and New Orleans all were trying to play their way into the postseason.)

In reality, the Patriots-Giants matchup mattered only because 16–0 was on the line. The Patriots had already clinched the top seed in the AFC. And the Giants were locked in as the five-seed in the NFC. The outcome of the game would have no bearing on anyone's hopes or chances in the playoffs.

Still, 16–0 is 16–0. And the football-watching world was enthralled. So much so, in fact, that the NFL Network, which had been caught up in a battle with cable TV providers throughout the season and remained unavailable to millions of Americans, cut a deal with NBC and CBS to simulcast the game.

Of course, Patriots fans who wanted to be part of the historic event didn't have to sit back and take in the TV broadcast. Or at least that was true of Pats fans with deep pockets. New Jersey was just a short drive away. And lots of Giants fans were more than happy to part with their seats—at prices of up to $1,600 per ticket.

And so the New England faithful were present in abundance to witness the final air show of the high-flying 2007 Patriots regular season. No one would claim they didn't get what they paid for.

With or without a reason to play, and mindful of the fact that no team should walk through an open door into football history, Giants coach Tom Coughlin conceded nothing. He played his starters from start to finish and did everything in his power to deliver a 15–1 finish to the Pats. He very nearly pulled it off too.

The Giants not only scored first but held the lead until the start of the second quarter, when Brady hit Moss with a four-yard touchdown pass, moving the Pats ahead 10–7. The lead proved extremely short-lived, however, as Giants return man Domenik Hixon took the ensuing kickoff 74 yards for a touchdown.

The Pats failed to score another touchdown in the first half—in frustrating fashion too, as a catchable 19-yard pass to Moss in the end zone late in the period bounced off the helmet of New York linebacker Gerris Wilkinson, leaving the Pats to settle for their third field goal—and went into halftime trailing 21–16. Patriots players became visibly agitated during the Giants' final scoring drive of the quarter, getting into post-play tussles with the Giants. Whether it was a desire to find their way into the history books or just a lack of familiarity with the very notion of losing, the Pats clearly were displeased with the way the game was unfolding.

Immediately on the other side of the break things got even more difficult. The Patriots got the ball to start the second half but went three-and-out, with Brady and Moss again failing to connect on a deep pass on third down.

A short punt set the Giants up to start their first drive of the half on their own 40. Seven plays later, Eli Manning hit Plaxico Burress with a magnificent 19-yard touchdown pass, putting the Giants ahead 28–16. It looked as if the football gods simply would not allow a 16-win regular season.

Then the Patriots offense started to wake up. With a 28-yard Brady-to-Welker pass and help from a pair of Giants penalties, they mounted a 73-yard drive that ended with a six-yard Laurence Maroney touchdown run.

Then, early in the fourth quarter, Brady dropped back to pass from the Patriots 35-yard line and found Moss in stride at the Giants 23. Moss took the ball into the end zone, giving himself a new NFL record for touchdown catches in a season (23) and Brady a new single-season record for touchdown throws (50). With a two-point conversion tacked on, the play also put the Patriots ahead 31–28.

A Manning interception and a 52-yard touchdown drive later, the Patriots were up 10. And although the Giants would score another touchdown of their own, the lead would hold. The Patriots came out on top 38–35. They had made it to 16–0.

Don Shula, coach of the undefeated 1972 Dolphins was suitably impressed. "Going undefeated during the regular season is a remarkable achievement," Shula said, following the game. "I know firsthand how difficult it is to win every game, and just as we did in 1972, the Patriots have done a great job concentrating on each week's opponent and not letting any other distractions interrupt that focus. If they go on to complete an undefeated season, I will be the first to congratulate Coach Belichick and the Patriot organization."

Brady's stats in that final game included 32 completions on 42 attempts for 356 yards and a pair of touchdowns. Brady earned a passer rating of 116.8 and was recognized for the fifth time in 2007 as the AFC Offensive Player of the Week.

The Patriots' 589 points for the season set a new league record. They also set new records with the 315-point differential between their 589 and the 274 they allowed, plus their 75 total touchdowns.

For the Books — 2007

League Records

Most Touchdowns	50
Most Consecutive Games with Five or More Touchdowns (tied with Daunte Culpepper)	2
Most Consecutive Games with Three or More Touchdowns	10
Most Wins in a Regular Season	16
Best Completion Percentage in a Playoff Game	92.9
Most Pass Attempts without an Interception in a Super Bowl	48

Team Records

Most Touchdown Passes in a Game	6

Honors and Career Milestones

NFL MVP
First-Team All-Pro
Pro Bowl, Fourth Career Selection
Offensive Player of the Year
AP Male Athlete of the Year

Brady's final numbers included NFL single-season records for best touchdown-to-interception differential (+42) and most games with three or more touchdown passes (12). He also recorded the league record for most touchdown passes in a month with 20 in October.

Brady was named NFL MVP, taking 49 of 50 votes. (The single dissenting vote, which went to Brett Favre, was cast by Frank Cooney, president of the SportsXchange. Cooney later explained that he felt Favre played a more instrumental role in leading an inexperienced Green Bay Packers squad to a 13–3 finish than Brady had in directing the more complete Patriots team to 16–0. His position was arguably flawed but hardly unreasonable.) Brady also was named NFL Offensive Player of the Year. And he finished the season having been named AFC Offensive Player of the Month twice.

For Brady and the Patriots, the work of putting together the greatest regular season in league history was over. All that remained was to win three more games and earn recognition as the greatest team in NFL history.

★ ★ ★

The fact that the Patriots would eventually fall short of that lofty goal can't help but color perceptions of the 2007 season, but it doesn't erase any of what the team or the quarterback achieved. Neither does it alter what was accomplished in the AFC playoffs.

In the Patriots' divisional-round matchup with the Jacksonville Jaguars, Brady completed 26 of 28 passes, setting an NFL record (postseason and regular-season) for completion percentage in a game, 92.9 percent. (Consider, too, that both of Brady's incompletions in the game were delivered into the hands of receivers who simply dropped the ball.) Brady set another postseason record by completing his first 16 passes of the game and was a perfect 12-for-12 in the first half.

Brady's accomplishments against the 12–5 Jaguars came despite a Jacksonville defensive game plan designed to take away the deep pass and knock the Patriots out of their offensive comfort zone. The Jags loaded up on Moss, covering him with multiple defensive backs throughout the game and challenging Brady to find a way to win without looking to his biggest, fastest, and most talented target.

The strategy worked, at least to an extent: Moss finished the game with just one catch for 14 yards—and that was the Patriots' third-longest passing gain of the night. The trouble for the Jaguars was that Brady hit every other pass-catcher on the field. He completed passes to eight different players—primarily Welker, who snagged nine balls for 54 yards and a touchdown—racking up 262 passing yards and three touchdowns. To top it off, Laurence Maroney came up huge, rushing for 122 yards and a touchdown and hauling in a pair of passes for 40 yards. The Pats came out on top 31–20, and Brady came away from the game with an astonishing postseason passer rating of 141.6.

And the Jags joined the long list of Patriots opponents who discovered that they could play their best football against New England and still end up losing. Like several others before them, they weren't happy about the lesson.

Jacksonville safety Reggie Nelson became the spokesman for his team's frustration after the game when he sneered at Brady's performance: "It was a dump-down game. Anybody can go 26-of-28 in a dump-down game."

As if Brady had somehow done something wrong by taking what the Jaguars defense gave him. As if Brady hadn't been masterful in selling a fake Statue of Liberty play that set up a six-yard touchdown pass to Welker. As if the play that broke Jacksonville's back hadn't been a beauty of a 53-yard bomb to Stallworth down the right sideline that Brady launched while darting away from heavy pressure by the Jacksonville pass rush.

Brady was characteristically understated in sizing up his record-setting performance, transferring credit to his teammates: "When they're open like that, it's my job to hit them. They were open every time, so it's easy to play quarterback."

★ ★ ★

Things didn't go nearly as smoothly in the AFC Championship Game—for the team or the quarterback. But, then, things seldom go smoothly for either team in an NFL semifinal game.

The Chargers came to Foxborough severely banged up from their divisional-round win over the Colts in Indianapolis but nonetheless eager to avenge their heartbreaking postseason loss to the Pats a year earlier.

Chargers players, for their part, were confident in their ability to pull off an upset. "Seventeen have tried, and it hasn't happened," San Diego quarterback Philip Rivers told the media. "We think it can happen." Perhaps it could have. But it didn't.

Brady had a difficult day against the Chargers' fifth-ranked defense. Though he completed 67 percent of his passes (22-for-33) and threw two touchdowns, Brady also was picked off three times in the game, including once in the San Diego end zone.

Fortunately for the Patriots, Brady had a better day than Rivers, who connected on just 19 of 37 pass attempts with two picks and no touchdowns.

Even so, it was one of those games in which Pats fans kept waiting for something awful to happen, a sense of dread building with every Chargers drive and little relief to be had even when the best San Diego could do was settle for a field goal.

Still, the New England defense played tough. And a 122-yard rushing effort by Maroney helped the Patriots post a 21–12 victory. New England earned a Lamar Hunt Trophy for the first time in three years. Brady reached 100 wins earlier in his career than any other quarterback in league history, besting Joe Montana's previous mark by a full 16 games. And the Pats advanced to the Super Bowl with a record of 18–0 and history very much in their sights.

★ ★ ★

As tough as things got in Super Bowl XLII, the Pats still had a bead on immortality until the very end of the game. Sure, the Giants pass rush came after Brady with a degree of ferocity it hadn't exhibited five weeks earlier. New York's defensive front forced Brady to hurry throws. They chased him out of the pocket. And before the first half was over, they'd sacked him three times.

Even as Brady appeared to be leading the Patriots on a patented end-of-the-half scoring drive, Justin Tuck shot through the New England offensive line and stripped the ball from Brady's hands. Osi Umenyiora recovered the fumble, and the Pats were denied a chance to go into halftime up 14–3.

Still, the Patriots started the second half leading 7–3. And they had a chance to extend their lead on the opening drive of the third quarter. Brady led the offense from the New England 21-yard line to the New York 25, completing eight of nine passes for 47 yards—and taking over as the record holder for career Super Bowl completions—before he took his fourth sack of the day. With the six-yard loss on the sack, the Pats were effectively pushed out of field-goal range. They elected to go for it on fourth-and-13 from the 31. And the Giants once again brought heavy pressure, forcing Brady to throw an incompletion over Gaffney's head in the back of the end zone.

But the Pats hung in. And although they trailed 10–7, they were still fighting for a spot in football lore midway through the fourth quarter when they took over at their own 20 following a Giants punt.

Brady looked as collected as ever on the ensuing drive in spite of the constant pressure he'd faced throughout the evening. He connected on 8 of 11 passes, covering a total of 71 yards through the air. And with 2:45 remaining on the clock, on third-and-goal from the Giants 6-yard line, Brady stood calmly in the pocket and rocketed a pass to Moss for the go-ahead score.

After that…well, that's where it famously fell apart. A fourth-and-one conversion. A missed opportunity by Asante Samuel to end the game with an interception. Manning's Houdini act and David Tyree's improbable catch. Then Burress' game-winning touchdown with 35 seconds left.

No unsurpassed glory for the Patriots. An indelible black mark on what was otherwise a season for the ages. You can try to pretend that ending didn't happen, but it doesn't work. Thing is, the same is true for all of the records set by Brady and the team. They're there. Many will be there for a long time to come, some perhaps forever.

The finish may have denied the team immortality, but nothing can undo greatness.

CHAPTER 18

★ ★ ★

Tom Brady vs. Jim Kelly

Jim Kelly is probably the most underrated quarterback in the Pro Football Hall of Fame. It's sort of a weird distinction, sure. But do you know how you get to be an underrated Hall of Fame QB? You start for the losing team in four consecutive Super Bowls. That way, everybody ends up looking at you as a guy who couldn't win on the big stage instead of seeing the better part of what you were: the only quarterback ever to lead his team to the Super Bowl in four consecutive years.

That's an amazing achievement. And it's a damned pity that no one outside of western New York seems able to appreciate it.

Consider that only one team other than the Bills has advanced to the Super Bowl in more than two consecutive seasons. One. The Miami Dolphins played in the championship game three years running, beginning with Super Bowl VI.

Two in a row happens, and more frequently than you might imagine. But not a lot. Nine teams have done it, and three of those have done it twice. With the Miami and Buffalo multiseason runs, that adds up to 17 instances of a team appearing in back-to-back Super Bowls. Seventeen across the scope of 50 games involving 100 teams.

If anything, that number seems high. When a team makes a return trip to the Super Bowl, it gets noticed. And for good reason. The very structure of the

Former Buffalo Bills quarterback Jim Kelly talks with Brady before a game between the Bills and the Patriots on September 14, 2009, in Foxborough.

NFL's single-elimination playoff system makes surviving through three or four rounds of postseason play in any single year incredibly difficult. And that's not to mention the fact that professional football is a ridiculously punishing sport. Any extra game played in any season amounts to that much more wear and tear that can't help but take its toll, even on the other side of the off-season. Start stacking up the 19- and 20-game schedules year after year, and things have a way of getting really tough.

So with that in mind, let's consider it again: From 1990 through 1993, the Buffalo Bills were the only AFC team to appear in the Super Bowl. Or, put another way, the Bills were the winners of four AFC Championship Games in a row.

In three of their conference title games, the Bills won decisively. Only the 1991 Denver Broncos were able to keep things close, losing 10–7 in a bone-crunching defensive struggle that took its toll on both Kelly and John Elway.

In the 1990 conference championship, Buffalo eviscerated the visiting Los Angeles Raiders. The Bills were dominant on both sides of the ball, but it was their 502 yards of total offense, including 300 passing yards and a pair of touchdowns by Kelly, that fueled the 51–3 blowout.

The wild-card 1992 Bills took on the Dolphins in Miami and came away with a 29–10 win behind a respectable 177-yard, one-touchdown effort by Kelly, who had suffered a knee injury in the last week of the regular season and missed Buffalo's first two playoff games. And in the 1993 playoffs, it was running back Thurman Thomas, not Kelly, who led the charge as the top-seeded Bills turned away Joe Montana's Kansas City Chiefs 30–13.

★ ★ ★

Things didn't go nearly as well for the Bills once they reached the Super Bowl, of course. Facing the best teams from the dominant NFC of their era, the Bills fell to pieces on three out of their four tries for the Lombardi Trophy. Only in their first attempt, against the New York Giants in Super Bowl XXV, did the Bills come close to earning a victory. And there, they were thwarted by a classic Bill Belichick defensive game plan. Then the Giants defensive coordinator under Bill Parcells, Belichick made a conscious decision to concede the run in order to allow his unit to focus on stopping the Bills' prolific passing attack. The team was finally undone by Scott Norwood's famously errant 47-yard field-goal attempt as time expired.

★ ★ ★ ★ ★ ★ ★

Winning consistently is one of the hardest things to do in the NFL. To see a guy be able to totally dominate year after year the way Tom [Brady] does, that's pretty unusual and pretty special.

—Jim Kelly

Kelly's performance in that 20–19 loss was his best in a Super Bowl, and it was pedestrian to say the least. Kelly completed 18 of 30 passes for 212 yards with no touchdowns and no interceptions, earning a passer rating of 81.5.

Super Bowls XXVI, XXVII, and XXVIII ranged from difficult to downright ugly. In Super Bowl XXVI, which was supposed to be a shootout between the league's two top-scoring offenses, Kelly completed just 28 of 58 passes for 275 yards. And though he put up a pair of touchdowns, Kelly also threw four picks and lost a fumble. His passer rating for the day was just 44.8. The Bills lost 37–24 to Washington.

Kelly's knee injury caught up with him in the second quarter of Super Bowl XXVII. But before he left the game, he had thrown two interceptions and given up a fumble that was returned for a Dallas Cowboys touchdown. Dallas came away with a 52–17 victory.

You Can't Argue with Figures

	Tom Brady	Jim Kelly
Regular-Season Record	172–51	101–59
Winning Percentage	.771	.631
Postseason Record	22–9	10–8
Winning Percentage	.710	.556
Overall Record	194–60	111–67
Winning Percentage	.764	.624
Passer Rating	96.4	84.4
Touchdown Percentage	5.5	5
Interception Percentage	1.9	3.7
TD/INT	2.9/1	1.4/1
Completion Percentage	63.6	60.1
Yards Per Attempt	7.4	7.4
First-Team All-Pro	2	1
League MVP	2	0
Super Bowl MVP	3	0
Super Bowl Record	4–2	0–4

The Bills lost to Dallas again in Super Bowl XXVIII, falling 30–13 in a game in which no Buffalo player on either side of the ball seemed to be able to do anything right.

In his four Super Bowl appearances, Kelly completed just 81 of 147 passes for 829 yards and two touchdowns, with seven interceptions. His Super Bowl passer rating was just 59.0. The thing about those results, though, is that they were well outside the norm, for both the Bills and their quarterback. The Bills didn't luck into any of their Lamar Hunt Trophies. They earned every one. And they did that substantially on the arm of their quarterback.

★ ★ ★

Oddly enough, Kelly didn't really want to play for the Bills. Though he was the third QB selected from the heralded quarterback draft class of 1983, going to Buffalo with the 14th overall pick, Kelly opted to play for the Houston Gamblers of the USFL. He would have stayed in the upstart league, too, if it hadn't folded around him. He was the most successful quarterback in the league's short history, leading a run-and-shoot offense that piled up 618 points in his rookie season. He was on track to eclipse even that high total a year later before he was sidelined with an injury.

And then there was no USFL. So Kelly reported to Buffalo, where he helped import the run-and-shoot to the NFL.

Beginning with his second season with the Bills, or at least after players returned to the field following a short strike, Kelly played under head coach Marv Levy. And together, the coach and quarterback led the franchise through the most successful period in its history. (The Bills won a pair of AFL championships in the mid-1960s but weren't able to sustain that success.)

Buffalo won the AFC East title six times during Kelly's 11 seasons with the team. They advanced to the AFC Championship Game five times (winning the aforementioned four and losing to the Cincinnati Bengals in 1988).

Kelly threw for 3,000 or more yards in eight different seasons, and it likely would have been nine had it not been for the 1987 strike (he compiled 2,798 yards in 12 starts after the players went back to work).

During their Super Bowl seasons, Kelly's Bills were consistently among the most productive teams in football. In 1990 they led the league with 428 total points. And even in the fast-paced, deep-ball-oriented Bills offense (Kelly averaged eight or more yards per attempt in three different seasons), Kelly maintained a career completion rate of more than 60 percent and, in his best season, 1990, led the league with a 101.2 passer rating.

Take the Super Bowl losses out of the equation, and Kelly's career stats are outstanding. But they're not elite. Kelly was more than the stereotypical regular-season stats machine who couldn't perform come January. He was good in the postseason too…right up to the point where he wasn't.

And while the failure to deliver a single Lombardi Trophy in four tries isn't all Kelly should be remembered for, the truth of the matter is that the greatest quarterbacks find a way to come up big in the biggest games.

Tom Brady has done it. Brady hasn't led his team to four straight Super Bowl appearances, but he did lead the Patriots to two straight Super Bowl victories, and three over the course of four years. Brady's Patriots have won the AFC East title with even more consistency than Kelly's Bills did. And in six of Brady's 14 seasons as a starter, the Patriots have appeared in the Super Bowl. Brady's Pats haven't won the championship game every time they've advanced to it, but they have won twice as many Super Bowls as they've lost. And Brady has racked up better regular-season and postseason statistics than Kelly. That's the difference between an underrated Hall of Famer and the greatest of all time.

CHAPTER 19

★ ★ ★

Settle Down, Already: 2008

There's nothing a Tom Brady hater loves to recall more than 2008, when New England, for all intents and purposes, went a full season without its future Hall of Fame quarterback.

But the anti-Brady crowd's reflective delight isn't about the memory of going a whole year without having to hear about Brady's latest accomplishments. That, surely, has been erased over the seven standout seasons since No. 12 returned to the field.

Neither is it about reliving the glee haters felt when Kansas City Chiefs safety Bernard Pollard delivered the cheap hit that tore up Brady's knee in the first quarter of the Patriots' first game of the season. (Well, it's probably a little bit about reliving that perverse pleasure; schadenfreude is highly addictive.)

The real joy Brady's detractors take from 2008 is that they imagine it offers concrete evidence of their most cherished belief: Brady really isn't that good. He's a system guy, a beneficiary of Bill Belichick's coaching prowess (they won't say "genius," not ever). And if you don't believe it, just look at how well the Patriots did with Matt Cassel in Brady's place.

It's true that the Patriots fared better with their backup quarterback than some other teams might have. New England's 11–5 record in 2008 was considerably better, for example, than the 2–14 the Indianapolis Colts landed on when they had to wage their 2011 campaign without Peyton Manning. (Whether the Colts' worst-in-the-league record was purely organic or "benefitted" at some point from a desire to land the first overall pick in the 2012 draft—and, with it, Andrew Luck—is another question altogether.) But that line of debate is specious at best.

It doesn't matter whether the Pats were better with Cassel than the Colts were with Curtis Painter, Dan Orlovsky, and Kerry Collins. All that ultimately proves is that New England is better at drafting and developing backup quarterbacks than their rivals in Indianapolis. (And, OK, that the Patriots are better coached than the Colts. And that New England has done a better job than Indianapolis of building a complete team rather than putting everything on the back of their starting QB.)

Cassel's a better quarterback than Painter, Orlovsky, or Collins. That's an easy point to concede. But it has absolutely nothing to do with whether Brady is a better quarterback than Manning.

What matters isn't how the 2008 Patriots stack up against the 2011 Colts, but how Cassel's Patriots measure against the most similar New England teams led by Brady: the Pats of 2007 and 2009. And the fact is, it's not even close.

The best comparison is with 2007, because outside of who played quarterback, there was little difference between that team and the 2008 squad.

Brady in '07 completed 398 of 578 passes (68.9 percent) for 4,806 yards and 50 touchdowns, while throwing just eight interceptions. His passer rating for the season was 117.2. The Patriots won all 16 regular-season games and the AFC Championship Game. They put up 589 points that season and outscored opponents by 315 points (nearly 20 per game).

★　★　★　★　★　★　★

A lot of us get to a place where we think we've arrived and we can put our feet up. Tom never gets to that place. He's always pushing himself to get better. It's not something many people can do. And maybe the best thing about Tom is that he has a way of pushing the players around him without them feeling like they're being pushed.

—Pat Kirwan

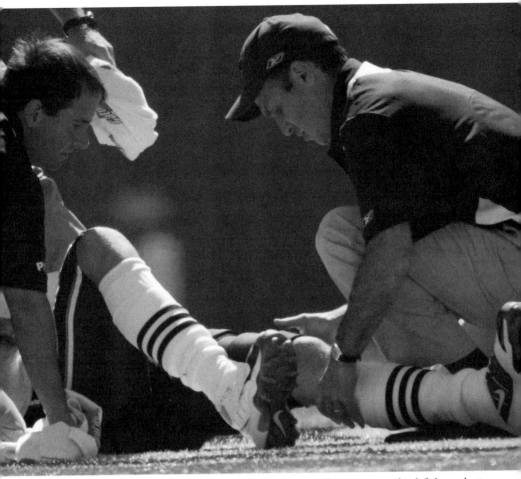

Brady is attended to by medical staff after he sustained an injury to his left knee during the first quarter against the Kansas City Chiefs on September 7, 2008. Though the Patriots defeated the Chiefs 17–10, the injury sidelined Brady for the remainder of the season.

Cassel, playing with the same team in the same system a year later, completed 327 of 516 pass attempts (63.4 percent) for 3,693 yards and 21 touchdowns, with 11 interceptions. That calculates out to a passer rating of 89.4.

The Patriots of 2008 tied for the best record in the AFC East but missed the postseason because they lost tiebreakers for both the division title and the final AFC wild-card spot. They scored 410 points and outscored their opponents by

101 points (just more than six per game). The numbers for Cassel and the 2008 Patriots are nothing to sneeze at, but they hardly compare to what the team accomplished in 2007.

Then, coming off an injury and complications of surgery that left his ability to start in doubt until early spring, Brady returned in 2009 to play under a different offensive coordinator on a team with a rebuilding defense. Rust and other impediments aside, Brady completed 371 of 565 passes (65.7 percent) for 4,398 yards and 28 touchdowns, with 13 picks. He finished the season with a passer rating of 96.2. And while the Patriots won only 10 games, they won them scoring 427 points and outscoring opponents by 142 (nearly nine points per game). They recaptured the AFC East championship.

So, sure, the Patriots had a better year than any team playing without its superstar quarterback could have any reason to anticipate. That's a testament to Cassel's talent and football intelligence. It's the reason the Patriots got a high second-round draft pick from the Kansas City Chiefs in exchange for Cassel's rights in the 2009 off-season and the reason Kansas City signed Cassel to a six-year, $62.7 million contract. Cassel isn't Brady, and no one ever expected him to be, but neither is he Dan Orlovsky.

And there's no way to know for sure what the 2008 Patriots might have achieved had Brady remained healthy. 15–1? 14–2? A return trip to the Super Bowl? Maybe. As always in the NFL, it's all a matter of how things break. But it's at least clear that it would have been somewhere to the north of 11–5 and an early start to the off-season. Only a committed Brady hater could possibly argue otherwise.

CHAPTER 20

★ ★ ★

Tom Brady vs. Troy Aikman

Three Super Bowl championships in four seasons. Accomplish that and you're in the conversation about great NFL quarterbacks, no matter what the rest of your career looks like. And Troy Aikman accomplished that—and maybe a little bit more (but just a little).

Aikman had a lot in common with Terry Bradshaw. Like Bradshaw, he was an outstanding college quarterback who was taken with the first overall pick in the NFL Draft. Also like Bradshaw, Aikman had a pro career that started and ended shakily but had a memorable sweet spot in the middle.

The most important similarity, though, was that, much like Bradshaw, Aikman was a quarterback who was at his best in the postseason.

Aikman never lit up the regular season. Once in his career, in 1993, he led the league in completion percentage (69.1); otherwise he was largely just a part of the pack. But he always performed well enough to help his team reach the playoffs. And once they were there—at least during his best seasons—he stepped up and did what it took to deliver championships.

Some of Aikman's success, certainly, had to do with landing in the right place at the right time. The Cowboys had sputtered through the final seasons of Tom Landry's 29-year stint as head coach. Landry had been reluctant to adapt his play calling as the game evolved. And that, coupled with a few years of poor management under bad ownership, had left the organization in shambles. In the months between the end of the 1988 season and the 1989 draft, however, the team was sold to Jerry Jones, who promptly fired Landry, hired Jimmy Johnson, and selected Aikman at the top of the draft.

Then, after the team got out to a 0–5 start in 1989, Johnson made the Cowboys the beneficiaries of the most lopsided trade in NFL history. He shipped running back Herschel Walker to the Minnesota Vikings in exchange for five veteran players and a raft of draft picks over three years, including three each in the first and second rounds. Johnson used those picks to stock his team with talent, and life got a whole lot easier for Aikman.

★ ★ ★

But things didn't turn around immediately. The Cowboys still managed to slide into a 1–15 record in 1989, with Aikman as the starting quarterback in 11 of their losses.

But in the 1990 draft, the team brought in running back Emmitt Smith. And in 1991 the Cowboys made their return to postseason play, earning a wild-card slot mainly on the legs of Smith, who led the league with 1,563 rushing yards.

A year later, the Cowboys returned to the Super Bowl. With Smith again the league's leading rusher (he racked up 1,713 yards and an NFL-best 18 touchdowns) and the Dallas defense playing lights-out football, the Cowboys didn't need to get all that much from their quarterback.

Just the same, they got plenty. In the regular season, Aikman completed 302 of his 473 passes, threw for 3,445 yards and 23 touchdowns, and earned a respectable passer rating of 89.5. In the postseason, he came on strong and kept getting better.

In a divisional-round matchup with Philadelphia, Aikman completed 15 of 25 passes for 200 yards and two touchdowns, earning both a 112.1 passer rating and a blowout 34–10 victory. He got better still when the Cowboys traveled to San Francisco for the NFC Championship Game, hitting 24 of 34 passes for 322 yards and another two touchdowns and walking away with a passer rating of 120.0.

You Can't Argue with Figures

	Tom Brady	Troy Aikman
Regular-Season Record	172–51	94–71
Winning Percentage	.771	.570
Postseason Record	22–9	11–4
Winning Percentage	.710	.733
Overall Record	194–60	105–75
Winning Percentage	.764	.583
Passer Rating	96.4	81.6
Touchdown Percentage	5.5	3.5
Interception Percentage	1.9	3.0
TD/INT	2.9/1	1.2/1
Completion Percentage	63.6	61.5
Yards Per Attempt	7.4	7.0
First-Team All-Pro	2	1
League MVP	2	0
Super Bowl MVP	3	1
Super Bowl Record	4–2	3–0

Against Buffalo in Super Bowl XXVII, Aikman made the most of a seemingly endless string of gifts from his defense. Twice in the first half, Aikman parlayed turnovers by the Bills in their own territory into short drives capped by touchdown passes. Aikman didn't necessarily need a short field to produce points, though. His two other touchdown passes came on drives from Cowboys territory. And he moved the ball effectively throughout the game. Aikman finished the championship game 22-for-30 (73.3 percent) for 273 yards and four touchdowns, earning a passer rating of 140.7. He was named Super Bowl MVP.

Everything clicked for the Cowboys again in 1993. Smith led the league in rushing for the third consecutive year. The *D* was ranked second in the league, allowing just 14.3 points per game. And Aikman, in spite of off-season back surgery that initially threatened to keep him sidelined for the first six games, turned in the best regular-season performance of his career. Over 14 starts, Aikman earned passer ratings of 100 or better eight times. He passed for 3,100 total yards and threw 15 touchdowns and just six interceptions.

Aikman continued to play well in the NFC playoffs. He threw for 302 yards and three touchdowns in a divisional-round victory over Green Bay. And in the conference championship against San Francisco, he played exceptional football, connecting on 14 of 18 passes for 177 yards and a pair of scores before taking a knee to the head that caused him to miss most of the second half with a severe concussion. That head injury limited Aikman's effectiveness in Super Bowl XXVIII, but he was still able to contribute, passing for 260 yards, as Dallas rallied from a 13–6 halftime deficit to beat Buffalo 30–13.

★ ★ ★

In spite of changes at offensive coordinator and head coach—an always rocky relationship between owner and coach finally came to a head, and Johnson was sent packing in favor of Barry Switzer—the Cowboys had a chance to reach a third consecutive Super Bowl following the 1994 season.

Aikman's regular season was uneven, and his output dropped significantly after he suffered an injury to the thumb of his throwing hand just before Thanksgiving. But in a divisional-round playoff game against Green Bay, he came up big yet again, completing 23 of 30 passes for 337 yards and two touchdowns to lead Dallas to a 35–9 rout of Brett Favre's team.

But Aikman's 380 passing yards (a record total at the time) and two touchdowns in the NFC Championship Game at San Francisco weren't enough. His three interceptions, including a pick six that killed the Cowboys' opening drive, helped Dallas dig a 21–0 hole that the team simply couldn't climb out of.

A year later, though, the Cowboys were back on top. Aikman once again was just good enough in the regular season to allow Dallas to make the most of Smith's league-leading rushing performance and another standout year for the D. Aikman's postseason play this time wasn't spectacular, but it was well above average. And that was enough to get Dallas past the Philadelphia Eagles in the divisional round and support a 150-yard, three-touchdown outing by Smith in the NFC Championship Game.

Aikman was a bigger factor in Super Bowl XXX, completing 15 of 23 passes for 209 yards and a touchdown. And that, in conjunction with a pair of key interceptions by Dallas cornerback Larry Brown, both of which led to touchdown carries for Smith, propelled the Cowboys to a 27–17 victory over the

Pittsburgh Steelers. The Cowboys became the first team in NFL history to take home the Lombardi Trophy three times in four seasons (a feat matched only by the 2001–04 New England Patriots).

★ ★ ★

Aikman was 10–1 in the postseason and, at age 29, still in the prime of his career. But then things started to go south. The Cowboys were good enough to win the NFC East title in 1996, and they got past the Minnesota Vikings in the wild-card round in spite of Aikman's failure to step up his play for the postseason for the first time in his career. But that would be their last win in the playoffs with Aikman behind center.

In the four seasons to follow, as injuries took their toll, Aikman's production fell off to the point where strong efforts from Smith and the defense weren't enough to get the team over the hump. And following a 2000 season in which concussions took a major toll, the club chose to release their onetime star rather than pay him a $7 million roster bonus. Unable to find another team willing to take a chance on an aging and oft-concussed quarterback, Aikman announced his retirement and moved on to a career in broadcasting.

Aikman remained the Cowboys' all-time leading passer with 32,942 career yards until Tony Romo overtook him late in the 2014 season. He has his rings. He has the distinction of having been a crucial part of an NFL dynasty. But his major accomplishment has been duplicated by Brady, who didn't stop with three Super Bowls in four years. Brady was 34, the age at which Aikman retired, at the end of the 2011 season. He'd already won more postseason games and more conference championships than Aikman then and he's added substantially to his resume since. And he's achieved a level of success in the regular season that Aikman never so much as approached.

Aikman doesn't owe anyone an apology for the crime of being a quarterback who was great when it mattered most. But it's not the same as being a quarterback who's just plain great.

CHAPTER 21

★ ★ ★

Brady, Come Back: 2009

You know you're doing OK as an NFL team when what qualifies as a disappointing season is a rebuilding year in which you finish 10–6, win your division, host a playoff game, and see a starting quarterback who's just back after missing a full season due to a major knee injury throw for nearly 4,400 yards and 28 touchdowns.

But there's the irony of the Tom Brady–era New England Patriots: everyone simply expects greatness, year in and year out, even when that expectation is entirely unreasonable.

By some accounts, it was unreasonable even to think Brady could start 16 games—or perhaps even as many as one—in 2009.

Late in 2008, as the Patriots were wrapping up a season in which they missed the playoffs despite finishing 11–5 with Matt Cassel starting at quarterback, new questions emerged about Brady's recovery from surgery on his left knee.

Brady's anterior cruciate and medial collateral ligaments had been torn when the quarterback took a low hit midway through the first quarter of New England's 2008 season opener. The ligaments were surgically repaired early in October. But late in that same month, it was revealed that Brady had undergone additional procedures to clean out infections in the knee, delaying his recovery process. A six-week course of intravenous antibiotics, prescribed to fight further infection, had set back Brady's rehab schedule even further. There was speculation even then that the ligament surgery might need to be redone.

Then, on December 28, Tom E. Curran of NBCSports.com, citing an unidentified league source, reported that Brady's 2009 season was indeed in jeopardy. Curran's panic-raising report claimed that Brady's repaired ligaments were "loose," that scar tissue had built up in the knee, limiting mobility, and that those conditions pointed to the need for another surgical procedure.

Curran wrote: "Even if Brady gets the scar tissue removed, regains greater mobility in the knee and is able to get the strength back in his quad, the looseness in the ligaments won't go away without a second surgery, the source said. At this point, deciding to have that second surgery would cost him the 2009 season because a second surgery wouldn't be recommended this soon after the first, especially with the current condition of the area."

Some New England sports fans panicked. Most simply held their breath. They were still holding it nearly two months later when Brady reported that his recovery was on schedule but couldn't say for sure when he'd be back on the field. Speaking during a charity event in support of the Boys & Girls Club of Allston, Massachusetts, Brady said, "Everything is progressing just as I expected." He reported that he'd been working with his trainer and throwing the ball but wouldn't speculate on when he'd be ready for game action.

Curran, or his source, had been wrong. Brady was on the mend. And as it turned out, his recovery progressed quickly enough that Brady was ready in time for the preseason. More ready, in some ways, than the rest of the organization.

The Patriots organization Brady returned to in 2009 wasn't the same one he'd been ripped away from a year earlier. The front office had seen the departure of longtime vice president of player personnel Scott Pioli, who left to become general manager of the Kansas City Chiefs. Josh McDaniels, the offensive coordinator who had called plays for the record-shattering 2007 squad, had left to take on the role of Denver Broncos head coach. Defensive stalwart Rodney Harrison had retired, while Ellis Hobbs and Mike Vrabel had been traded. Cassel, too, had been traded. And Jabar Gaffney and long-snapper Lonie Paxton had followed McDaniels to Denver.

The changes kept coming during the preseason too. Russ Hochstein, who had been part of the offensive line that protected Brady in two Super Bowl seasons, was traded to Denver. Linebacker Tedy Bruschi, an icon of the Patriots' Super Bowl dynasty, opted to retire after the third game of the preseason rather than force the team to release him. And finally, two days after the final game of the preseason, defensive end Richard Seymour was shipped off to Oakland for a first-round draft pick in 2011.

2009

By the Numbers

Total Yards	4,398
Yards Per Game	274.9
Attempts	565
Completions	371
Completion Percentage	65.7
Yards Per Attempt	7.8
Touchdowns	28
Interceptions	13
Passer Rating	96.2
Games Rated Higher Than 100	6
Best Single-Game Rating	152.8

Still, the Patriots had their world-class signal caller back. That was reason enough to hope, if not for a championship season in 2009, then at least for a bright future.

★ ★ ★

When the Patriots hosted the Buffalo Bills in the inaugural Monday night game of the 2009 campaign, Brady looked about as sharp as anyone could have expected from a player who hadn't been involved in a real game in 372 days.

There were signs of rust, of course. Brady at times looked reluctant to step into his throws. And, partially as a result of that, he missed on some passes he would otherwise have been expected to complete, failed to find the end zone in the first three quarters, and fell victim to a pick six by Bills defensive end Aaron Schobel (who was a thorn in Brady's side for his entire nine-year NFL career).

But Brady also found ways to exhibit his toughness and demonstrate the health of his knee. He absorbed some hard hits. He scrambled for nine yards on a broken first-down play. And late in the fourth quarter, with the game on the line, he officially reentered the Brady zone.

With 5:25 remaining and the Patriots trailing 24–13, Brady started a drive from the New England 19-yard line and moved the offense all the way to Buffalo's end zone, passing on every down. Brady went 9-for-11 on the drive, capping it with an 18-yard strike through three defenders and into the hands of tight end Benjamin Watson.

An errant pass thrown on the run on the two-point attempt that followed ended up in the hands of Bills linebacker Bryan Scott. But a fumble on the ensuing kickoff gave New England the ball back at the Buffalo 31, and Brady wasted no time finding Watson in the middle of the end zone yet again. The Pats missed again on a two-point conversion, but it didn't matter; the 16-yard touchdown had put them in front of the Bills by a point with less than a minute to play.

The Patriots finished the evening 1–0. Brady finished 39-for-53 for 378 yards and two touchdowns. His completion percentage during the game was 73.6, his passer rating 97.8. Brady delivered the ball 12 times each to Randy Moss and Wes Welker, for 141 and 93 yards respectively. (Welker, however, aggravated a knee injury, which would force him to miss Weeks 2 and 3.) The quarterback earned his 13th career AFC Offensive Player of the Week award for his efforts.

Watching that opening game wasn't quite like witnessing the unstoppable offensive onslaught of 2007, but it was a good bit more encouraging than, say, seeing a team struggle while its quarterback started his season on the PUP list.

The results the following week in New Jersey weren't quite so encouraging. The New York Jets, under new (knuckle)head coach Rex Ryan, implored their fans to create a hostile environment for the Pats. The Jets fans came through, as did the New York defense. The Patriots committed an uncharacteristic 11 penalties—including back-to-back delay-of-game penalties by Brady that effectively killed a promising third-quarter drive—and failed to score a touchdown for the first time since December 10, 2006. Although the Jets offense didn't have much to offer, they still managed to pull off a 16–9 victory. Brady finished the afternoon 23-for-47 with no touchdowns and an interception.

★ ★ ★ ★ ★ ★ ★

Tom puts players in a better position to execute, and they relish someone who can put them in that position.

—Gino Cappelletti

And so the season went, up and down, the Patriots and Brady alike looking one week as if they were starting to turn it on, the next as if it was all they could do to try to find their way.

★ ★ ★

Though career highlights for Brady were few and relatively far between, the season wasn't without its standout moments.

In Week 6 Brady and the Pats celebrated the AFC's 50th anniversary season in spectacular fashion. Taking advantage of a snow-covered field and a weak Tennessee Titans squad (in Houston Oilers throwback uniforms), they put on an AFL-style air show for the fans in Foxborough.

Brady threw for six touchdowns overall and set an NFL record by passing for five of them in a single quarter. Those touchdowns included strikes of 40 and 28 yards, all on Brady's arm, to Moss; a 38-yard catch-and-run connection with Kevin Faulk; and a pair of very pretty scoring passes to Welker, one from 30 yards out, the other from a mere five yards away.

The Pats' 45–0 lead at halftime was the biggest in NFL history. And the 59–0 final score tied the record for largest margin of victory since the 1970 AFL-NFL merger (set by the 1976 L.A. Rams in a win over the Atlanta Falcons).

Brady finished the day with 29 completions on 34 attempts for 380 yards. He earned a near-perfect passer rating of 152.8. His completion percentage, 85.3, was the best in Patriots regular-season history (though not quite on par with the 92.9 Brady had achieved against Jacksonville in the 2007 postseason). The effort earned Brady his second AFC Offensive Player of the Week nod of the season.

In a Week 12 loss to the Saints in New Orleans, Brady became the Patriots' all-time passing leader, eclipsing Drew Bledsoe's 29,657 career yards.

He picked up his third and final AFC Offensive Player of the Week Award in a Week 16 blowout win over the Jaguars in Foxborough. Brady completed 23 of 26 passes in the game, breaking his own team record for best regular-season completion percentage (88.5), and earned a passer rating of 149.0. Three of Brady's four touchdown passes during the game went to Moss.

With the 35–7 win, the Patriots clinched the AFC East championship. It was the ninth consecutive season in which New England had finished at least tied

For the Books   2009

League Records
Most Touchdowns in a Quarter   5

Team Records
Highest Regular-Season Single-Game Completion Percentage   88.5
Most Career Touchdown Passes   225

Honors and Career Milestones
Comeback Player of the Year
Pro Bowl, 5th Career Selection
Patriots All-Time Passing Leader

for the best record in the division and the Pats' sixth straight division title, and seventh overall, in seasons with Brady starting behind center.

★ ★ ★

The Patriots' postseason came to a crashing halt at the hands of the Baltimore Ravens in the wild-card round. New England suffered a 33–14 loss that wasn't nearly that close as Brady turned in the poorest playoff performance of his career, completing just 23 of 42 passes and throwing three interceptions en route to a dismal 49.1 passer rating.

The idea that the team might have fared even better if not for the fact that Welker, Brady's most reliable and most productive target, was lost to a devastating knee injury in Week 17 is probably more than a bit romantic. The Ravens owned the Patriots from the very first snap. Sure, Welker might have helped the Pats keep it closer, but no one who actually witnessed the steamrolling the Patriots took would ever attempt to argue that New England was one key player away from winning.

It was a disappointing conclusion, to be sure, but only in the context of the Patriots' incredible achievements during the Belichick-Brady era could 2009 possibly be considered a disappointing season.

Brady's total passing yardage, 4,398, was the second-highest of his career at the time (though he's surpassed it three times since). His passer rating, 96.2, also was the second-best of his career up to that point (though he bettered that in five of his next six seasons). And his 28 touchdowns matched what was then his second-highest single-season total (though, again, in the seasons to follow, Brady has made that stat appear pedestrian).

Brady's numbers looked even more impressive after reports surfaced that he had played the final three weeks of the regular season with a broken finger on his throwing hand and three broken ribs.

And no one was surprised in the least when on January 6, 2010, the Associated Press named Brady its 2009 NFL Comeback Player of the Year.

CHAPTER 22

★ ★ ★

Tom Brady vs. John Elway

John Elway very probably will always be the NFL quarterback who retired best. That's not some backhanded compliment. It's not as if retiring well was Elway's greatest achievement. Far from it. But it's the case, nonetheless, that Elway's final decision as a professional football player speaks to his intelligence, dignity, and foresight perhaps better than any move he ever made on the field.

Elway is one of a very few star players in the history of professional football—really, in the history of professional sports—who elected to go out on top. He announced his retirement in May 1999, three months after leading the Denver Broncos to victory in Super Bowl XXXIII. He had put in 16 seasons as an NFL starter, during which he threw for 51,475 career yards, led 35 fourth-quarter comebacks, and became the first quarterback in history to start in five Super Bowls (a feat that has been topped only by Tom Brady). And, finally, after years of effort and frustration, he had won a pair of championships back-to-back.

There was nothing left for Elway to prove. So he walked away while walking was still an option. He didn't try to squeeze another season out of his shoulder and knees. Didn't wait until the Broncos had to tell him it was time for them to move on. Didn't finish his career with another team, striving desperately to return to glory, never quite succeeding, leaving everyone to wonder why and to wish, if only quietly, that he'd just call it a career.

You can't help but admire that decision, particularly when you consider that it takes a fierce competitor to battle through 16 years in the NFL, 10 of them elongated by playoff berths. Star players tend to stay too long in their careers because they can't back off of the very desire to win that drives their success. Elway found a way to do it.

In a sense, Elway chose to end his career in the same way he'd begun it: on entirely his own terms. Elway was selected by the Baltimore Colts with the first overall pick in the 1983 NFL Draft. Most star players coming out of college would have viewed the Colts' choice as an honor. To Elway's mind, it was something of a slap in the face. The Colts hadn't simply been bad enough in the strike-shortened 1982 season to secure the first pick in the '83 draft, they'd been nothing but awful for the preceding five years. Elway didn't think the Colts organization was capable of turning things around, and he'd stated prior to the draft that he would not play for Baltimore. The Colts picked him anyway, and Elway informed the team that their choices were to trade him or to watch him go off to play center field for the New York Yankees. The team chose to get some value for him by shipping him to Denver.

Elway was 22 years old, had never taken a single snap in the NFL, and already he'd dictated the path his career would take: he was going to succeed, but he was going to do it his own way.

★ ★ ★

Success—in the regular season, at least—came fairly quickly. Elway struggled through his rookie season. Splitting time with Steve DeBerg, just as Joe Montana had done in San Francisco early in his career, Elway finished the 1983 season with a 47.5 percent completion rate and a 4–6 record as a starter. By his sophomore campaign, though, Elway had figured out the pro game. He was the starter in 12 of the Broncos' 13 wins, raised his touchdown percentage from 2.7 to 4.7, and dropped his interception percentage from 5.4 to 3.9.

In 1986 Elway led the Broncos to an 11–5 regular-season record, then made a memorable run through the playoffs to Super Bowl XXI. Elway had established a reputation for leading fourth-quarter comebacks by the time the '86 season

You Can't Argue with Figures

	Tom Brady	John Elway
Regular-Season Record	172–51	148–82–1
Winning Percentage	.771	.643
Postseason Record	22–9	14–7
Winning Percentage	.710	.667
Overall Record	194–60	162–89–1
Winning Percentage	.764	.645
Passer Rating	96.4	79.9
Touchdown Percentage	5.5	4.1
Interception Percentage	1.9	3.1
TD/INT	2.9/1	1.3/1
Completion Percentage	63.6	56.9
Yards Per Attempt	7.4	7.1
First-Team All-Pro	2	0
League MVP	2	1
Super Bowl MVP	3	1
Super Bowl Record	4–2	2–3

wrapped up. He cemented that image for all time in the AFC Championship Game with "the Drive," in which he moved the Broncos 98 yards to score a game-tying touchdown during the final five minutes of regulation.

Elway's performance in the Super Bowl wasn't good enough to win, but it was perfectly respectable. He threw for one touchdown, rushed for another, and finished with an 83.6 passer rating as the Broncos fell 39–20 to the New York Giants.

Elway was downright awful when the Broncos returned to the Super Bowl a year later. He threw three picks to just a single touchdown and came away with a 36.8 passer rating as Denver was crushed 42–10 by Washington.

When the Broncos faced Montana's 49ers in Super Bowl XXIV, things got even worse. Elway completed just 10 of 26 passes for 108 yards, threw for no touchdowns (though he rushed for one), and was intercepted twice, for an abysmal passer rating of 19.4. And the Broncos were clobbered 55–10 by the Niners.

It looked very much like Elway was another one of those quarterbacks who could achieve great things in the regular season but would never find a way to succeed with everything on the line.

★ ★ ★

Certainly, Elway offered no evidence to the contrary as he slogged through the bulk of the 1990s. In some seasons, the Broncos missed the playoffs entirely. And in others, they got there only to fall flat, all too frequently behind a subpar day from their quarterback.

The Broncos advanced to the AFC Championship Game in 1991 but lost 10–7 to Jim Kelly and the Buffalo Bills. Once again, Elway struggled under the postseason spotlight. He was sacked three times, completed just 11 of 21 passes, and threw a pick six that allowed Buffalo to take a 7–0 lead late in the third quarter. Elway eventually left with a thigh injury, leaving backup quarterback Gary Kubiak to engineer Denver's only scoring drive of the game.

In 1993 Elway led the league in pass attempts, pass completions, and passing yardage. And he turned in a solid performance in Denver's lone playoff appearance, throwing for 302 yards and three touchdowns. But all of those scores came in the first half. And in the second, with the Los Angeles Raiders offense running up and down the field, Captain Comeback was unable to rally the troops around him, and the Broncos fell 42–24.

The Broncos finished the 1996 season with the best record in the NFL, 13–3, but were upset in their first playoff game by the wild-card Jacksonville Jaguars. Elway had a decent day statistically and led a touchdown drive that brought the Broncos to within a field goal late in the game, but the team ran out of time and was unable to get any closer. And then came the Super Bowl championship seasons and a satisfying conclusion to a great NFL career.

The thing is, Elway can really only claim responsibility for one of those championships. The best anyone can honestly say about Elway in Super Bowl XXXII is that he didn't prove to be an obstacle to victory. Elway completed just 12 of 22 passes for 123 yards, with no touchdowns and an interception. His passer rating for the game was 51.9. And although Broncos owner Pat Bowlen dedicated the win to Elway, it was running back Terrell Davis' 157-yard, three-touchdown day and an outstanding performance by the Broncos defense that produced the 31–24 victory.

Super Bowl XXXIII was another matter, as was the entire 1998 season. Elway led the Broncos to a 14–2 regular-season record. Though he threw for just 2,806 yards, the third-lowest single-season total since his rookie year, he finished with 22 touchdowns to just 10 interceptions and posted career bests in yards per attempt (7.9) and passer rating (93.0).

And in Denver's Super Bowl XXXIII matchup against their former head coach Dan Reeves and the Atlanta Falcons, Elway finally had a standout game when it mattered most. He earned a 99.2 passer rating, completing 18 of 29 passes for 336 yards with one touchdown and one interception. And he added a fourth-quarter rushing touchdown that put the game out of reach for Atlanta.

Elway was able to lift the Lombardi Trophy again and to claim the title of Super Bowl MVP. He also was able to walk away and leave NFL fans with a great last impression.

It was a great ending to a very good story. And perhaps the day will come when Brady will borrow a play from Elway's book and walk away at the top of his game. But however he leaves the NFL, Brady will leave with at least one more Super Bowl start than Elway, at least two more wins, and at least two more MVP nods, not to mention a list of regular-season accomplishments that far exceeds Elway's.

CHAPTER 23

★ ★ ★

It's Unanimous: 2010

A second consecutive one-and-done postseason. The year Randy Moss finally flamed out. The year of the Logan Mankins holdout. Those are the negatives—the important ones, anyhow—for the New England Patriots of 2010. And the connection between the first two is undeniable.

The Patriots' early exit from the playoffs at the hands of the hated New York Jets can't realistically be separated from Moss' early exit from Foxborough. What the Jets were able to do to the Pats in their divisional-round matchup—limiting offensive productivity by funneling the passing game to the middle of the field—couldn't have been achieved with a productive Moss in the lineup. If the most talented wide receiver ever to put on a Patriots uniform (perhaps the most talented ever to wear pads) had been on the field and playing like the Moss of 2007, or even of 2009, the Jets secondary would have been forced to work outside the numbers—and the Patriots might well have hosted Pittsburgh in the AFC Championship Game.

But Moss wasn't on the field. He'd talked his way out of town early in the season. And while the Patriots, even without him, had turned in one of the most impressive offensive seasons in their history, the team's lack of a vertical threat was a constant concern. It provided the Jets with a weakness to exploit—and that was enough to rob New England of a solid chance to go the distance.

What the Pats left on the table as a result wasn't just a league-best 14–2 record but one of the finest single seasons of Tom Brady's career.

Brady's achievements during the season, which included throwing 36 touchdowns and just four interceptions, not only earned him a second career nod as NFL MVP, they made him the first player ever to be given that award by unanimous consent of the 50-member voting panel. Brady was also a unanimous All-Pro selection and was named Offensive Player of the Year.

At the very least, Brady's outstanding performance made it clear that he was all the way back from the devastating knee injury that had derailed his 2008 season and slowed him down in 2009. As the season progressed, it also became ever more apparent that Brady's favorite target, Wes Welker, also would make a full recovery from his own severe knee injury. And with the emergence of rookie tight ends Rob Gronkowski and Aaron Hernandez as key targets who caught a combined 87 balls for 1,109 yards, it seemed Brady and the Patriots were just a player or two away from becoming an unstoppable offensive force once again.

★ ★ ★

Though Brady wouldn't truly hit his stride until after Moss' departure in early October, he got things cranking with Welker from the get-go. Brady hit Welker with a five-yard pass over the middle on the Patriots' first offensive play of the season. And although the play that propelled the Pats' opening drive against the visiting Cincinnati Bengals was a 45-yard hookup with Hernandez, Brady found Welker again to cap the effort, throwing a swing pass to the left that Welker advanced nine yards to the Bengals end zone.

Welker, whom many had assumed would miss as much as half the season after he tore his ACL and MCL in Week 17 of 2009, finished the day with eight catches for 64 yards and two touchdowns. Brady found six other receivers, including Moss, during the game to come away with 258 yards, three touchdowns, and no picks for a passer rating of 120.9. And the Patriots came out on top 38–24.

But the story of the week was Moss, who was unhappy about being in the final year of his contract and was determined to let the world know about it. The receiver, who had been on his best behavior since arriving in New England in April 2007, started exhibiting signs of his previous malcontent nature the week before the season opener. Moss complained in the press that his contract status made him feel unwanted, though he promised he'd play through his emotional discomfort and pledged not to become a distraction.

That promise didn't hold up long. As soon as Moss took to the microphones for his league-mandated press conference following the win over Cincinnati (in which he had caught five passes for 59 yards but hadn't logged a touchdown), the receiver launched into a speech about his ongoing negative feelings.

"If you do a good job and think that you're doing a good job, you want to be appreciated," Moss told the media. "I really don't think that—me, personally—that I'm appreciated."

In response to questions from the

By the Numbers	2010
Total Yards	3,900
Yards Per Game	243.8
Attempts	492
Completions	324
Completion Percentage	65.9
Yards Per Attempt	7.9
Touchdowns	36
Interceptions	4
Passer Rating	111.0
Games Rated Higher Than 100	12
Best Single-Game Rating	158.3*
(*Perfect)	

press, Moss tied those feelings to his contract situation. "This is the last year of my contract," he said. "Nothing has been discussed. There's not been anything said. Not a letter. Nothing." He went on to point out that he wasn't willing to wait until the end of the season to discuss a new deal. "For me to be offered a contract after this season is over, I think that would be a smack in my face," he said.

Moss officially had become a distraction. He also, it turned out, had resigned himself to leaving the Patriots. Weeks later, the *Boston Herald* reported that following that Week 1 victory, Moss instructed his agent to contact the Pats and request a trade. The consummation of that desire wasn't terribly long in coming.

Moss' contributions over the following three games were uneven at best. In Week 2, when the Pats lost 28–14 to the Jets in the Meadowlands, Moss was targeted 10 times but made only two catches (though one of them, a one-handed grab in the end zone, was not only one of the prettiest touchdown catches of his career but his 150th touchdown overall). Brady, meanwhile, threw a pair of picks while trying to force deep passes to his squeaky wheel of a receiver.

Moss caught a pair of touchdown passes in a 38–30 home win over the Buffalo Bills in Week 3, but they were the only two passes that went to him all afternoon. And it was with throws to Hernandez and Welker that Brady kept the chains moving and earned a passer rating of 142.6.

Moss' Patriots career reached its nadir and its finishing point in a trip to Miami in Week 4. New England won 41–14, mainly on the strength of huge defensive and special teams plays in the second half. And Brady became the fastest quarterback in the Super Bowl era to achieve 100 career regular-season victories, getting there in 131 games—eight fewer than the previous record holder, Joe Montana. But Moss was a nonfactor on the field and, reportedly, a source of significant tension in the locker room.

Brady attempted one throw to Moss in the Monday night game. When the Patriots reached the Miami 12-yard line with 18 seconds remaining in the first half, Brady faked a spike then lobbed the ball to Moss on the left side of the end zone. Moss got his hands on the slightly high, wobbly pass but couldn't hold on. And the Patriots, who had to settle for a field goal, went into halftime trailing 7–6.

Apparently angry at a game plan in which he felt he was underused, Moss reportedly confronted de facto offensive coordinator Bill O'Brien during the break. The blowup didn't get Moss any more involved in the game, but it likely helped get him shipped out of town.

Two days later, with the Patriots in their bye week, the team announced that Moss had been traded to the Minnesota Vikings, the team with which he had begun his NFL career. New England shipped Moss and a 2012 seventh-round draft choice to Minnesota in exchange for a third-round pick in 2011.

The Patriots and Brady alike officially expressed their gratitude to Moss and wished the receiver well in the rest of his career. Behind closed doors, everyone involved likely breathed a sigh of relief. At the very least, the Pats hadn't let Moss become the ongoing morale killer he had reportedly been at the end of his first stint in Minnesota and his subsequent tenure with the Oakland Raiders. At best, the Pats had parlayed a fourth-round pick in 2007 and a seventh-rounder in 2012 into one record-breaking season and two more productive seasons from an incredibly talented receiver, plus a third-round draft pick.

Of course, not everyone thought the decision to deal Moss was a wise one. Patriots fans worried that the loss of a deep threat would derail the season. And analysts, including Moss' onetime Vikings teammate Cris Carter, expressed certainty that Brady's productivity would suffer.

"There's no way you take Randy Moss away from any quarterback in this league and that quarterback gets better," Carter told *The New York Times*. In the long term, Carter may have been right, at least to a degree. In the short term, he could hardly have been farther off the mark.

★ ★ ★

It only took Brady a couple of weeks to begin putting the lie to Carter's pronouncement. Brady's first start without Moss in the lineup was a mixed bag. He threw for 292 yards and a pair of touchdowns in a home game against the Baltimore Ravens, but he connected on only 27 of 44 pass attempts and threw a pair of interceptions. And the Patriots needed a field goal in overtime to edge the Ravens 23–20.

Still, there were plenty of positive signs to be found in the victory, not the least of which was that the game marked a solid homecoming for wide receiver Deion Branch. The Patriots traded a fourth-round pick in 2011 to the Seattle Seahawks in exchange for Branch (whose trade from New England to Seattle four years earlier had brought the Pats a 2007 first-round choice). And after a bit of a slow start, Branch and Brady picked up where they had left off, connecting on seven passes for 75 yards and a touchdown in the fourth quarter and overtime. Hernandez, Welker, and Danny Woodhead also had productive days catching the ball against the Ravens' third-ranked defense.

Brady threw for just a single touchdown per game over the next two weeks, but his play was good enough to help the Patriots overcome the Chargers in San Diego and the Vikings in Foxborough. Against Minnesota, Brady earned a passer rating of 100.8, his first of more than 100 since Moss' departure.

The purple-clad Moss, meanwhile, caught just one pass for eight yards in his return to New England. And on the heels of a bizarre postgame rant in which he praised the Patriots and criticized his new team and coach Brad Childress—and a meeting with team owner Zygi Wilf, in which he reportedly called for Childress to be fired—Moss was released by the Vikings the following day.

★ ★ ★

The Browns caught the Patriots off guard in a Week 9 matchup in Cleveland, taking advantage of defensive miscues, special teams blunders, and fumbles by Gronkowski and Sammy Morris to win 34–14.

For the Books ★ 2010

League Records

Consecutive Games with Two TD Passes and No Interceptions	9
Fastest to 100 Career Wins (Games)	131
Best Touchdown-to-Interception Ratio	9/1
Most Seasons Undefeated at Home	5

Team Records

Most Career Touchdown Passes	261

Honors and Career Milestones

NFL MVP, Second Career Selection*
First-Team All-Pro, Second Career Selection
Pro Bowl, Sixth Career Selection
AFC Offensive Player of the Year, Third Career Selection

(Only Unanimous MVP in League History)

But that would be the last regular-season game the Patriots would lose. As the distance between the Moss era and the 2010 Patriots continued to increase, so too did Brady's productivity and the team's success.

The Patriots squared off against the 6–2 Steelers, a team that featured the best defense in the NFL, and came out on top 39–26. The victory was won behind a stellar performance by Brady, who completed 30 of 43 passes for 350 yards and three touchdowns—earning a 117.4 passer rating—and added a rushing touchdown.

On their return home, the Pats held off a late-game comeback attempt by Peyton Manning and the Indianapolis Colts to prevail 31–28. The victory was the 25th consecutive home win for Brady, which tied a league record held by Brett Favre.

In a Week 12 visit to Detroit, Brady went 21-for-27 for 341 yards and four touchdowns without throwing an interception, earning a perfect passer rating for the second time in his career.

In Week 13 he threw another four touchdowns and came away with a 148.9 passer rating as the Patriots humiliated the Jets in Foxborough. The win gave Brady sole possession of the record for consecutive regular-season home wins and earned him a second straight AFC Offensive Player of the Week Award.

In Week 15, Brady rallied the Patriots in a comeback win over the eventual Super Bowl–champion Green Bay Packers. After New England fell behind 27–21 early in the fourth quarter, Brady engineered a drive that put the team in field-goal range and another that ended with a 10-yard touchdown pass to Hernandez. It was the 23rd fourth-quarter comeback of Brady's career. The game also was the seventh in a row in which Brady passed for at least two touchdowns without throwing an interception, breaking a record Don Meredith had held since 1966.

Brady's interception-free streak hit yet another mark a week later in Buffalo, when he threw his 309th pass without a pick, breaking a record Bernie Kosar had held for 19 years. (It's interesting to note that Kosar's streak came in 1990–91, when he was a member of the Cleveland Browns under head coach Bill Belichick.)

In the season finale, a 38–7 home win over the Dolphins, Brady extended his run of two-touchdown, zero-interception games to nine. It was Brady's 11th consecutive game without a pick, the longest such streak since the 1970 AFL-NFL merger.

★ ★ ★

In the first four games of the season, with Moss in the lineup, Brady had completed 85 of 122 passes for 911 yards with nine touchdowns and two interceptions, earning a passer rating of 109.0 Over the remaining three-fourths of the season, he went 239-for-370 for 2,989 yards, with 27 touchdowns and two picks, for a passer rating of 111.6.

Contrary to Carter's opinion, Brady's performance had unquestionably improved once Moss was removed from the roster. But it was just as certain, however, that that Pats could have used Moss—the good Moss, anyhow—in the postseason.

The loss to the Jets in the Patriots' only game of the playoffs—in which Brady went 29-for-45 for 299 yards, throwing two touchdowns and an interception—necessarily raised the question of whether Brady might have fared even better if Moss had been able to overcome his most insane instincts.

But that leaves out the fact that Moss didn't simply lose his cool in New England. Nor did he merely go on to wear out his welcome in Minnesota in record time. After the Tennessee Titans claimed him off waivers, Moss accomplished all of nothing. Over eight games with the Titans, Moss caught six passes for 80 yards and no touchdowns.

The Patriots may have parted ways with Moss simply because he had lost touch with the Patriots Way, but it may have had just as much to do with a recognition that the receiver had lost a step or two. After spending the 2011 season out of football, Moss returned in 2012 with the San Francisco 49ers, turning in one final lackluster season before hanging up his cleats for good.

Brady, on the other hand, clearly had lost nothing. His passing total of 3,900 yards was far from the best of his career. Indeed, it was some 900 yards fewer than he'd put up in 2007 and nearly 500 yards less than he'd managed coming off his injury in 2009. But his passer rating, 111.0, was the second-best of his career (behind only his ridiculous 117.2 from 2007) and was at the time the fifth-best in league history. Brady was the first quarterback ever to finish two seasons with a passer rating of better than 110.0.

Brady's 9.0/1 touchdown-to-interception ratio for the season shattered his own record of 6.25/1 from 2007. His 0.8 interception percentage was the third-lowest of all time and the lowest ever by a quarterback who started 16 games. (Onetime Brady backup Damon Huard finished the 2006 Kansas City Chiefs season with a 0.4 interception percentage, but he started only eight games. And Joe Ferguson finished the Buffalo Bills' 1976 season with a 0.7 but started just seven games. Josh McCown and Nick Foles both joined the all-time list with limited starts for Chicago and Philadelphia respectively in 2013.) Brady was only the sixth quarterback ever to throw at least one touchdown pass in every game of a 16-game season.

In addition to being unanimously voted MVP and All-Pro, he was named to the Pro Bowl and topped every notable list of the season's best offensive players.

If only he could have capped it with a Super Bowl championship, or even an AFC championship, 2010 would have been one of those seasons no one ever stopped talking about.

CHAPTER 24

★ ★ ★

Tom Brady vs. Brett Favre

The football world probably needed a few years away from Brett Favre before it was ready to see him for the great quarterback he was. And it seems as if 2016, the year of Favre's induction into the Pro Football Hall of Fame, has proven to be the year we all came back around.

It's not as if anyone who was paying attention during Favre's 20 seasons in the NFL didn't get it, at least on some level. But for a while there it was hard for many to find the brighter side of Favre under the thick layer of personality tarnish that formed over his image in the final years of his career.

It wouldn't be entirely accurate to call Favre the anti-Elway. To do so would at least imply that—unlike the Broncos legend, who left football on the heels of his greatest career achievement—Favre was one of those athletes who insisted on playing long after he had lost his ability to compete. That didn't happen.

Sure, Favre's final season in the NFL, 2010, was marred by injury and inconsistency. And the Minnesota Vikings, the team with which Favre spent his last two seasons, paid the price, sputtering to a 6–10 finish. But just a year earlier, Favre had led Minnesota to a 12–4 record and a spectacular battle with the New Orleans Saints in the NFC Championship Game. And there's reason to wonder now whether Favre and the Vikings might have moved on to a berth in Super

Bowl XLIV if not for the illegal bounty system that saw Favre targeted for injury by the Saints defense.

But Favre was certainly the antithesis of Elway in the manner in which he handled his protracted departure from the NFL. As if Favre's subornation of the incessant media speculation about retirement that started in 2002 and colored his final two seasons with the Green Bay Packers hadn't been enough, there was the seemingly endless cycle of retirement and unretirement that followed—from 2008 to 2010. There was the trading of recriminations with the Green Bay front office that accompanied Favre's first decision to unretire in 2008. And, of course, there were the accusations of sexual harassment from New York Jets employees and contractors that followed his departure for Minnesota.

By the end, it didn't matter how great a football player Favre had been. It didn't matter how much fun he was to watch on the field. It didn't matter that you never felt a Favre-led team was out of a game. Or that he was tough and competitive, big-armed and elusive. By the end, there were two kinds of football fans: Favre loyalists, who could never so much as consider a negative, and everyone else—those of us who just wanted him to move the hell on already. If it took a shoulder injury and a concussion to bring out that result, well, it didn't seem like that huge a price to pay.

But that feeling has faded with time. Favre will never be many fans' favorite NFL personality, and many of us will never excuse his misogyny. But he appears to have regained the status of a player whose career we can marvel at unselfconsciously. And that's probably a good thing, because what Favre accomplished on the field of play was really worthy of admiration.

★ ★ ★

Many of Favre's records are attributable to the length of his career—and to the extreme toughness that kept him from missing a single start from September 27, 1992, to December 5, 2010. That's 297 consecutive starts. It's the most in history by a quarterback. And there's almost no chance it won't still be the most ever by a quarterback 100 years from now.

When you play 16 games per season for most of a 20-year career, you're going to pile up some pretty big numbers. Favre's 71,838 career passing yards far outdistanced anyone who played before him. Only Dan Marino came within 10,500 yards of that mark. And Favre's passing yards record stood until Peyton Manning overtook it halfway through his 17th full season. Manning finished 2015, his final season, with 102 more career passing yards than Favre. Drew Brees and Tom Brady are closing in, but it's not certain that either will get there. Brees needs at least two more seasons playing at a high level to catch Favre; Brady needs at least three. For quarterbacks who will enter the 2016 season at ages 37 and 39 respectively, nothing is guaranteed.

Favre held the NFL record for regular season wins, 186, until Peyton Manning tied it in his final regular season game. And he held the record for combined regular season and postseason wins, 199, until Manning logged his 200th combined win in Super Bowl 50, the last game of his career. (Brady, with 172 regular season and 194 combined wins to his credit through 2015, seems likely to move past both Favre and Manning, and to do so with considerably fewer total starts than either.)

You Can't Argue with Figures

	Tom Brady	Brett Favre
Regular-Season Record	172–51	186–112
Winning Percentage	.771	.624
Postseason Record	22-9	13–11
Winning Percentage	.710	.542
Overall Record	194–60	199–123
Winning Percentage	.764	.618
Passer Rating	96.4	86.0
Touchdown Percentage	5.5	5.0
Interception Percentage	1.9	3.3
TD/INT	2.9/1	1.5/1
Completion Percentage	63.6	62.0
Yards Per Attempt	7.4	7.1
First-Team All-Pro	2	3
League MVP	2	3
Super Bowl MVP	3	0
Super Bowl Record	4–2	1–1

Favre surrendered the record for career passing touchdowns to Manning in 2014. His 508 remain second most all time, however, with only Brees and Brady (428 each) as much as two-plus standout seasons away. (Of course, Favre, who was famous for taking stupid chances with the football, also holds the record for career interceptions at 336. No one is closing in on that mark, and given that it's rare for a quarterback who throws a lot of picks to continue as a starter over a long period, it's likely no one ever will.) Heading into the 2016 season Favre appeared to be at little risk of surrendering the records for career pass attempts (10,169) and completions (6,300). And it will be a long time, if ever, before anyone can take away his record for seasons with 3,000 or more passing yards, 18.

Others of Favre's many distinctions aren't related to his longevity. Favre was the NFL MVP for three years running, winning the award outright in 1995 and 1996 and sharing it with Barry Sanders in 1997. He is the only player in league history to take MVP honors in three consecutive seasons.

Favre's teams won their divisions eight times and qualified for the postseason 12 times during his 19 years as a starter. He led the Packers to the NFC Championship Game four times and got there a fifth time with the Vikings. And, of course, he played in back-to-back Super Bowls, beating Drew Bledsoe and the Patriots in Super Bowl XXXI and losing to John Elway's Denver Broncos in Super Bowl XXXII.

In 2007, the last of his 16 seasons in Green Bay, Favre rebounded from a terrible 2006 campaign to lead the Packers to a 13–3 record and all the way to the conference championship game. He passed for 4,155 yards, his third-highest career total at the time, and 28 touchdowns. He finished 10 games during the regular season with a passer rating of 100 or more. When the Packers hosted the Seattle Seahawks in the divisional round of the playoffs, Favre completed 78

★ ★ ★ ★ ★ ★ ★

[Brady] strives for perfection. If he throws one interception or makes one bad throw—to him, that's a bad game. He's very hard on himself. That's why he is who he is.

—Wes Welker

percent of his passes and threw three touchdowns en route to a 42–20 victory. He earned a 137.6 passer rating for the effort. Though his overall performance in the NFC Championship Game against the eventual Super Bowl–champion New York Giants was good, Favre threw a pick in overtime that set up the Giants' game-winning field goal.

★ ★ ★

Favre had one last great season in him, and he played it out in a Minnesota Vikings uniform. In 2009, the year he turned 40, Favre led the Vikings to a 12–4 record, completing a career-high 68.4 percent of his passes (363 of 531) for 4,200 yards and 33 touchdowns. He also finished that season with just seven interceptions, by far the fewest in any single season of his career. Once again finishing 10 games with a passer rating of 100 or better, Favre finished the season with the best single-season passer rating of his career: 107.2.

And once again, Favre started the postseason with a bang. Hosting the Dallas Cowboys in the divisional round, he threw for 234 yards and four touchdowns in a 34–3 blowout win, earning a passer rating of 134.4.

But in the conference championship game at New Orleans, Favre was picked off twice. And the second of those interceptions was easily the worst of his career. With the score tied 28–28 and 19 seconds left in regulation, the Vikings faced third-and-15 at the Saints' 38-yard line. Favre rolled out right, pumped, and, instead of taking the 10 yards he could have picked up running, tried to force a pass to Sidney Rice in the middle of the field. He put the ball directly in the hands of New Orleans cornerback Tracy Porter.

That bad decision not only cost the Vikings a chance to win in regulation, but it effectively cost them the opportunity to advance to the Super Bowl. The Saints won the coin toss in overtime and kicked the winning field goal on their first possession.

Ultimately, it was that kind of play, that kind of decision-making, that separated Favre from the game's truly elite quarterbacks. Favre's desire to compete and win was always there. His physical abilities endured for far longer than any quarterback has ever had the right to expect. His football intelligence, however, was never great. Favre could never make the distinction between a daring play and a stupid one. It's why he threw so many interceptions over the years. It's also why he went to five conference championships but only two Super Bowls.

Brady says he plans to play into his forties. He's currently under contract to play until age 42. Whether he can pull it off remains to be seen. If he can do it, and continue to play well, Brady will make a run at the volume records held by Favre and Manning alike. No matter what happens, Brady has the edge in accuracy, intelligence, and championships. And no matter how he finally leaves the game, Brady almost certainly will do it with more class and less public angst than Favre.

CHAPTER 25

★ ★ ★

Could Have Been More, Should Have Been Less: 2011

Eric Wilbur had himself a good old-fashioned temper tantrum. The Patriots had just lost the Super Bowl to the New York Giants in heartbreaking fashion—for the second time in four years—and the *Boston Globe* sports columnist was frustrated. No, more than frustrated. Wilbur was enraged.

He let his negative energy spill out onto the servers at Boston.com. In a column that was hastily written and posted while Pats fans were still in the early stages of grief, Wilbur seethed and pointed an accusing finger at Tom Brady.

"Sorry, Tommy Boy, this one's on you," Wilbur snarled. "Your hideous performance led to the Giants' 21–17 Super Bowl title win. How embarrassing for your coach, your teammates, and your fans."

As Wilbur saw it, Brady lost the game for his team on the Patriots' first offensive play. The defense had forced the Giants to punt on the game's opening possession, but a perfectly placed kick pinned the Pats deep. On first down from the New England 6-yard line, Brady dropped back to pass, waited, waited, and still had no one open. With the pocket breaking down, Brady saw Giants defensive

Against the Raiders on October 2, 2011, Brady demonstrates the intensity that got him this far…and will carry him into the record books as the undisputed greatest quarterback of all time.

end Justin Tuck break through the offensive line and come barreling toward him. He launched the ball deep down the middle of the field—toward nobody.

The throw to avoid the sack drew a flag for intentional grounding. And intentional grounding in the end zone results in a safety. That meant two points and possession of the ball for New York.

In Wilbur's opinion, the NFL might just as well have called Super Bowl XLVI right then, six minutes into the first quarter, because New England's fate was sealed.

"The safety killed the Patriots. Killed them," Wilbur raged. "And there's nobody to blame but Tom Brady."

He was right about the last part, anyhow. There was no one but Brady to blame for the safety. You could wonder about the play call if you liked. Most teams facing first down at their goal line will go with a running play to try to get some breathing room. But Brady doesn't make a lot of mental errors. Going with a pass play was more likely to catch the Giants off guard than it was to...well, lead to the kind of result it produced.

You could also talk about the offensive line not holding up in a critical situation if you really wanted to. But to do so would be an insult to Tuck, a monster of a football player who was relentless in his efforts during a slow-developing play and finally bullied his way into the backfield. And even if the offensive line deserves some criticism, the fact is that Brady is a veteran quarterback who knows the rules and ought to have known that he needed to slide three steps to his right before getting rid of that ball.

So, yes, Brady bears responsibility for the safety. His error put points on the board for New York and, more important, put the New England defense back on the field on impossibly short rest. Consequently, by the next time Brady touched the ball, the first quarter was nearly over and the Patriots were trailing 9–0.

But the safety didn't cost the Patriots the game. Brady didn't cost the Patriots the game. It was facing a more balanced, more talented team—a team that had struggled with injuries before getting healthy and coming on at the end of the regular season then battling its way past the 15–1 Green Bay Packers and 13–3 San Francisco 49ers in the playoffs—that cost the Patriots the game.

It was the ball bouncing New York's way throughout the night—coffin corner punts; a pair of potentially devastating fumbles that, by pure chance, landed back in the Giants' hands; a third fumble that was recovered by the Patriots only to be negated by a penalty; a game-ending Hail Mary that saw the ball bounce off a sea of Patriots and Giants to fall just one or two gut-wrenching inches beyond Rob Gronkowski's reach—that cost the Patriots the game.

It was an unlikely trio of dropped passes—by Wes Welker at the Giants 20-yard line on a drive that could have put the Pats up by nine with little time remaining, by Deion Branch at the New England 40, and Aaron Hernandez at the New England 30 on what might have been a game-winning drive in the final minute—that cost the Patriots their second chance to secure a fourth Super Bowl championship.

It was the fault of Brady and Welker and Branch, Gronkowski and Hernandez, Rob Ninkovich and Antwaun Molden. It was the fault of Bill Belichick and his coordinators, Bill O'Brien and Matt Patricia. It was all of their fault. And it was none of their fault.

Because Brady didn't just make a bad decision and give up a safety. He also completed 27 of 41 passes for 276 yards and two touchdowns and earned a passer rating of 91.1. He completed a Super Bowl–record 16 consecutive passes while leading scoring drives of 96 and 79 yards at the end of the first half and the start of the second, putting the Patriots ahead 17–9. He continually evaded a relentless and ferocious Giants defensive front, the same pass rush that had brutalized league MVP Aaron Rodgers in Green Bay three weeks earlier. He played tough after a sack by Tuck aggravated a shoulder injury he sustained at the end of the regular season. Tuck's sack and Brady's reaction to it looked bad enough that Pats backup QB Brian Hoyer was briefly seen warming up on the sideline.

In short, Brady more than made up for his game-opening error. He gave his team the chance to win one of the most competitive Super Bowls ever played. And he did it with lots of help. From Welker, who caught seven balls for 60 yards. From Hernandez, who snagged eight catches for 67 yards and a touchdown. From Gronkowski, who gave everything he could playing with a high ankle sprain that required surgery less than a week after the game. From Branch, Danny Woodhead, BenJarvus Green-Ellis—even Chad Ochocinco, who'd been invisible for most of the season. And from a defense that struggled through much of the season but came up big in every playoff game.

Wilbur was wrong. And he was still wrong two days later when, in the face of a furious backlash from Patriots fans—some questioned Wilbur's reasoning and conclusions, others went way over the top, leveling everything from vicious personal insults to threats of violence—he issued a halfhearted apology. Wilbur took back many of the absurd insults he'd slung at Brady following the loss. He conceded that the safety hadn't been a back-breaker for New England. But he maintained, "I still think Brady was most at fault for the loss."

★ ★ ★

That Wilbur wasn't willing to let go of his opinion probably indicated, more than anything else, that he had emerged from Super Bowl XLVI like everyone else who went into the game hoping the Patriots would be able to accomplish the one task left unfinished by the 2007 squad: incredulous.

If the loss in Super Bowl XLVI was less shocking, less gut-wrenching, than the loss in Super Bowl XLII, it was also somehow more confusing and more deflating. There was no perfection on the line this time. No chance to stop the corks from popping annually in Miami. No opportunity to see a group of athletes transform before our eyes into a new NFL pantheon.

But what was there, and what was lost, seemed nonetheless profound. The Patriots were supposed to turn it around. They were *supposed* to win. Mainly because they were supposed to lose.

That was the thing, wasn't it? The Patriots in 2011 were in so many ways the opposite of what they had been the last time they reached the Super Bowl.

They were a high-flying offensive team again, that's for certain. They weren't nearly the juggernaut they'd been four years earlier—they scored 513 points as compared to their league-leading, record-shattering 589 points from 2007—but they had managed to outpace 29 teams in the league in total points. And they'd scored consistently enough to come out ahead in 13 regular-season games in spite of a middle-of-the-pack defense that gave up 21 points per game and allowed more total yards than 30 of the league's other 31 teams.

And to a great extent it was the defense that had defined expectations. Heading into the season, defensive weaknesses were as much a part of the conversation as offensive strengths. The Patriots had what appeared to be a one-man pass rush, a linebackers corps with more than its fair share of questions, and a patchwork secondary.

The consensus among experts was that the Patriots possessed enough offensive muscle to carry the AFC East once again (though some had the division crown going to the New York Jets, who had been to two consecutive AFC Championship Games, winning neither of them, and had knocked off the top-seeded Patriots in the divisional round of the 2010 postseason) but didn't have the talent, experience, or depth on the defensive side of the ball to advance far into the playoffs. There was a chance the Steelers would get to the Super Bowl for a second year in a row. Barring that, it was probably time for the Ravens, Chargers, or Jets to step up.

★ ★ ★

The regular season did little to alter perceptions of the Pats. While Brady and the offense racked up yards and points—with Gronkowski emerging as the best tight end in the NFL; Hernandez showing the versatility to function as tight end, wide receiver, and even running back by turns; and Welker continuing his long run as the most productive and valuable receiver in football—the defense gave up yards. Week in and week out, the defense bent and bent. And though it didn't often break, its habit of giving up big yards and allowing big plays fed into the notion that the Patriots would fall as soon as they ran into an opponent with a high-octane offense or a *D* that could hold Brady and company to fewer than 30 points.

In their season-opening game, a Monday nighter in Miami, Brady passed for 517 yards and four touchdowns. That single-game total not only shattered Drew Bledsoe's team record of 426, it also topped Joe Montana's 22-year-old *Monday Night Football* record of 458. It ranked at the time as the fifth-best passing performance in NFL history.

Brady's outing included the longest play from scrimmage in Patriots history, a 99-yard touchdown hookup with Welker—who did most of the work, catching the ball at the Patriots 19, shaking off tackles, and sprinting all the way to the end zone—late in the fourth quarter. The touchdown also tied an NFL record that is fundamentally unbreakable, given that 99 yards is the maximum that can be gained on a play from scrimmage.

The only negative for Brady was that he threw an interception, snapping his NFL record streak of 358 pass attempts without a pick. Nonetheless, he finished the game with a passer rating of 121.6.

The defense, meanwhile, allowed Miami quarterback Chad Henne to pass for 416 yards. And although the final score, 38–17, made it look like a blowout, in reality the game was close until late in the third quarter.

Brady came up huge again six days later when the Patriots hosted the San Diego Chargers. Throwing for 423 yards and three touchdowns, he set a new NFL record for most passing yards in the first two games of a season, with 940. It was the first time in league history that a quarterback who had thrown for 500 yards in a game followed that effort by passing for more than 400. And it marked the 10th consecutive regular-season game in which the Patriots scored at least 30 points. Brady completed 31 of 40 passes (77.5 percent) and earned a passer rating of 135.7. He also earned his second consecutive AFC Offensive Player of the Week Award, making him the first player ever to take the honor in both of the first two weeks of a season.

The defense did its part, picking off Philip Rivers twice and recovering a pair of fumbles. But along the way it gave up 378 passing yards—allowing pass plays of 36 and 29 yards—and 470 total yards of offense.

It was clear that while the *D* could contribute, the Patriots' fate once again would be in Brady's hands. The Pats knew it, too, as Matt Light made clear after the game.

"He's the leader of our offense," the veteran left tackle said. "When he's doing well, we're all good."

It turned out that Brady didn't just have to do well for the team to be "all good." He needed to be on fire.

By the Numbers — 2011

Total Yards	5,235
Yards Per Game	327.2
Attempts	611
Completions	401
Completion Percentage	65.6
Yards Per Attempt	8.6
Touchdowns	39
Interceptions	12
Passer Rating	105.6
Games Rated Higher Than 100 (Includes One Postseason)	13
Best Single-Game Rating	135.7

Brady completed 30 of 45 passes for 387 yards and four touchdowns when the Pats visited Buffalo in Week 3. His 1,327 total passing yards for the season were the most ever thrown by an NFL quarterback in any three consecutive outings.

Nice day for the record books. For the Patriots win-loss record, not so much. Brady matched his touchdown total with picks. And the defense couldn't overcome the challenge posed by those turnovers, allowing 448 yards, 369 of them through the air. The Patriots suffered their first loss of the season, 34–31.

It appeared the preseason predictions had been right. The Pats would only go as far as Brady could carry them. The attendant concern was that for the third consecutive season, New England was headed for a one-and-done postseason.

★　★　★

If there wasn't much relief to be had from that worry as the season wore on, neither was there overwhelming occasion for outright angst.

The Patriots rebounded nicely after the loss to Buffalo, beating the Raiders handily in Oakland, as Brady posted his 13th consecutive game with at least two passing touchdowns, tying Peyton Manning's record. They then returned home to topple the Jets and hold off the Cowboys.

Brady led the Pats to victory over Dallas in the final two and a half minutes, orchestrating an 80-play touchdown drive in which he completed eight of nine passes for 78 yards and picked up the other on a quarterback sneak on third-and-one from the Cowboys' 29-yard line. With an eight-yard strike to Hernandez that put the Pats ahead 20–16 with 22 seconds remaining, Brady completed his 32nd career game-winning drive.

The win was Brady's 31st consecutive regular-season victory in Foxborough and the 116th regular-season win for the coach-quarterback combination of Belichick and Brady, which tied the league record held by Don Shula and Dan Marino.

The Patriots went into their bye week with a record of 5–1 and a quarterback who had thrown for an astonishing 2,163 yards, which put him on track to finish the season with more than 5,800.

Only, there's no keeping that kind of pace. That's why Marino's single-season record, 5,084, had stood for 26 years. The weather gets cold. The injuries pile up. Defenses hit their stride. Yardage totals dip as the season wears on. It happens every year.

And the trouble for the Patriots was that they needed Brady to stay hot. The *D* still hadn't gelled. They'd held the sputtering Jets in check, but they'd allowed Tony Romo to throw for 317 yards and a touchdown, including plays of 33, 32, and 20 yards (twice). Inevitable or not, an offensive slowdown, assuming it came, was going to be a major problem.

★ ★ ★

That slowdown arrived on the other side of the two-week break. Facing a relentless Steelers pass rush in Pittsburgh, Brady was unable to get anything going. He took three sacks and threw for just 198 yards. Ben Roethlisberger, meanwhile, racked up 365. The game ended when Brady was strip-sacked while attempting to mount a comeback drive in the final seconds of the game. The ball bounced through the Patriots' end zone, giving the Steelers a safety and a 25–17 victory.

A week later, it happened at home. The visiting Giants became the first team to topple the Brady-led Patriots in Foxborough since 2006. Just as they had done in Super Bowl XLII, the Giants combined tight coverage and a high-octane pass rush, creating difficult conditions and forcing Brady to make uncharacteristically bad decisions. Brady threw a pair of picks and lost a fumble.

Still, in the clutch, Brady did what he could to deliver a win. On fourth-and-nine from the Giants' 14-yard line with 1:36 to play, he stepped up in the pocket and threw a strike down the middle of the field to Gronkowski, putting the Pats ahead 20–17.

But the defense couldn't hold the lead. Eli Manning marched his offense up the field quickly, completing a 28-yard pass to tight end Jake Ballard on third-and-10 from the Giants 39 and finally adding a one-yard touchdown pass to Ballard that gave the Giants a 24–20 advantage with just 19 seconds remaining.

In his postgame press conference, Brady promised improvement. "There's no quit in this team," he vowed. "We're going to keep battling. We've got half a season to go. We'll see what this team is made of this week."

Brady's confidence—and the fact that the loss to New York would prove the Patriots' last of the regular season—notwithstanding, the game ensured that the Pats' ability to win tough games would be questioned right to the last.

★ ★ ★

The Patriots cruised through their next four wins, beating the Jets, Chiefs, Eagles, and Colts, while Brady added 1,213 passing yards and 10 touchdowns without throwing a single interception. The team held off a fourth-quarter comeback attempt by Washington in Week 14, while Brady passed for another 357 yards and three touchdowns.

And in Week 15, in front of a massive, Tebowmania-fueled TV audience, the Pats overcame an awful start—in which they gained just four yards in the entire first quarter and fell behind 16–7—to embarrass the Broncos in Denver. By the

For the Books 2011

League Records

Consecutive Regular-Season Home Wins	32
Consecutive Pass Attempts without an Interception	358
Consecutive 400-plus-Yard Passing Games	2
(Tied with six other players)	
Touchdown Passes in a Playoff Game	6
(Tied with Steve Young/Daryle Lamonica)	
Touchdown Passes in a Half/Playoffs	5
Super Bowl Starts	5
(Tied with John Elway)	

Team Records

Most Passing Yards in a Season	5,235
Passing Yards in a Game	517
Longest Pass Play	99-Yard TD
Consecutive Games with Two TD Passes	13
Most Career Touchdown Passes	300
Most 3,000-Yard Seasons	9

Honors and Career Milestones

Career Touchdowns	300
Pro Bowl, Seventh Career Selection	

time the game was over, Brady had completed 23 of 34 passes for 320 yards and a pair of touchdowns for a passer rating of 117.3. Brady's touchdown strikes in that game increased his season total to 35 for the second consecutive year, a feat achieved previously only by Brett Favre (who did it in three straight seasons).

With the 41–23 victory, the Patriots clinched the AFC East title for the third straight season—and the eighth straight in which Brady was healthy.

Brady completed only one touchdown pass in New England's Week 16 home win over the Dolphins—he flicked the ball to Deion Branch at the back of the end zone while running away from heavy pressure on third-and-goal—but it was a big one. With that score, Brady became the first quarterback in NFL history to log at least 36 touchdowns in three different seasons. (In addition to his record 50 in 2007, he had thrown 36 in 2010.) The win, in which Brady also scored a pair of rushing touchdowns, ensured the Patriots would get a first-round bye in the postseason.

While the result was satisfying, the game itself was anything but comfortable. Giving up huge plays on the ground and through the air, the defense spotted Miami a 17-point halftime lead. It was the second week in a row that Brady and the offense had been forced to dig the team out of a deep hole. A third was forthcoming.

Week 17 brought the Bills to Foxborough for what should have been a relatively easy game as division matchups go. These weren't the better-than-advertised, sharp, and highly motivated Bills who had handed the Pats their first loss back in September. These were the banged-up Bills who had lost nine of 12 games following their 3–0 start. While New England was in a race for home-field advantage through the playoffs, Buffalo was rounding out a season that had long since gone in the tank. The Bills were in no shape to do any kind of harm. Or so one might have thought.

Then the Bills scored a touchdown on their first possession of the game. The Patriots went three-and-out on theirs. The Bills scored another touchdown. The Pats went three-and-out again. And once again, the Bills drove down the field and put up seven. With 48 seconds remaining in the first quarter, the Bills were ahead 21–0. And in the process of getting there, they'd burned the Patriots defense on pass plays of 22 and 21 yards and touchdown passes of 18 and 15 yards. Buffalo also benefited from a 47-yard pass-interference call against Molden.

Perhaps it was the deficit and its implications—forget that it had been 11 years since the Patriots were swept by an AFC East team, home field in January was in serious jeopardy—or perhaps the corresponding boos from the crowd in Foxborough, but something roused New England from its slumber early in the second quarter.

The offense scored seven on a balanced 73-yard drive that included a 21-yard run by Stevan Ridley and a 27-yard pass from Brady to Hernandez. The *D* managed to keep Buffalo on its own side of the field for the first time in the game. And the offense scored again with an 81-yard drive, capped when Brady found Hernandez open on an out down the right sideline for a 39-yard touchdown. The offense kept scoring through the rest of the afternoon, and the defense clamped down, intercepting Bills quarterback Ryan Fitzpatrick four times.

The 49–21 victory clinched the top seed in the AFC and made Belichick the only head coach in NFL history to lead a team to 13 or more victories in five different seasons.

For Brady, the win marked 32 consecutive games with at least one passing touchdown, keeping him in the mix, along with New Orleans Saints quarterback Drew Brees, to threaten Johnny Unitas' longstanding record, 47.

Brady also finished just behind Brees in total passing yards for the season with 5,235 (Brees wrapped up with 5,476). Both players finished ahead of the previous single-season record, 5,084, set by Marino in 1984. Four seasons later, Marino, Brady, Brees, Matthew Stafford, and Peyton Manning are still the only quarterbacks in NFL history to throw for more than 5,000 yards in a season. Chances are, however, by 2020 a 5,000-yard season, though still meaningful, will have lost its luster.

Records, streaks, and seedings aside, however, Brady and his teammates knew they had issues to address over the two weeks before their first playoff game.

★ ★ ★ ★ ★ ★ ★

Tom Brady is the ultimate professional football player. He constantly strives to be the best and will not be satisfied until he leads his team to another Super Bowl championship.

—Bob Hyldburg, author, *Total Patriots*

"I'd love to be able to see what it looks like when we put together 60 great minutes of football," Brady told the media. "Today was 45, but it was better than 30 last week."

Better, but still not nearly enough. It was one thing to recover from shaky starts against the overrated Broncos, overmatched Dolphins, and understaffed Bills. But failing to show up for even as much as a quarter was likely to have disastrous results in the tournament. The Pats continued to look like a team that could take advantage of weak opponents in the regular season but that was destined to collapse when it faced an opponent good enough to qualify for the playoffs.

★ ★ ★

Whether that theory was tested in the divisional round is open to debate. Instead of an anticipated showdown with the 12–4 Steelers, the Pats got a rematch with the 8–8 Broncos.

Denver backed into the playoffs, winning the AFC West title despite ending their regular season on a three-game losing streak. In their wild-card playoff game against the Steelers, the Broncos took advantage of a severely injured Ben Roethlisberger to build a two-touchdown lead at halftime but still needed overtime to complete the win after Roethlisberger rallied his team in the fourth quarter.

The Broncos were 13-and-a-half-point underdogs when they arrived in Foxborough six days later. The result wasn't nearly so close. Denver was never in the game. New England got the ball first and drove 80 yards in five plays, scoring on a seven-yard pass from Brady to Welker. The Pats scored again on their second drive, this time with a 10-yard pass from Brady to Gronkowski. And although the Broncos tightened things up briefly with a touchdown of their own early in the second quarter, by halftime Brady had thrown for five touchdowns, a team postseason record, and the Pats were ahead 35–7.

The Patriots slowed it down in the second half, scoring only twice, with a 17-yard touchdown pass from Brady to Hernandez and a Stephen Gostkowski field goal. But the defense made sure Tim Tebow and the Broncos could do nothing, and the Pats prevailed 45–10.

Brady's six touchdown passes in the game tied a postseason record held jointly by Steve Young and Daryle Lamonica. (Gronkowski's three touchdown catches also tied a league playoff record and broke the Patriots' postseason record of two, set by Stanley Morgan during the organization's first Super Bowl run in 1985.) The touchdowns also moved Brady up the list of players with the most postseason touchdown throws. Brady went into the game fifth on that list with 30 scoring passes in his postseason career and came out of it third with 36, having passed Kurt Warner (31) and Dan Marino (32). (Brady would finish the playoffs with 38 touchdowns, trailing only Brett Favre's 44 and Joe Montana's 45.)

The game also was Brady's 18th consecutive postseason appearance with at least one touchdown pass, the second-longest streak of all time behind Favre (20).

And the win made Brady and Belichick, already the coach-quarterback combination with the most regular-season victories (124), the most productive combo in the postseason as well, at 15 wins.

Brady's final stats from the game: 26-for-34 for 363 yards, six touchdowns, and an interception, for another amazing postseason passer rating of 137.6. There was no pretending the performance put in by the Patriots as a team, and Brady in particular, were anything but impressive.

Broncos cornerback Champ Bailey, who'd personally put an end to the Patriots' hopes of winning a third straight Super Bowl with an end-zone interception of Brady six years earlier, summed up Brady's abilities succinctly following the game: "He's been around the block a few times. He knows how to win games. If you're not ready to punch him in the mouth, he's going to eat you up all night."

That the New England defense, too, had come up big was an encouraging sign. But there was still the fact that the Broncos arguably didn't belong in the playoffs to begin with. Even playing at home, there was no way the Patriots could hope to have such an easy time of things in the AFC Championship Game.

They didn't.

★ ★ ★

The Baltimore Ravens came to town equipped with one of the most impressive, most punishing defenses in the league—and an offense that wasn't elite but was certainly much better than Denver's—and forced the Patriots to earn a win. The Ravens limited Brady to 239 yards, held him without a touchdown pass, and intercepted him twice.

The quarterback did manage to engineer the drive that put the winning points on the board early in the fourth quarter. He scored the go-ahead touchdown himself with a dive over the line, on which he took a nasty hit from Baltimore linebacker Terrell Suggs. He exhibited toughness throughout the game. And he led the offense to 23 points against a defense that had allowed fewer than 17 per game during the season.

But real credit for the victory belonged to the Patriots defense. The *D* shut down the Ravens on the ground and through the air for most of the game and held off what could have been a game-winning drive at the end of the fourth quarter with spectacular plays by the secondary.

Brady certainly didn't spare himself in his assessment of the game. "Well, I sucked pretty bad today, but our defense saved us," he said in a postgame interview.

However the win came, it represented some impressive achievements for the QB and his coach. Brady tied Montana's record for career postseason victories, 16, and became only the second quarterback, along with John Elway, to reach five Super Bowls.

Belichick and Brady became the first coach-quarterback combination to make it to five Super Bowls.

★ ★ ★

In many ways, all of that only managed to make the loss in Super Bowl XLVI that much more disappointing.

The Patriots had won the conference championship despite a subpar performance from their quarterback. They had seen the defense step up in successive games, first to accentuate a blowout and second, and most important, to hold off a significant challenge.

The Giants had peaked at exactly the right moment, just as they had done four years earlier. But this time it appeared the Patriots were peaking at the right time too.

A fourth Super Bowl victory would tie Brady with Montana and Terry Bradshaw for the most in a quarterback's career. It would put Brady ahead of Montana for most postseason victories. It would, in spite of any attempts by fans of Montana and the 49ers to circle the wagons, render Brady inarguably the greatest ever.

And for the first time all season, one could feel reasonably sure that the defense was ready to rise to the occasion. The unit, at long last, appeared to have gelled.

So it didn't matter that the sentiment among expert observers was that the Giants were bound to prove more than that Patriots could handle. It didn't matter that the New York pass rush, in two consecutive meetings with New England, had chased Brady all over the backfield and fatally disrupted the Patriots' passing game. It didn't matter that Eli Manning indisputably had come into his own as an NFL quarterback—had, in many ways, surpassed his brother—and that he had possibly the best trio of receivers in the league to work with in Hakeem Nicks, Victor Cruz, and Mario Manningham.

Super Bowl XLVI was going to play out as the inverse of Super Bowl XLII. It would be the Patriots who would exceed expectations and come out victorious. That was just how it was going to work. Until it didn't.

But Patriots Nation's disappointment and Wilbur's apoplexy notwithstanding, the loss didn't undo Brady's legacy. Nor did it undo the 2011 Patriots' achievements. The Pats, behind Brady, had overachieved all the way to the Super Bowl. An offense without a legitimate deep threat had dinked and dunked and run its way to 6,848 yards and 513 points. It had carried a rebuilding defense through the season, giving it a chance to rise up down the stretch.

In the Super Bowl, the Pats defense found ways to contain Manning and the Giants offense through most of the game despite having been put in difficult situations. And Brady, playing against an outstanding Giants *D* and with one of his most important targets visibly hobbled by a high ankle sprain, finished with stats that were effectively identical to those of the Super Bowl MVP, Manning.

In three consecutive games stretching back to Super Bowl XLII, the Giants had made Tom Terrific look merely human and had gotten the better of the Patriots as a result. That was frustrating.

Still and all, Brady had emerged from the 2011 campaign as the winningest quarterback in NFL history, in both the regular season and the playoffs,

There was also the fact that Brady's 878 yards in the 2011 postseason set a new team record, surpassing Brady's previous mark of 792 from 2003.

And though the ending put a damper on what had felt like a fresh start for the Pats in 2011, the team headed into 2012 with an abundance of salary cap space, three picks in the first two rounds of the draft, and a quarterback who was showing no signs of slowing down as he reached his mid-thirties. By the day after Super Bowl XLVI, New England had been installed by the oddsmakers in Las Vegas as the favorite to win Super Bowl XLVII. There was plenty of reason to believe that Brady still had time to earn the fourth championship that would remove all doubt about his place as the greatest of all time.

CHAPTER 26

★ ★ ★

Tom Brady vs. Dan Marino

Dan Marino's legacy as an NFL quarterback was solidified before he even took the first snap of his second full year as a starter.

That's not a bit of an exaggeration. If Marino had suffered some kind of Joe Theismann–style career-ending injury in the Miami Dolphins' 1985 season opener, the only thing that would have changed is the way we talk about Marino. Instead of discussing him as the greatest quarterback who never won a Super Bowl, we'd talk about the greatest loss of potential in NFL history. We'd hypothesize about how many championships he might have won and how many league MVP honors he might have earned.

Because for everything Marino accomplished during his 17-season NFL career—and the list is long—nothing he did from 1985 through 1999 ever eclipsed the glory Marino achieved in 1984. That's not a slight, either. The fact is, very few quarterbacks have ever had a season on par with Marino's 1984. Indeed, if the Dolphins hadn't fallen flat in Super Bowl XIX, you'd be able to argue that no one ever had equaled, or likely ever would, the heights Marino achieved in the '84 campaign.

Not that Marino's capabilities as a quarterback took anyone by surprise, even in his sophomore season with the Dolphins. Marino had been an outstanding college quarterback at the University of Pittsburgh for three seasons, beginning in his freshman year. He struggled a bit in his senior season, and heading into the 1983 draft, there were some doubts about the condition of his knees and unsubstantiated rumors about drug use. The combination was enough to cause Marino to slide to the bottom of the first round, where Don Shula and the reigning AFC champion Dolphins were all too happy to grab him.

Marino took over as Miami's starting quarterback six games into his rookie season and led the team to seven victories in nine starts. Marino threw 12 touchdown passes in his first five games as a starter, brought Miami back from a 17–7 third-quarter deficit in a Week 14 game at Houston, and finished the season with a passer rating of 96.0. He was off to a good start.

But that proved to be nothing. When Marino got ahold of the reins for a full season, he lit up the league. With an incredible ability to read defenses, great poise under pressure, and a lightning-fast release, Marino made opposing defenses look

You Can't Argue with Figures

	Tom Brady	Dan Marino
Regular-Season Record	172–51	147–93
Winning Percentage	.771	.613
Postseason Record	22–9	8–10
Winning Percentage	.710	.444
Overall Record	194–60	155–103
Winning Percentage	.764	.601
Passer Rating	96.4	86.4
Touchdown Percentage	5.5	5.0
Interception Percentage	1.9	3.0
TD/INT	2.9/1	1.7/1
Completion Percentage	63.6	59.4
Yards Per Attempt	7.4	7.3
First-Team All-Pro	2	3
League MVP	2	1
Super Bowl MVP	3	0
Super Bowl Record	4–2	0–1

foolish. He opened the 1984 season with a 311-yard, five-touchdown outing in Washington. In that game, he completed 75 percent of his passes, averaged 11.1 yards per attempt, and earned a passer rating of 150.4. It was the first of nine games during the season in which Marino would finish with a passer rating of 100 or better.

Behind consistently jaw-dropping performances by Marino, the Dolphins won their first 11 games. The team finished the season with the AFC's best record: 14–2 (just one win fewer than the NFC's San Francisco 49ers). And Marino finished with a bundle of records that together made up the greatest single-season performance by a passer in NFL history.

Marino threw 48 touchdown passes during the season, shattering the previous league record of 36 that had been set 23 years earlier by George Blanda (and matched in 1963 by Y.A. Tittle). Marino's record stood for two decades before it was finally broken by Peyton Manning in 2004.

Marino's total has since fallen to fourth on the all-time list behind Manning's 49 in 2004, Tom Brady's 50 in 2007 and Manning's 55 in 2013. But that's it. In 31 years only two players have been able to exceed Marino's mark.

It took until 2011 for Marino to lose the single-season passing yardage record of 5,084 that he set during the 1984 campaign.

Marino also set single-season records for games with 300 or more passing yards (nine), games with 400 or more passing yards (four), and games with four or more passing touchdowns (six)—all of which have since been broken or tied. Marino earned a passer rating of 108.9 for the season. He was named MVP of the league.

And he continued to play excellent football in the AFC playoffs, throwing for 262 yards and three touchdowns in a divisional-round win over the Seattle Seahawks and shredding the Pittsburgh Steelers with a 421-yard, four-touchdown effort in the AFC Championship Game (for which Marino's passer rating was 135.4).

In Super Bowl XIX, however, Marino's output was limited by a powerhouse performance from the 49ers defense. Though he completed 29 of 50 passes for 318 yards and a touchdown, Marino was sacked four times and intercepted twice. On the other side of the ball, Joe Montana picked apart the Miami defense for

331 yards and three touchdown passes (plus a rushing touchdown). And Marino's great season ended in frustration as the Dolphins fell 38–16.

★ ★ ★

At the time, the question most frequently debated wasn't about whether Marino and the Dolphins would get back to the Super Bowl but how often they'd get there and how many titles they could be expected to win. No one suspected that the final answers would be *never* and *none*.

Marino's career after 1984 wasn't devoid of postseason success. The Dolphins qualified for the playoffs eight more times over the succeeding 15 seasons. And Marino threw a touchdown pass in 13 consecutive playoff games, which was a record at the time (it's since been surpassed by Brett Favre, with 20, and Brady, with 18). The Dolphins returned to the AFC Championship Game in 1985 but were upset by the Cinderella Patriots. And when they reached the conference title game again in 1992, they were once again toppled by a wild-card team, the Buffalo Bills.

Marino never stopped playing well and turning heads during the regular season. He was the first player in league history to reach both the 50,000- and 60,000-yard career passing marks. He led the league in passing yards in five seasons, which is tied for the all-time record with Sonny Jurgensen. And he continues to hold several records, including most seasons leading the league in completions (six) and fewest games needed to reach both 100 touchdown passes (44) and 200 TD passes (89).

★ ★ ★

The other side of the coin, though, is that, spectacular as 1984 was, it was the only season in Marino's career in which he ever earned a passer rating of higher than 100. And while Marino's personal achievements were considerable, he didn't consistently lead his team to great success.

The simple reality is that the Dolphins weren't a substantially better team during Marino's career than they'd been in the years before he arrived. If anything, they were less impressive in spite of Marino's gaudy stats.

The Shula-coached Dolphins of the early 1970s had been champions with Bob Griese and Earl Morrall starting behind center. Even as Griese aged, the

Dolphins continued to finish at the top of the AFC East standings. The team won the division title with eighth-round draft choice David Woodley and fifth-round pick Don Strock splitting time in 1981. And in the strike-shortened 1982 season, the team went all the way to Super Bowl XVII with Woodley at quarterback (though, in fairness, it was the defense, not Woodley, that was most responsible for Miami's success).

In Marino's career, which included 13 seasons playing under Shula and four with Jimmy Johnson as Miami's head coach, the Dolphins captured only five AFC East titles, rarely made it past the divisional round of the playoffs, and three times were eliminated from the postseason after just one game. They were a .500 team in four different seasons and had a losing record in one, 1988.

In many ways, Marino embodied the difference between a great passer and a great quarterback. Though his career passing statistics are better than those of his fellow class of '83 draftees and fellow Hall of Famers John Elway and Jim Kelly, Marino didn't play in five Super Bowls and win two as Elway did, nor did he lead his team to four Super Bowls like Kelly.

Though success in the NFL turns on great performances by individual players, the final measure isn't about individual achievement. It's about winning as a team. Marino's Dolphins didn't do that in the Super Bowl, didn't do it in the playoffs by and large, and sometimes didn't even do it in the regular season.

That left Marino, at the end of his impressive career, with only individual records to mark his place in NFL history. Those have fallen over time to a number of players, quite often including Brady, who also has won far more AFC East titles and AFC championships than the great Marino, not to mention four Super Bowls titles to Marino's none.

Brady isn't just a better quarterback than Marino was. According to the measurements that matter most—yards per attempt, touchdown percentage, touchdown-to-interception ratio—he's a better passer than Marino was too. And that's a distinction very few players have ever been able to claim.

CHAPTER 27

★ ★ ★

Pretty Good, Anyhow: Aaron, Russell, Ben, Eli, Drew, and Joe

Sooner or later, there's going to be an NFL quarterback who's better than Tom Brady. That's just the way it works. Sammy Baugh had his moment until Bart Starr came along. And then Starr was supplanted by Joe Montana. And then came Brady.

And so it will pass that a quarterback will come into the league who will shatter Brady's records, who will win and win and win some more, who'll pile up championships and gaudy stats and inspire some people to say, "Yeah, but he isn't as good as Brady," and others to point out that, actually, yes he is.

Is that quarterback playing professional football right now? Ummmmm...you know, probably not. (If you're reading this while watching Russell Wilson lead the Seahawks to victory in Super Bowl LI, pretend that instead of "probably not" what I actually wrote just there was "you never know.")

Still, it's worth taking a moment at least to look at the other guys in the league who have rings.

★   ★   ★

Aaron Rodgers

How good is he?

It's an interesting question. And the answer sort of depends on how you gauge excellence. If you go just by passer rating, he's astonishingly good. If you go by overall regular season performance, still top of the line. If you go by postseason performance, Rodgers still has a lot to prove.

No matter how you look at things, it's astounding that Rodgers, who was an exceptional college talent and could have been the first overall pick in the 2005 draft, fell to Green Bay at pick No. 24. Shocking and fortunate for the Packers. Rodgers has far outplayed Alex Smith, whom the 49ers took at the top of that draft.

More than that, Rodgers has outplayed most quarterbacks in the league. He has passed for more than 4,000 yards in five of his eight seasons as the Packers' starting QB, missing that measure only once in a season in which he started all 16 games. He holds the NFL record for best single-season passer rating, 122.5, and has twice led the league in that important stat. He's posted a passer rating of 100 or better in six seasons. Rodgers has averaged 8 yards per attempt over his career, which is tied with Steve Young for fifth best all time. In 2011, he led the NFL with an amazing 9.2 yards per attempt, despite throwing the ball 502 times. He has twice led the league in TD percentage. He has a career record of 80–39 for a winning percentage of .672.

Rodgers currently has the best career passer rating of all time, 104.1, and the best career interception percentage, 1.6. His career touchdown-to-interception ratio is an incredible 4/1.

Rodgers was named MVP of Super Bowl XLV, a game in which he completed 24 of 39 passes for 304 yards and three touchdowns without throwing a single pick (passer rating: 111.5). He's a two-time NFL MVP.

How good can he get?

Probably not much better. But that ain't bad. Rodgers has the advantage of having come of age in an incredible era for NFL passers. Years of rules tweaking designed to open up the passing game and an ever-increasing emphasis on player safety have made it more difficult than ever to defend the pass. And Rodgers would be a great passer in any era. He has a great arm. He's incredibly accurate. He's mobile. And he has a good head for the game. He doesn't really need to get better. If he can continue to perform at the same high level, he'll rack up stats and earn opportunities to succeed in the postseason.

But not better than Brady?

Not if the question is one of greatness. In the end, greatness is a product of ability and achievement. In sports, that means championships. And given that Rodgers will turn 33 during the 2016 season, it's difficult to imagine he has time to reach three more Super Bowls, let alone win that many. There's also the fact Rodgers has encountered some difficulty staying healthy, which hasn't always limited his starts, but has at times undermined his effectiveness late in the season and in the postseason. Rodgers has an overall postseason record of 7–6 and only twice has led the Packers past the divisional round. Anything's possible, of course, but it seems unlikely that Rodgers will accomplish what Brady has on the big stage.

★ ★ ★

Russell Wilson

How good is he?

Wilson is the best young quarterback in the league. And it looks for all the world as if he's the current QB with the best chance to knock Brady off the throne. At 27 (he'll turn 28 during the 2016 season), and just four seasons into his career, Wilson already has led the Seahawks to back-to-back Super Bowls, winning the first of them. Seattle's victory over Denver in Super Bowl XLVIII made Wilson the third youngest Super Bowl–winning QB ever.

The Seahawks have qualified for postseason play in each of Wilson's four seasons, twice as NFC West champions and the conference's No. 1 seed. Wilson has compiled a record of 46–18 (.719). His career passer rating, 101.8, is the second best of all time behind Rodgers. His 110.1 passer rating in 2015 was best in the league. His career interception percentage, 2.0, is the third best all time behind Rodgers and Brady. And his 8.1 yards per attempt rank fourth all time and best among active quarterbacks.

As a read-option quarterback operating in a run-oriented offense, Wilson hasn't put up big-volume passing numbers. He's topped 4,000 yards in a season just once and has averaged less than 3,500. And he's averaged fewer than 27 touchdowns a season. But he's also run for an average of 582 yards and four TDs a season.

Most important, Wilson has great football intelligence. And he typically makes good decisions under pressure (his ill-fated throw at the end of Super Bowl XLIX notwithstanding). Those are qualities that usually point to success.

How good can he get?

Extremely good. Wilson's major challenges as his career progresses will be to stay healthy—not always an easy task for a running QB—and to develop a stronger ability to operate effectively from within the pocket. Wilson doesn't need to become a different quarterback. His style has served him well. He simply needs to adapt as he ages. He's shown that he has the head to make the transition. The big question will be whether, at 5'11", he has the physical attributes to match. Wilson also benefitted early in his career from the fact that the Seahawks had a team stacked with young, affordable talent. If he's to continue to succeed, he'll need to show a Brady-like ability to alter his game as the salary cap forces changes to the talent around him.

But not better than Brady?

Well, maybe. Wilson's got plenty of time to build on in already impressive 7–3 postseason record. He may yet get to six Super Bowls. And he certainly has shown an ability to win more than he loses. Had he completed the game-winning pass in Super Bowl XLIX, you'd have to say he was already well on his way to topping the man who was ultimately named MVP of that game. But he didn't. And as a result, Wilson heads into his fifth NFL season with little left to prove, but much still to accomplish.

★ ★ ★

Ben Roethlisberger

How good is he?

Ultimately, Roethlisberger has proven to be an uneven quarterback. From season to season, sometimes from game to game, Roethlisberger fluctuates between outstanding and...shrug. And while it's tempting (really tempting at times) to look at Roethlisberger as something of a modern-day Terry Bradshaw—a decent quarterback who's gone further than one might really expect his raw talent to carry him because he plays on a team with a crushing defense—that's not exactly the case.

Certainly Roethlisberger has a bit of Bradshaw in him, both for better and for worse. Like Bradshaw, Roethlisberger is big-armed, strong, fearless, and a dozen degrees past tough. But also like Bradshaw, he has a penchant for making bad decisions, which is reflected in a tendency to throw interceptions. Roethlisberger isn't nearly as given to the pick as Bradshaw was (he throws 1.9 touchdowns for every interception, whereas Bradshaw threw 1-for-1), but he knows how to make them hurt. Like in Super Bowl XLV, when his pick-six late in the first quarter let the Packers take a 14–0 lead and his second interception, toward the end of the second quarter, set up a short scoring drive that put Green Bay ahead 21–3.

Even so, Roethlisberger has been to three Super Bowls, and he's been on the winning side of two of them. That's not an easy thing to accomplish. He's 11–6 overall in the playoffs. And while he's never been the league's greatest passer (in 12 years, he's led the league in passing yards once, passing touchdowns never, and interceptions once), Roethlisberger is virtually impossible to sack and has a career yards-per-attempt average of 7.9, which is the kind of stat that tends to produce wins.

How good can he get?

Roethlisberger has 12 seasons behind him. He goes into 2016 at 34 years old. If getting better means improving statistically, it's probably safe to say that Roethlisberger has reached his plateau. Roethlisberger isn't the kind of player who's likely to produce a flashy set of stats in any given season. He's largely the same player now that he was as a rookie, and that's not likely to change. Except perhaps for the worse. Roethlisberger's toughness and fearlessness have proven his undoing more than once in his career, as mounting injuries have taken their toll and led to an early exit from the playoffs for his Steelers. And football players rarely become less susceptible to injury as they age. Roethlisberger plays for a team that typically fields an outstanding defense. So he may yet have an opportunity to extend his career just as Peyton Manning did in Denver, letting D and a strong run game lead the way. Otherwise, Roethlisberger may turn out to be one of those quarterbacks who makes a transition from asset to liability seemingly overnight.

But not better than Brady?

Roethlisberger's two rings and three Super Bowl appearances mean he at least has a chance to catch up with Brady. But he'll need to double his postseason win total in the process, even if Brady never wins another game in the playoffs. And he's not going to catch Brady in areas like career win-loss record, career touchdowns, or career passing yards. Roethlisberger's a winner and probably a future Hall of Famer. But unless the final years of his career include something truly spectacular, he isn't likely to crack many lists of the top 10 all-time greatest quarterbacks, never mind reach the top spot.

★ ★ ★

Eli Manning

How good is he?

It isn't really sufficient to say that Eli Manning is a two-time Super Bowl champion. Or that he's a two-time Super Bowl MVP. Those distinctions are as fine as they are rare. But they don't paint a complete picture of who Manning is when he's at his best.

The whole truth about Manning is that he may be the best big-game quarterback in NFL history. At the very least, he occupies a spot near the top of the all-time list. Consider this: Bill Belichick has been part of eight Super Bowl teams, two as defensive coordinator for the Giants and six as head coach of the Patriots. Over those eight games, seven starting quarterbacks have gone up against Belichick's defenses: John Elway, Jim Kelly, Kurt Warner, Jake Delhomme, Donovan McNabb, Eli Manning, and Russell Wilson. And not only is Manning the only one of those QBs to come away with a win, but he's done it twice. Those other six quarterbacks combined for 10 touchdowns and seven interceptions; Manning threw three TDs and just a single pick. Most important, in both of the Giants' Super Bowl wins over Belichick's Patriots, Manning took the field in the final minutes of the fourth quarter with his Giants trailing and moved the team into position to put the go-ahead score on the board.

★ ★ ★ ★ ★ ★ ★

I think Tom has taken from the previous generation that it's like going to law school. Quarterbacking has a true element of cerebral reflexive memorization. If you have control of all the information, if you know what everyone's doing reflexively, now you can put your attention on the 11 guys across from you and pinpoint them. That's where Tom is now. He's dictating the defenses. That's where Tom is well beyond anybody else.

—Steve Young

Yes, getting the job done took a circus catch the first time around and one of the greatest catches in Super Bowl history in the second meeting. And yes, Tom Coughlin had something to do with both wins. But it remains that Manning accomplished twice what no one else to date has been able to do once. That's how good he is.

How good can he get?

Well, he's not done yet, which means he could win a third Super Bowl. Maybe he'll even do it against Belichick's Patriots once again. And if he does, he'll have shown that he can win it all without Coughlin. That would be something special. Barring another title, though, it's difficult to see Manning finding a way to build on his legacy. He turned 35 in January 2016. And while his passing stats in 2014 and 2015 were excellent, his Giants still stumbled to 6–10 finishes in both seasons. His career win-loss record is barely above .500. And he's not likely to set any career records as a passer. Still, three rings would make him hard to ignore.

But not better than Brady?

Certainly not. The head-to-head thing is impressive, and it's something Giants fans can (and do) crow about. But just as Brady's head-to-head record against Peyton Manning's teams doesn't automatically make Brady the better quarterback in that rivalry (there are other, more important factors in Brady's favor there), Eli's Super Bowl victories don't make him the better QB. (And Manning supporters can't have it both ways. If Eli is better than Tom, then Tom is better than Peyton, which means Eli is better than Peyton. And no one's taking *that* argument to dinner with Archie and Olivia, are they?)

Manning has never posted a single-season passer rating higher than 93.6. That's not bad, but Brady's best is 117.2 and he's been up over 100 four times. Brady's career passer rating, 96.4, is better than Eli's best single season. Brady is one of the most accurate passers in league history. Eli is a guy with a bad habit of throwing picks and a touchdown-to-interception ratio of 1.5/1 to show for it. Manning is 8–3 in the playoffs, 4-0 in both of his championship seasons, 0-3 otherwise. When he doesn't win the Super Bowl, he either misses the postseason entirely or loses in his first game. Better than many? Sure. Better than most? Eh, maybe (sometimes). Better than Brady? Not a chance.

★ ★ ★

Drew Brees

How good is he?

Brees is an extremely talented athlete who played excellent football in spite of mediocre coaching and a dysfunctional front office during his four seasons as a starter in San Diego and who has risen to the top of the pile since joining the New Orleans Saints in 2006.

In 2011, Brees was one of three NFL quarterbacks, along with Tom Brady and Matthew Stafford, to throw for more than 5,000 yards. Brees, however, was the league leader. His 5,476 yards shattered Dan Marino's 27-year-old record of 5,084. (Peyton Manning in 2013 topped Brees' record, by exactly one yard.) Brees is the only quarterback in league history to pass for 5,000 or more yards in more than one season, and he has done it four times. (Through 2015, Brees accounted for half of the eight 5,000-plus passing yard seasons in NFL history.) Brees is currently ranked fourth all-time in career passing yards with 60,903 and, barring disaster, appeared certain to overtake Dan Marino (61,361) for third early in the 2016 season. He likely needs slightly more than two seasons to challenge Brett Favre (71,838) and Peyton Manning (71,940).

Brees is tied with Brady for fourth all time in passing touchdowns, 428. He holds the record for consecutive games with a TD pass, 54. He has led the NFL in touchdown passes in four of his 15 seasons. He is one of just eight quarterbacks ever to have thrown seven touchdown passes in a game. His 8,085 career pass attempts are fourth most all time, and his 5,365 completions are third.

Brees' career completion percentage, 66.4, tops the all-time list. That could change, of course, as he ages and his skills diminish. But it doesn't seem likely to move by much given the accuracy Brees has demonstrated throughout his career. Brees holds both the best and second-best all-time single-season completion percentage marks, 71.2 in 2011 and 70.6 in 2009.

How good can he get?

He probably can't get any better. Brees appears at the very least to have hit the top of the curve, and he's shown some signs in recent seasons that he may have begun to decline, if only by a few degrees. That said, the Saints have experienced a couple of down seasons. A turnaround at some point before the end of Brees' career is hardly out of the question. And if Brees is a factor in that turnaround, especially if it results in a second Super Bowl win, it can't help but reflect well on the aging quarterback.

But not better than Brady?

Brees has been a consistently great individual achiever. But his teams haven't been consistent winners—in the postseason or the regular season. Brees has a regular-season record of 124–92 (.574) and a postseason record of 6–5. He's a Super Bowl champion and a Super Bowl MVP, but he's also a guy who has been a starter in the NFL for 14 seasons, has posted losing records five times, .500 records twice, and qualified for the playoffs just six times. He's a great player and one of the all-time great passers, but, no, he's not better than Brady, and he's not ever going to be.

★ ★ ★

Joe Flacco

How good is he?

Not half as good as he thinks he is. Flacco has a ring. No one can take that away from him. Moreover, he was named MVP of Super Bowl XLVII, a game in which he completed 66.7 percent of his passes while throwing for 287 yards and three touchdowns. And that was just the final stride in an amazing run through the 2012 playoffs, which included a 28–13 victory over the Patriots in Foxborough in the AFC Championship. He will always have that. But at least for the moment, Flacco has little more on which to stake his repeated claim that he is an "elite" NFL quarterback.

How good can he get?

At just 31 years old heading into the 2016 season, Flacco indubitably has the opportunity to grow as a quarterback and build his resume. It's not a given, however, that he can pull it off. Eight years into his career, Flacco has yet to lead the NFL in any meaningful passing statistic for a season. He started with a bang, winning a playoff game in each of his first five seasons and posting 62 wins over his first six regular seasons. But he hasn't yet thrown for 4,000 yards in a season. His top single-season passing touchdown total is 27. And he throws entirely too many interceptions, two for every three touchdowns. Those aren't the numbers of a quarterback who's on the brink of setting the league on fire.

But not better than Brady?

Not by a longshot. Flacco may well be the best quarterback to play in Baltimore since Johnny Unitas. But that wasn't exactly a difficult ladder to climb. And the fact is, Flacco's no Unitas. And even Unitas was no Brady.

CHAPTER 28

★ ★ ★

As Goes Gronk: 2012

It doesn't make sense to label 2012 a hangover year for the Patriots.

Sure, teams suffering Super Bowl hangovers don't always fold in on themselves. Sometimes they only barely miss the playoffs, the way the Patriots did in 2002. Sometimes they struggle to get started and come on too late. Sometimes they start strong only to limp to the finish line. And, yes, sometimes they straight out collapse.

But something hangover teams never do is win 12 games, capture a fourth straight division title, and advance to a second straight conference championship game.

That's not only the opposite of a hangover. It's a performance that a lot of teams would be overjoyed by, a result nearly every team would view as "something to build on."

Not every team is the Patriots.

And not every quarterback is Tom Brady.

Just as most teams would be happy with a 12–4 regular season and a trip to the semifinals, most quarterbacks would look at what Tom Brady accomplished in 2012 as something to be proud of. For many, it would have been a career year. Brady put up close to 5,000 passing yards, throwing 34 touchdowns to just eight interceptions. He wrapped up the regular season with a passer rating of 98.7. And his postseason run featured back-to-back 300-plus-yard games.

Not bad. But when you're Brady, it's also not anything to get particularly worked up about.

So, yeah, not a hangover. But also not a high. And a good part of a reason the Patriots wound up somewhere in the middle is that not every tight end is Rob Gronkowski.

If you need to categorize the Patriots' 2012 season, you might be wise to look there. You could call it the first of Gronk's injury years. Because even though that doesn't tell the whole story of the 2012 Patriots, it's the most efficient way of capturing the way the story ends.

★ ★ ★

The way the story begins, appropriately enough, is with an unbalanced offseason.

And the way the 2012 offseason began was with the commencement of a difficult, and ultimately fruitless, contract negotiation with Wes Welker. A month to the day after their loss to the New York Giants in Super Bowl XLVI, the Patriots announced that they had opted to apply the franchise tag to Welker, who had been scheduled to hit free agency with the start of the 2012 league year. The move guaranteed Welker a one-year salary of $9.5 million and gave the team and the player four months to reach a long-term deal. When Welker signed his franchise tender in May, it seemed a sign that a new contract would soon follow. But the anticipated agreement never came. Welker wanted three years and $22 million; the team's best offer was two years, $16 million. And by the time the deadline for signing new contracts with franchised players passed, it was well and widely understood that the failure of those negotiations meant that 2012 would be the last year in a Patriots uniform for the player who had been Brady's most frequent and most reliable target since 2007.

Still, Welker was on the roster for the season ahead. And that seemed a good sign for an offense that had put up 513 points in the previous season with Welker as its leading receiver.

With Welker and the dual tight end threats of Gronkowski and Aaron Hernandez, the Patriots passing game appeared to be in solid shape. And while the success of any receiver added to the Patriots' roster is always dependent on his ability to sync with Brady, there was ample reason to hope that free agent

Brandon Lloyd, who signed with the Patriots in March, would provide the deep threat that had been missing since Randy Moss's flameout two years earlier.

The only truly notable loss among offensive skill players was BenJarvus Green-Ellis, who left for Cincinnati in free agency. (Sentimental favorite Kevin Faulk also had played his last snaps with the team in 2011, but that came only after Faulk's career effectively ended with an ACL in the second week of the 2010 season.) Green-Ellis had been the Patriots' leading rusher in 2010 and 2011, and its touchdown leader in 2010 (he finished second behind Gronk in 2011). And 2011 third-round draft pick Stevan Ridley had already shown that he was capable of filling Green-Ellis's shoes.

By the Numbers — 2012

Total Yards	4,827
Yards Per Game	301.7
Attempts	637
Completions	401
Completion Percentage	63.0
Yards Per Attempt	7.6
Touchdowns	34
Interceptions	8
Passer Rating	98.7
Games Rated Higher Than 100 *(Includes One Postseason)*	10
Best Single-Game Rating	144.5

On the other side of the ball, while the Patriots did little in free agency to improve their middling defense of 2011, they added a pair of exciting young players to their defensive front in the first round of the draft, trading up in both cases to acquire defensive end Chandler Jones and linebacker Dont'a Hightower. Both of those picks—and the Patriots 2012 draft—appeared to bode well for the D in the long term. But neither appeared likely to transform it in a single offseason. So once again, it was clear that the Patriots were likely to go only as far as Brady and the offense could take them.

★ ★ ★

The first round rookies called that assumption into doubt early in the second quarter of the season opener in Tennessee, however. With the Titans facing third-and-long deep in their own territory, Jones strip-sacked quarterback Jake Locker at the goal line and Hightower finished it off by scooping and scoring to give the Patriots a 14–3 lead.

The 34–13 win over the Titans also saw Brady throw his 301st career touchdown, breaking a tie with John Elway to take sole possession of seventh on the all-time leader board.

A week later, though, the Patriots dropped a home opener at Gillette Stadium for the first time ever in a frustrating game against the Arizona Cardinals. Neither Brady nor anyone else on the New England squad could seem to get anything right. And in the end, the only real positive to come out of the game was that near the end of the fourth quarter, Brady finally completed what would be his sole touchdown pass of the day, keeping his streak of games with at least one passing TD alive at 34.

The offense played better in a week three visit to Baltimore, and Brady made it 35 straight games with a touchdown pass. But the D wasn't there. And the Patriots slipped to 1–2 for the first time since 2001.

While Brady was racking up passing yards—he'd thrown for more than 300 in both of the Pats' losses—touchdown passes had been difficult to come by. Brady had thrown only four TDs in New England's first three games, and just one in each of the losses. His streak appeared to be hanging by a thread. More important, it didn't appear the Patriots were likely to win many games unless Brady figured out how to find the end zone more frequently.

Brady appeared to solve that problem in a week four visit to Buffalo, throwing for three TDs en route to transforming a 21–7 third quarter deficit into a 52–28 win. By throwing a touchdown pass in a 36th consecutive game, Brady tied Brett Favre for the third longest streak all time.

★ ★ ★

He moved past Favre into sole possession of third a week later when the Patriots hosted the Denver Broncos. Brady's 37th straight game with a TD pass came on the same day that Drew Brees threw for a touchdown in his 48th consecutive game, breaking the record that had been held by Johnny Unitas for 52 years (and that had long been considered unbreakable). New England's week five game also was notable in that it marked the first matchup between Brady's Patriots and the Peyton Manning–led Denver Broncos. Brady played well enough in the match, completing 23 of 31 passes and earning a passer rating of 104.6, though it was the running game, led by Ridley, along with a defense that forced and recovered three fumbles, that gave New England a 31–21 win.

The Patriots' bumpy ride continued over the two weeks to follow, with a tough loss at Seattle followed by an overtime win against the Jets in Foxborough. But New England went into their bye week on a high note, crushing the St. Louis Rams in front of 84,000 fans at London's Wembley Arena. Brady's four touchdown passes were the most he'd thrown in a single game all season, and the most in any regular season game since week three of 2011 (though he'd thrown six in the Patriots' postseason dismantling of the Broncos in January). Brady also became the third QB in NFL history (after Unitas and Brees, of course) to throw at least one TD pass in 40 straight games.

The Pats got right back to frustrating fans after the bye, however, struggling to hold off the Buffalo Bills in Foxborough. It was another one of those games in which Brady and the offense played well enough—Brady put up 237 yards and a pair of TDs, and the offense posted 37 points—but the defense couldn't hold off the opponent. The Bills were in the game until the very end, losing only by virtue of Devin McCourty's interception of a poorly thrown Ryan Fitzpatrick pass in the Patriots end zone in the closing seconds.

Not that McCourty's effort wasn't appreciated, but it was clear the Patriots couldn't get their recent trade acquisition, cornerback Aqib Talib, on the field soon enough. The defense needed help.

Fortunately, Talib was ready to go from the moment he stepped on the field. In his first game in a Patriots uniform, Talib took an interception of Indianapolis Colts rookie quarterback Andrew Luck 59 yards for a touchdown that gave New England a 21–14 lead in the second quarter. The game from there was all Patriots. Brady finished with 331 yards and three touchdowns. And the Pats came out on top 59–24.

But while the win over the Colts was big, it wasn't entirely good. Late in the game, while blocking on an extra point, Gronkowski suffered a break to his left forearm. The injury would keep Gronk off the field for the next five weeks. And his hurried return for the end of the season would ultimately backfire on the Patriots.

★ ★ ★

The Pats fared OK in the immediate aftermath of Gronkowski's injury.

They won back-to-back road games over the division rival Jets (in the infamous Butt-Fumble game) and Dolphins, with Welker and Hernandez accounting for the bulk of receptions.

And when the 11–1 Houston Texans came to Foxborough for a week 14 Monday nighter, full of themselves and resplendent in their newly issued high school style letterman jackets, the Patriots made a point of taking them down several pegs. New England's 42–14 blowout of the supposedly Super Bowl–bound visitors saw Brady throw for 296 yards and four touchdowns before being pulled late in the fourth quarter.

But six days later, Brady and the Patriots alike struggled against the visiting San Francisco 49ers. Brady threw a pair of picks and the Patriots dug themselves a 31–3 hole before rallying in the third and fourth quarters to tie the score. But they couldn't complete the comeback and ultimately dropped the game 41–34. Brady's 443 passing yards were his second most in a single game at the time. But he threw just a single touchdown pass and completed only 55 percent of his deadly 65 attempts (which remain the most in a single game in Brady's career; second most in Patriots history behind Drew Bledsoe's NFL record 70).

Brady's lone touchdown pass against the 49ers did extend his streak to 46 games, just one behind Unitas for second longest all time. It also gave him 30 touchdown passes on the season, marking his third straight season throwing at least 30 TDs and making him the fifth player in NFL history to throw 30 or more touchdowns in each of four seasons.

If either the streak or the milestone meant anything to Brady, he didn't show it. Neither did he spend any time gleaming a week later when he tied Unitas. Instead, Brady's focus following the week 16 game in which the Patriots struggled to achieve a 23–16 win over the Jaguars in Jacksonville, was on venting his frustration.

Though he might easily, and legitimately, have excused the lackluster effort he and his teammates put in against the pitiful, two-win Jacksonville squad as a product of exhaustion, or by copping to overconfidence, Brady would have none of that. Following a game in which he threw as many interceptions as touchdowns (2) and managed to complete just 58.5 percent of his passes, Brady put his displeasure on display.

For the Books   2012

League Records

Most Division Titles by a Quarterback	10
Most Career Postseason Wins by a Quarterback	17
Most Career Postseason Passing Yards	5,949

Team Records

Consecutive Games with a TD Pass	48
Most 3,000-Yard Seasons	10
Most Career Touchdown Passes	334

Honors and Career Milestones

Third Consecutive Season with 30 or More TD Passes
Pro Bowl, Eighth Career Selection

"It was a bad 60 minutes of football," Brady said in his postgame press conference. "We got out-competed, out-fought, and we're lucky to win."

That the Texans also found a way to lose in week 16 meant the Patriots were still alive for the AFC two seed and a bye in the first round of the playoffs. But at 11–4, they were still going to need some help. And they were going to need to help themselves with a week 17 win over Miami. That meant everyone, including Brady, was going to have to play like they meant it.

They did. With Gronk returning to the field in limited action—he caught just two passes, though one of them was for his 11th touchdown of the season—the Patriots put the Dolphins away 28–0. The Texans obliged by dropping their second straight game, their fourth of the season, and giving the Patriots a bye week to start the postseason to go with their 12–4 record. And Brady's first touchdown pass of the game, a nine-yard hookup with Welker in the first quarter, extended Brady's streak to 48 games, one more than Unitas and six behind Drew Brees, whose run had been broken at 54 games. Brady also became the only quarterback in NFL history to throw for at least one touchdown in every game in three consecutive seasons.

★ ★ ★

But, as usual for the Belichick-Brady–era Patriots, success in the regular season wasn't the goal. The Patriots had work left to do. They had a chance to advance to the Super Bowl for a second straight year. And with Gronk back on the field, a week off for the entire team to rest, and the guarantee of at least one home game in the playoffs, it appeared they had solid chance to make it happen.

And that chance improved when the Patriots drew Houston in the divisional round. Five weeks after the takedown in Foxborough that had thrown their season into a tailspin, the Texans would have to return to Gillette Stadium. And this time they'd find the Patriots offense—the unit that had dropped 42 points on them in their previous meeting—with one of its best pass-catching weapons back on the field.

Things couldn't have lined up better for New England.

But the way things line up doesn't always correspond with the way things shake out.

The Patriots won again. So there's that. It wasn't quite the blowout that New England had enjoyed in the regular season. This time they only put up 41 points, while allowing 28. And Brady threw for 344 yards and three touchdowns (passer rating, 115.0). But in the process of winning the game, the team once again lost Gronk. Early in the first quarter as he attempted to haul in a pass along the right sideline, Gronkowski tumbled out of bounds and landed on his surgically repaired forearm, snapping the bone in a second place. Watching the replays, one didn't need a medical degree to know the Patriots had seen the last of their great tight end for the postseason.

It was some consolation that the Patriots were able to overcome the Texans even without Gronk, and without pass-catching running back Danny Woodhead, who'd left earlier in the game with a thumb injury. And for those clocking individual accomplishments, the fact that the win was Brady's 17th in the postseason, breaking a tie with Joe Montana and giving him sole possession of the NFL record for playoff victories by a quarterback, accorded more than a little bit of meaning to the moment. Brady also became the first quarterback to complete 500 passes in the postseason.

But neither the Patriots win nor Brady's records were sufficient to assuage fears about the team's path forward. The Baltimore Ravens had upended the Broncos in Denver a day earlier, which meant they were headed to Foxborough for an AFC Championship rematch. And the Patriots, who hadn't been able to overcome the Ravens with Gronk on the field during the regular season, clearly were in for a difficult match.

For the most part, the game went as expected.

Brady hit Welker with a one-yard TD pass late in the second quarter—the last time one of the most successful quarterback-receiver tandems in NFL history would ever connect on a scoring play—and the Patriots built a 13–7 halftime lead in spite of Gronkowski's absence. But the New England offense spent the third quarter stuck in the mud. And in the fourth quarter, the Patriots found it impossible to score—and difficult even to hold on to the ball.

Ridley gave up a fumble after being knocked unconscious by a brutal hit from Ravens safety Bernard Pollard early in the final period, giving the Ravens offense a short field that they converted into their fourth touchdown.

Then, trailing by 15 points, the Patriots three times failed to score after driving deep into Baltimore territory. On their first attempt to pull closer, the Patriots failed on three tries to pick up four yards from the Ravens 19-yard line, turning the ball over on downs. On their second, the Patriots moved from their own 40-yard line to the Ravens' 24 in a single play, a deep pass from Brady to Welker, only to come away empty after a Brady pass over the middle was tipped at the line and intercepted at the Baltimore 16. Finally, with just over a minute remaining, the Patriots set up on the Ravens' 22-yard line, but Brady underthrew Lloyd in the end zone and was picked off once again.

The championship game saw Brady surpass Brett Favre for the all-time lead in postseason passing yardage. Beyond that, there wasn't much for anyone associated with New England to feel remotely good about.

Neither was there much to say. Unless maybe it was to concede that the importance of Gronkowski to the Patriots could not be overstated.

Brady arguably already had established himself as the greatest quarterback of all time. But effective offenses aren't built around a single player, no matter how great. The Patriots' plans turned on the expectation that Brady would have a one of the league's most fearsome pass-catching weapons to throw to. Compensating for the loss of a player as good as Gronkowski on the fly isn't easy in the regular season; it's all but impossible in the postseason. So it was clear: No matter how well he played, Brady without Gronk was only ever going to be able to carry the Patriots so far.

CHAPTER 29

★ ★ ★

So Go the Patriots: 2013

It's tempting to say that the Patriots 2013 season ended on June 17.

That's the day tight end Aaron Hernandez executed his "friend" Odin Lloyd in an industrial park a mile away from Hernandez's home in North Attleboro, Massachusetts. And, while everything about that murder is more important than its effect on a football team, it's true nonetheless that it brought an end to the career of a player who had emerged as a key component of the Patriots' offense.

So, yes, tempting. But probably not accurate.

To begin with, it's become fairly clear that Hernandez had long been tracking toward flaming out in some spectacular manner. Hernandez was a great football player whose versatility on the field made him a perfect fit in the Patriots offense, but he was/is a despicable human being, a cold-blooded killer for certain, a sociopath in all likelihood. Lloyd allegedly was not the first person Hernandez ever shot. He was simply the last. Sooner or later, Hernandez's personal life was going to destroy his professional life.

The Patriots were always going to need to deal with that eventuality. But even if you could set aside the emotional and intellectual difficulty that came from the recognition that Pats had spent three seasons with a murderer in their midst, even if you could move beyond the human tragedy of Lloyd's death, from a purely pragmatic standpoint, the timing of Hernandez's self-destruction could hardly have been worse for the team. The Patriots barred Hernandez from their facilities as soon as it became clear that he was the prime suspect in Lloyd's murder. They dropped him from their roster on June 26, less than two hours after he was arrested and charged with the killing. And all of this came just a month before the Patriots opened training camp, and 10 weeks before start of the regular season. It was far too late in the offseason for the team to have any hope of replacing Hernandez.

The loss was a factor, for certain. But it wasn't *the* factor.

★ ★ ★

In truth, there was no single factor that set up New England's disappointing season. (And, again, we're talking about Belichick-Brady–era Patriots disappointing, rather than standard-issue disappointing. That's disappointing in the form of a second straight 12–4 regular season, a fifth consecutive AFC East title, and a third straight appearance in the AFC Championship, but no trip to the Super Bowl.) There were several contributing factors, and they started lining up not in June of 2013 but a full year earlier.

When the Patriots and Wes Welker failed to reach agreement on a long-term deal in the summer of 2012, leaving Welker to play the season under the franchise tag, one didn't need inside sources to know that Welker would be departing Foxborough with the start of the next league year. Not that there appeared to be significant bad blood. It was just one of those situations in which team and player had different ideas about value. And differences on that subject tend not to be reconciled in the course of an additional season.

So while fans held out hope that the Patriots would be able to retain Welker for another year or two after 2012, and while many expressed dismay when Welker signed a two-year, $12 million deal with Denver at the start of the 2013 league year, no one who'd been paying attention was truly shocked to see him go.

Still, watching the player who had been Tom Brady's go-to receiver since his arrival in Foxborough six years earlier head off to join Peyton Manning's Broncos was neither easy nor comfortable.

And Welker's decision to leave was only the start of a troublesome offseason for the New England offense.

Two days after Welker was signed away, pass-catching running back Danny Woodhead inked a free agent deal with the San Diego Chargers. The loss of Woodhead didn't cause the same degree of hand-wringing as Welker's departure, but it surely wasn't welcome news.

And though no one was surprised, and few were terribly disappointed, when the Patriots released deep-threat Brandon Lloyd on March 16, the move still raised questions about how exactly the team was going to replace Lloyd's 74 catches for 911 yards.

The Patriots had signed Danny Amendola away from the St. Louis Rams in an apparent attempt to replace Welker. And if you assumed the talented receiver/return man would be able to establish a rapport with Tom Brady quickly (never a safe bet), you could think your way around an outright panic attack. That was helpful.

It was a relief, too, when Julian Edelman, who'd shown promise in limited opportunities filling in for Welker, agreed to return to the Patriots on a one-year deal in early April.

But even with that re-signing, the questions for the 2013 Patriots loomed large. Guys who had accounted for 250 of Tom Brady's 401 completions in 2012 were no longer on the roster. And the offense included just two tested, proven pass-catchers with significant experience working with Brady: Hernandez and Gronkowski.

And Gronkowski's availability was in question.

Gronk had broken his left forearm in the middle of the 2012 season. He'd returned to the field at the end of the season only to break the arm a second time in the Patriots' first playoff game. During the winter and spring, he underwent a series of medical procedures aimed both at repairing the broken bone and clearing up infections associated with the metal plate that had been inserted to help stabilize the bone.

And when news broke in mid-May that Gronkowski not only needed a fourth operation on his arm, but also needed surgery to repair a damaged disc in his back, it raised questions about whether he would be available for the start of the season. The idea of Gronk missing significant time was almost too much to bear. Though he'd only played 11 games in 2012, Gronkowski had pulled in 55 catches for 790 yards and 11 touchdowns (catching very nearly a third of Brady's 34 total

TD passes on the season). That kind of production would have been difficult to do without even if the rest of the offense had remained intact. Under the existing circumstances, it was hard to imagine the Patriots succeeding on any level without Gronk on the field for any extended period of time.

In that context, the day Hernandez was removed from the offensive mix really did feel like the end of the road for New England.

The outlook for the season became a bit less gloomy when the Patriots elected not to place Gronkowski on the physically unable to perform list heading into the season. And it lightened again when Gronk returned to the practice field a week before the start of the regular season.

There was hope, at least, that the best tight end in football would be able to return to game action sometime in the first quarter of the season.

★ ★ ★

It didn't work out that way. Gronkowski's recovery kept him on the sidelines through the Patriots' first six games of the season.

Still, the Pats during that stretch somehow managed to go 5–1.

The team's success was tied in part to the emergence of Edelman. When Amendola left the season opener at Buffalo after aggravating a groin injury he'd suffered in training camp, Edelman became the only healthy, experienced receiver on the Patriots offense. The team needed him to step up. He delivered.

Brady completed 29 passes for 288 yards in the Bills game. Amendola and Edelman accounted for 17 catches and 183 yards between them, with tailback Shane Vereen snagging another seven catches for 58 yards. With 2013 second round draft pick Aaron Dobson absent due to a hamstring injury (the first in a career-defining string of injuries), and fourth round pick Josh Boyce a non-factor, that left undrafted rookie free agent Kenbrell Thompkins and blocking tight end Michael Hoomanawanui to round out the day's catch count. Hoomanawanui caught a single pass. Thompkins managed four catches—on 14 targets.

Brady finished the day having completed less than 56 percent of his passes. And it was later reported that Vereen had broken a bone in his wrist and would be lost for several weeks while recovering from surgery.

The season was off to exactly the rough start one might have anticipated. Except that the Pats got a win. And Brady extended his streak of games with at least one touchdown pass to 49. (He threw two scoring passes in the game, connecting with Edelman on both.) Brady was five games away from tying the record Drew Brees had set in the previous season—and two ahead of the mark that had kept Johnny Unitas at the top of the all-time leader board for the previous 52 years.

In a week two Thursday night matchup with the Jets, with Amendola and Vereen missing and heavy rain pounding the field in Foxborough for much of the game, Brady managed to complete just 19 of 39 pass attempts (48.7 percent) for 185 yards. Edelman caught 13 of Brady's passes that day, on 18 targets. Dobson, the Patriots' next most productive receiver, was good for three catches on 10 targets.

By the Numbers 2013

Total Yards	4,323
Yards Per Game	271.4
Attempts	628
Completions	380
Completion Percentage	60.5
Yards Per Attempt	6.9
Touchdowns	25
Interceptions	11
Passer Rating	87.3
Games Rated Higher Than 100	4
Best Single-Game Rating	151.8

Still, Dobson did make one crucial play. With the Patriots facing third-and-two at the New York 39-yard line on their opening drive, Brady took the snap from under center, turned right, and faked a handoff to Stevan Ridley. The Jets defense bit hard on the play fake, ignoring Dobson's delayed release and allowing the receiver to dart uncovered outside the numbers on the right side of the field. Brady flipped a pass that Dobson took in stride at the 31 and carried the rest of the way to the end zone.

That lone Patriots TD proved the difference in a 13–10 defensive struggle. It also made Brady the second quarterback in NFL history to complete a touchdown pass in 50 straight games.

Brady spread the ball around more in the Patriots' week three game against a challenged Tampa Bay Buccaneers squad, completing passes to six different players. Brady finished 25 of 36 for 225 yards and two touchdowns, both of them to Thompkins. Edelman and Dobson hauled in seven catches each on the day. And Brady's touchdown streak grew to 51 games.

The streak hit 52 games in a visit to Atlanta when Brady threaded the ball through a pair of Falcons defenders in the end zone to connect with tight end

Matthew Mulligan, a street free agent signed in early September to help fill out the injury depleted roster. Mulligan was one of three tight ends on the field for the Patriots in the goal-line scoring play, along with Hoomanawanui and undrafted free agent rookie Zach Sudfeld (whose inability to field an onside kick late in the same game would lead to his release four days later).

Al Michaels and Cris Collinsworth, in the *Sunday Night Football* booth, summed up the moment perfectly.

"They just keep pulling guys in off the street, don't they?" Michaels mused after calling the Mulligan TD.

"They really do," Collinsworth said over replay footage. "But this was a play where Brady had to go back to option number two. How 'bout this: Zach Sudfeld, option number one; Matthew Mulligan, option number two?"

In other words, Brady once again was finding ways to spin straw into gold.

Brady's impressive effort on the night wasn't limited to throwing scoring passes to workaday tight ends, though. He also completed six passes to Thompkins for 127 yards and another seven to Edelman for 118. And there were more spectacular passing plays in the mix than NBC could possibly have asked for.

Late in the second quarter, after starting a drive at their own 7-yard line, the Patriots lined up on first down at their 19. Brady dropped back to the 12, shook off Atlanta defensive end Malliciah Goodman, stepped up to the 14 and launched the ball to the Atlanta 35, where Thompkins, in double coverage, went up over safety William Moore to make a spectacular catch before falling to the 32.

With the scored tied at 10 in the third quarter, Brady again made a key connection with Thompkins that moved the ball from the Patriots' 14-yard line to their 32.

Brady's next two passes went to Edelman: a 17-yard hookup that moved the Patriots close to midfield, followed immediately by a 34-yard completion, all in the air, that brought New England to the Atlanta 18.

And early in the fourth quarter, with the Patriots up 20–13 and looking to put the game away, Edelman took a short pass on the left side of the field in Patriots territory and carried the ball to the Atlanta 18-yard line for a 44-yard pickup. Brady and Thompkins paid it off on the next play with a perfectly placed pass that dropped into Thompkins' hands just as he crossed the goal line.

Brady finished the night having completed 20 of 31 passes for 316 yards and two TDs. The Patriots came out with a 30–23 win and a 4-0 record.

It might have felt like a perfect way to end September, except that the team lost Vince Wilfork for the season with a ruptured Achilles tendon.

★ ★ ★

Oddly enough, though the Patriots started October with Amendola back in the offensive lineup and Wilfork absent from the D, it was the offense that struggled when the Patriots visited Cincinnati. The defense held the Bengals to 13 points. The O managed to put up only six. And Brady, who took four sacks, finished a dismal 18 of 38 (47.4 percent) for 197 yards. His touchdown streak was snapped at 52 games, two shy of Brees' record.

Brady was sacked all over the field again the following week in a win over the visiting 5–0 New Orleans Saints that somehow managed to be sloppy, costly, and spectacular by turns. Although the New England offense struggled throughout the game, the D was able to do just enough to keep the Patriots' hopes alive.

The New England defense suffered yet another blow late in the game when linebacker Jerod Mayo left with what turned out to be a season-ending pectoral tear. With Wilfork gone and Mayo out, the D had to operate not only without two of its best and smartest players, but without two players whom the team counted on to provide crucial on-field leadership.

Somehow, though, the D came up big twice in the closing minutes of the game.

Trailing 24–23 with 2:50 remaining, the Patriots attempted to convert fourth-and-six at their own 24 and failed. The D responded by holding the Saints to three yards of offense, surrendering only a field goal.

On the first play of the ensuing possession, Brady attempted a deep pass to Edelman that was intercepted at the New Orleans 30-yard line. Fans began filing out of the stadium. The game appeared to be over. But then, once again, the D held strong, knocking the Saints back two yards over the next three plays and forcing a punt.

And with 1:13 remaining, the Patriots took possession at their 30-yard line trailing 27–23.

The drive New England mounted was no more the most masterful of Brady's career than it was the most meaningful. But it did produce a memorable result.

After opening with a 23-yard strike through the air to Edelman in the middle of the field (while under heavy pressure once again from the New Orleans pass rush), Brady hurried the offense to the line, took a snap out of the shotgun and delivered another completion up the middle, this time to wide receiver Austin Collie, who had been signed by the Patriots just 10 days earlier.

Four plays later, with his team facing fourth-and-four at the Saints' 26-yard line, Brady found Collie once again for a nine-yard pickup and a first down. Brady hustled his offense to the line of scrimmage and spiked the ball with 10 seconds left on the clock.

Finally, on second down from the New Orleans 17, Brady again took the snap out of the gun. He stepped up into a collapsing pocket, fired to the left side of the end zone, and found Thompkins for the game-winning touchdown over the head of cornerback Jabari Greer.

The moment likely will be remembered forever by fans in New England for local radio color commentator Scott Zolak's bizarrely enthusiastic response.

"Brady's back!" Zolak exclaimed. "That's your quarterback! Who left the building?! Unicorns! Show ponies! Where's the beef?!"

It was difficult to decipher parts of Zolak's call. But it would have been impossible not to understand his excitement.

The Saints game seemed in some meaningful way to encapsulate the Patriots' season. It had been messy throughout. It had been horribly frustrating at times. But somehow a battered defense and a quarterback who didn't know how to quit had found a way to make it work in the end. It gave Patriots Nation hope. The team never seemed to stop crumbling around him, but it felt like anything was possible if Tom Terrific could continue to work miracles.

★ ★ ★

The football gods wouldn't allow that feeling to linger, however.

In a game against the Jets in New Jersey seven days later, Brady suffered ligament damage to his right hand. He soldiered through, but the injury limited his effectiveness. Brady completed less than half of his passes and failed to throw a touchdown for the second time in three games.

Still, he did enough to force overtime. And the Pats lost only after a questionable penalty call against defensive tackle Chris Jones gave New York kicker Nick Folk a second shot—from 15 yards closer to the goalpost—at a field goal he initially missed.

The loss had an undeniable silver lining, however: Gronkowski finally made his return to the lineup. And he came back in style, with eight catches for 114 yards. The loss was tough to take, and had Brady not been hiding his hand injury, fans likely would have panicked. But Gronk's return was the first positive development involving an injured Patriots player all season. That, it seemed, had to be cause for at least cautious optimism.

★ ★ ★

Gronk wasn't much of a factor in the Patriots' ugly home win over the Dolphins a week later. He wasn't alone.

Brady, whose swollen throwing hand was captured by CBS TV cameras, raising questions about how he could hold a football let alone throw one, managed just 13 completions on 22 attempts, passing for all of 116 yards. Brady did find a way to connect with Dobson for a 14-yard touchdown in the third quarter, however. The scoring throw was the 343rd of Brady's career, which moved him past Fran Tarkenton into fourth place all time (along with Brees, who also threw career TD 343 that same day).

Brady's injured hand would continue to bother him for the rest of the season, though at least he was able to play through it. Sebastian Vollmer wasn't so fortunate. The broken leg suffered by the Pats' outstanding right tackle in the Miami game brought an end to his season.

Brady and Gronkowski both regained their momentum the following week in a 55–31 home win over the Pittsburgh Steelers. Brady had his best day of the season, completing 23 of 33 passes for 432 yards and two touchdowns and earning a passer rating of 151.8. And Gronk, who hauled in nine catches for 143 yards and a TD, was one of three Patriots to finish the day with more than 100 receiving yards—along with Dobson and Amendola.

Following their bye, the Patriots lost another game to the refs in a Monday night visit to Carolina.

After the Panthers scored a go-ahead touchdown with 69 seconds left in the game, Brady dug deep and led his team into Carolina territory. With three seconds left, he attempted a pass to Gronkowski in the end zone that was intercepted by safety Robert Lester. The interception, however, was set up by a blatant and egregious act of pass interference against Gronk by linebacker Luke Kuechly. It appeared the Patriots would get another chance from the one-yard, but officials picked up the flag, inexplicably ruling that the pass was uncatchable. They were wrong. But there was nothing the Pats could do about it.

If nothing else, New England at least came away from Carolina with more (though still rare) good injury news. Vereen had returned to the field and had led the Pats with eight catches for 65 yards. It didn't make up for the loss, but it was something.

★ ★ ★

Then the 9–1 Broncos came to Foxborough for a Sunday night game that turned out to be yet another classic.

Early on, the game appeared to be shaping up as a disaster for the Patriots.

On New England's first possession, Ridley, who had developed a bad habit of coughing the ball up, fumbled at the Denver 40-yard line. The ball was picked up and returned for a touchdown by linebacker Von Miller.

Two plays later, Miller came up big for the Broncos yet again with a strip sack of Brady at the New England 21. The fumble was recovered by defensive tackle Terrence Knighton and returned to the Patriots' 10, setting up a two-play touchdown drive for the Denver offense.

On the ensuing New England possession, the Patriots were able to hold onto the ball for all of two plays before LeGarrette Blount put it on the ground at the Pats' 44. The D held Denver to a field goal, but that still translated to a 17–0 first quarter lead for the visitors.

The Patriots stopped giving the ball away after that, but were still unable to get much done offensively. And the teams went into halftime with the Broncos leading 24–0.

New England turned it around in the second half.

Brady, who had gone 10 of 17 for 81 yards in the first half, opened the second with a drive on which he was a perfect 7 of 7 for 76 yards and a touchdown.

And when the Broncos decided it was their turn to start giving the ball away, the Patriots took full advantage.

With their first two possessions of the half, New England cut their deficit from 24 points to 10. With their third, the Patriots officially made it a game again. Brady led the Patriots from their own 35-yard line to the Denver 6 in four plays with most of the yardage coming in a single play. On first down at the New England 49, Brady took the snap from under center, dropped back seven steps to the 40, bought time, slid up into the pocket with excellent protection and let fly to Edelman, who had broken free of cornerback Chris Harris and was wide open deep in Denver territory. Edelman made the catch at the Broncos 16 and advanced the ball to the 8 before he was knocked out of bounds.

Three plays later, Brady fired over the middle to Gronkowski, who muscled out of a hold by linebacker Jeremy Mincey in the end zone to make the touchdown grab. The scoring play put the Patriots solidly back in the game. It also made Brady the fifth player in NFL history to record 350 career passing TDs.

Manning made it easier for the Patriots to capture the lead by throwing an interception at the Broncos' 30-yard line on Denver's next possession. And Brady and Edelman made the comeback even more fun to watch when they connected for their second TD of the game.

On a first-down play at the Denver 14, Brady found Edelman on a hitch at the 10, and the receiver took it from there, spinning away from Harris, evading linebacker Danny Trevathan with the help of a nice downfield block by Mulligan, zipping between safety Mike Adams and linebacker Shaun Phillips and diving into the end zone, arms stretched in front of him, giving him the appearance of Superman in flight.

The TD put the Patriots ahead 28–24.

The Pats ultimately needed overtime and a critical error by Denver's Tony Carter on a punt return to nail down the win. But they got it, winning 34–31 on a Stephen Gostkowski field goal.

Brady finished the day having completed 34 of 50 passes for 344 yards and three touchdowns for a passer rating of 107.4. Edelman officially won over Patriots fans with his spectacular touchdown and with the fact that he significantly outperformed Welker, catching nine passes for 110 yards and two TDs to Welker's four catches for 31 yards and no TDs. And Gronk continued to show

For the Books ★ 2013

League Records

Most Division Titles by a Quarterback	11
Most Career Postseason Wins by a Quarterback	18
Most Career Postseason Appearances by a Quarterback	26
Most Career Postseason Passing Yards	6,424

Team Records

Consecutive Games with a TD Pass	52
Most Career Touchdown Passes	359
Most 3,000-Yard Seasons	11

Honors and Career Milestones
Pro Bowl, Ninth Career Selection

how valuable he was to the team, pulling in seven catches for 90 yards, including the TD he produced through shear Gronk power.

With a one-game lead on both Cincinnati and Indianapolis and a relatively weak lineup of opponents in front of them, the Patriots had the inside track in the race for the AFC two seed. And sitting just a game behind Denver in the standings, but with the head-to-head win giving them a tie-breaker advantage, the Pats also had a shot at overtaking the Broncos for the one seed.

★ ★ ★

They might have made it happen, too, if it hadn't been for those meddling Cleveland Browns.

The Patriots followed their win over Denver with another comeback victory, again winning 34–31 in a road game against the less-than-impressive Houston Texans. Gronk's six catches for 127 yards and a touchdown were instrumental in the win.

While it didn't present much to get excited about, the victory at Houston did mark the first time in 2013 that Brady finished consecutive games with a passer rating of 100 or better. It also made for the first time in the season that Brady had thrown for 300 yards or more in back-to-back outings. Gronkowski was rounding into form and it was paying dividends for the Pats and their quarterback.

Brady threw for 418 yards (his sixth career game with 400 or more passing yards) in yet another comeback victory the following week, this time with the Patriots hosting the Browns. The game was considerably more competitive than it should have been, and far more costly than New England could afford.

After falling behind 12–0 five minutes into the second half, the Patriots started from their 20-yard line and advanced to their 45 with a trio of runs and help from a pass interference call against Cleveland. On first down, Brady lofted a pass to Gronkowski, who had beaten linebacker D'Qwell Jackson in coverage. Gronk made a sweet catch over his right shoulder at the Cleveland 38 and turned up field. But as Gronk crossed the 35, safety T.J. Ward charged in and made a hard dive at the tight end's knees. Ward struck just as Gronkowki's right foot planted on the turf. And the force of the blow tore Gronk's ACL and MCL, bringing an end to his season.

Gronkowski had seen the field for only six and a half games and had made 39 catches for 592 yards and four touchdowns. His average of 84.6 receiving yards per game was a career high.

Brady and the Patriots had found a way to get by without Gronkowski in the early part of the season. Against Cleveland, they went on to complete a comeback win over even after falling behind 19–3 near the end of the third quarter, mainly as a result of a huge effort by Vereen (12 catches for 153 yards). But it was still hard to imagine that the team could successfully navigate the postseason without Gronk.

★ ★ ★

A loss to the Dolphins in Miami the following week appeared to confirm fears about the Pats prospects without Brady's biggest target. The Pats fell behind yet again and trailed for most of the game. They managed to take a 20–17 lead late in the fourth quarter, only to surrender it with a minute and change remaining.

On New England's final possession, Brady moved the offense 61 yards to the Miami 19-yard line in 48 seconds with passes to Edelman, Vereen, and Amendola. But the Pats couldn't complete the drive as Brady's first three attempts at the game-winning TD pass fell incomplete and his final desperation throw was intercepted.

Brady's fourth straight 300-yard passing effort was wasted. Likewise Edelman's 13 catches for 139 yards and a touchdown, and Amendola's 10 catches for 131 yards.

Perhaps the worst part of the loss to Miami was that it represented a failure to capitalize on Denver's loss to San Diego in a Thursday night game three days earlier. There remained an outside chance that the Broncos might lose to the 2–12 Texans or the 4–10 Raiders, but it didn't seem likely. The reality was that the Patriots last best hope at capturing the one seed and home-field advantage through the postseason slipped away with their inability to get into the end zone at the end of the Dolphins game.

Brady, in his postgame press conference, came off as thoroughly defeated.

"We didn't do a good job getting in the red area. We didn't do a good job finishing drives," he said. "It just wasn't a good day."

"We had plenty of chances all day," Brady said when asked about the final drive. "We made some good plays. We made plenty of shitty plays."

Watching the presser, and seeing the QB looking worn out and shell-shocked, one couldn't help but wonder if the unrelenting bad fortune of the season had finally caught up with Brady and the team.

One also couldn't help but think that the game would have turned out much differently had Gronk been on the field.

★ ★ ★

A balanced effort in a blowout win at home against the Ravens in week 16 helped restore hope. Maybe the running game and the D could make up for the hole Gronkowski's injury had left in the passing attack. That idea seemed even more plausible after Blount came up huge (189 yards and two TDs) the following week in the usual Patriots dismantling of the visiting Bills.

The season finale saw the Patriots clinch the two seed and with it a bye and at least one home game in the postseason. The Pats had won the AFC East for the fifth straight season. They'd posted double-digit wins in 11 consecutive seasons, and had won at least 12 games and earned a first-round bye in four straight. And

Brady had notched his 148th career regular season win, tying him with John Elway for third most all time.

Brady's 4,343 passing yards were his fewest since 2010. His 25 TDs were his fewest since 2009. But they also put him at sixth and 11th in the league respectively. Not bad for a quarterback who'd had just one of his top three receiving weapons available to him for more than half the season, and who'd been forced once again to forge working relationships with a group of newcomers on the fly.

The Patriots offense finished third in the league with 27.8 points per game.

★ ★ ★

Those accomplishments in spite of the obstacles the team faced would have been all the more impressive if the team had been able to win a championship, or even to reach the Super Bowl. But in reality, when the team reached the AFC Championship for a third straight year it was already more than anyone had a right to expect.

Brady didn't have all that much to do with New England's win over the visiting Indianapolis Colts in the divisional round. But with Blount rushing for 166 yards and four touchdowns, Ridley adding 52 yards and a pair of TDs, and the defense picking off Andrew Luck four times, Brady's 13 completions for 198 yards were more than enough.

Brady's day did include a key hookup on a deep pass to Amendola. Early in the third quarter, after the Colts narrowed the Patriots' lead to a single score, 21–15, the Patriots started a possession at their own 12-yard line. On first down, Brady took the snap from under center, faked a handoff, fooling no one, dropped back to the 5, and fired deep down the right side of the field where Amendola had got behind a pair of Colts defenders. The ball found Amendola at the 50, and the receiver fought his way to the 35 before going down. The play set up Ridley's first touchdown of the day, a score that effectively ensured a Patriots win.

Simply by appearing in the game, Brady broke a tie with Brett Favre to take sole possession of the record for postseason games by a quarterback, 25. With the victory, Brady extended his NFL record for most postseason wins to 18.

When the Patriots traveled to Denver for the AFC Championship, Brady was able to extend his record for postseason passing yards to 6,424, and to edge closer to Favre and Montana in postseason passing TDs (Brady's 43 put him one behind Favre for second and two behind Montana for most all-time). But that was about all the day had to offer.

It would be wrong to say the Patriots offense played poorly. They managed 320 yards of total offense and kept plugging even after falling behind 23–3 at the start of the fourth quarter. It was simply that the Pats didn't have enough left in them to keep up with the Broncos.

Brady completed 24 of 38 pass attempts for 277 yards and a touchdown. He also picked up a five-yard rushing TD with the game out of reach late.

And even years later, questions lingered regarding whether the Patriots defense would have been able to contain Manning and the Broncos if not for Welker's takeout hit on Talib at the start of the second quarter (at which point the Broncos led 3–0).

Still, Talib did leave the game. And Manning put up 400 yards and a pair of touchdowns en route to a 26-16 Denver win.

The loss left Patriots fans with a bad taste in their mouths—which was only slightly relieved by the outright beatdown the Broncos suffered at the hands of the Seattle Seahawks in Super Bowl XLVIII.

But there was no pretending the Patriots hadn't overachieved in 2013, a season marked from well before it began by a series of unfortunate events that would have destroyed most teams. Neither were the reasons for New England's unlikely success a mystery. Once again, the game's best coach and greatest-ever quarterback had found a way to carry their team to the threshold of the Super Bowl.

And as long as there was Belichick, and as long as there was Brady, there was always next season.

CHAPTER 30

★ ★ ★

Tom Brady vs. Steve Young

Steve Young is without question the most underappreciated quarterback in NFL history. Not underrated—underappreciated.

Those who saw Young play the game couldn't help but recognize him as an incredible athlete. Those who care about the NFL and its history know that his career as a starter, while short, was astonishing. And the record books reveal him not only as one of the league's all-time great passers but as a great ball-carrying quarterback.

And still, every story about Young begins with Joe Montana and ends with Young's inability to stay healthy and his failure to lead the San Francisco 49ers to more than one Super Bowl. The result is that football fans don't always fully appreciate the middle of the tale, the part about Young's dominance at the height of his career.

Young did spend his early seasons in San Francisco as Montana's backup, of course. And before that he spent two seasons with the USFL's Los Angeles Express and another two awful seasons with the hapless Tampa Bay Buccaneers, where he split time, and shared a 4–28 record, with Steve DeBerg. All things considered (which is to say, given that he had a 3–16 record as a starter and threw 10 more interceptions than touchdowns while in a Bucs uniform), Young was

247

fortunate that Bill Walsh was willing to invest a second- and a fourth-round draft pick to acquire his rights in a trade with Tampa.

Walsh saw something he liked in Young. He also saw that Montana was getting increasingly dinged up as his career wore on. So he took a chance. And from 1987 through 1990, Young mostly stood on the 49ers sideline and watched Montana lead the team to a pair of Super Bowls. When he did play during those seasons, Young played well. Coming off the bench and making spot starts while Montana healed from one injury and then the next, he completed 193 of 324 passes for 23 touchdowns and six interceptions. Young compiled a record of 7–3.

When Montana was lost for the year with an elbow injury in the 1991 pre-season and Young got his first chance to start for real, the results were mixed. Young's personal stats were solid—his 101.8 passer rating was the best in the league, as was his yards-per-attempt average of 9.0—but Young missed several games with a knee injury, and the 49ers, though they finished 10–6, missed the playoffs for the first time in nine years.

Young started all 16 games of the 1992 season, as Montana's elbow continued to be a problem. The Niners surged to a 14–2 record. And Young led the league in passer rating for a second consecutive year with a 107.0 finish. This time, he also topped the lists in yards per attempt (8.6), completion percentage (66.7), touchdowns (25), touchdown percentage (6.2), and interception percentage (1.7). While Young was named NFL MVP as a result of his great season, he wasn't able to get the 49ers back to the Super Bowl. Young played fairly well in the playoffs but not at the level he'd exhibited through the regular season. And the 49ers were unable to get past Troy Aikman and the Dallas Cowboys in the NFC Championship Game.

In 1993 the 49ers officially became Young's team, as Montana was traded to the Kansas City Chiefs. Young once again played great football during the regular season. He became the first player in history to lead the NFL in passer rating for three consecutive seasons, wrapping up the year at 101.5. And again he led the league in yards per attempt (8.7), touchdowns (29), and touchdown percentage (6.3). But again Young couldn't get the 49ers over the hump in the playoffs. Though the team blew out the New York Giants in the divisional round, they fell to Dallas in the conference championship for a second year in a row. Young's performance in that final game, 27-for-45 with one touchdown and a

You Can't Argue with Figures

	Tom Brady	Steve Young
Regular-Season Record	172–51	94–49
Winning Percentage	.771	.657
Postseason Record	22–9	8–6
Winning Percentage	.710	.571
Overall Record	194–60	102–55
Winning Percentage	.764	.650
Passer Rating	96.4	96.8
Touchdown Percentage	5.5	5.6
Interception Percentage	1.9	2.6
TD/INT	2.9/1	2.2/1
Completion Percentage	63.6	64.3
Yards Per Attempt	7.4	8.0
First-Team All-Pro	2	4
League MVP	2	2
Super Bowl MVP	3	1
Super Bowl Record	4–2	1–0*

*As a starter. Young went to two additional Super Bowls as a backup.

pick (for a passer rating of 76.8), caused many to conclude that they could add his name to a long list of NFL quarterbacks who could produce great results in the regular season but couldn't win big games.

★ ★ ★

Young needed just another year to lay those doubts to rest. And he did it with a season for the ages.

Young's 1994 campaign included 12 games in which he posted a passer rating of 100 or better. In seven of those, he topped 120. His 112.8 passer rating for the season not only was the best in the league that year, but was the best in league history at the time. (Young's 1994 rating currently sits fourth on the all-time list behind Aaron Rodgers' 122.5 from 2011, Peyton Manning's 121.1 from 2004, and Tom Brady's 117.2 from 2007.) His 70.3 percent completion rate was the best in the league and the best of his career. He also led, once again, in yards per attempt (8.6), touchdowns (35), and touchdown percentage (7.6).

The 49ers stormed through the NFC playoffs and reached Super Bowl XXIX, in which Young turned in the greatest quarterbacking performance in Super Bowl history. Young completed 24 of 36 passes for 325 yards and a Super Bowl–record six touchdowns, threw no interceptions, and finished the game with a passer rating of 134.8. He led the 49ers to a 49–26 victory over the San Diego Chargers.

The Niners never got back to the Super Bowl during Young's career. Injuries started to take their toll beginning in 1995, when Young was able to start only 11 games. And though San Francisco qualified for the playoffs in every year through 1998, the 49ers only made it past the divisional round once, losing to Brett Favre's Green Bay Packers in the 1997 NFC Championship Game.

Young suffered a severe concussion that cost him most of the 1999 season, his last in the league. He retired with a long list of accomplishments to his credit. He is one of only two players, along with Sammy Baugh, ever to lead the league in passer rating in six seasons. He is the only player to lead in that category in four consecutive seasons (1991–94). He also led again in back-to-back seasons in 1996 and 1997. (Consider that, in league history, only six other players ever have led in passer rating in any two consecutive seasons.) Young also finished six different seasons with passer ratings of 100 or better, a distinction matched only by Peyton Manning and Aaron Rodgers. (And it's only been done 80 times in league history.) Young's career passer rating, 96.8, is the best ever among retired players. Aaron Rodgers (104.1), Russell Wilson (101.8), and Tony Romo (96.9) are the only current players with career passer ratings higher than Young's.

Young led the league in passing touchdowns in four seasons, which is tied for most all-time with Johnny Unitas, Len Dawson, Brett Favre, Manning, Tom Brady, and Drew Brees, all of whom had considerably longer careers as starters than Young. He also led the league in completion percentage for four consecutive seasons, 1994–97, which is the second-longest streak in league history behind Dawson's six. Young's NFL record for rushing touchdowns by a quarterback, 43, stood for 16 years until it was tied by Cam Newton in week 17 of the 2015 season.

★　★　★

It's impossible to consider Young's accomplishments without noting that he appears to have benefitted at least to some degree from salary-cap cheating on the part of the 49ers' front office. At the end of Young's career, the team was under investigation by the league for violating cap rules. And in 2000 that investigation led to a $300,000 fine and the forfeiture of draft picks for the team and a $400,000 fine for Carmen Policy, who had been team president from 1991 through 1998. It was those violations, in part, that allowed San Francisco to build and maintain a superior team around Young.

It's silly to think, though, that Young wouldn't have succeeded without the help. Young brought incredible talent and leadership to the football field. He succeeded because he was a great player.

What Young wasn't was a multiple-time champion. As a starter, he qualified for one Super Bowl and lost more conference championships than he won.

Young didn't turn out to be one of those quarterbacks who *couldn't* win the big games. But he was, nonetheless, for all the talent around him, a quarterback who more often than not *didn't* win the big games. And that—winning when it matters most—is one of the things that separates the great from the greatest.

Tom Brady isn't going to finish his career having led the NFL in passer rating six times. Nor is Brady any more likely than anyone else ever to best Young's four straight seasons leading in that category. Neither will Brady top Young's career 96.8 passer rating. Brady will, however, finish his career with at least three more Super Bowl victories as a starting quarterback than Young. Brady also will finish with at least five more conference championship victories and nine more conference championship appearances than Young. He'll almost certainly finish with both a better regular-season winning percentage and a better postseason winning percentage than Young. Brady's career passing stats are better in some places than Young's and worse in others; and they're close virtually everywhere. But with everything on the line, Brady more often than not has found a way to win. That's something Young only truly managed once.

CHAPTER 31

★ ★ ★

Don't Dream It's Over: 2014

Four games into the 2014 season, Tom Brady was done. Fork stuck. Lights turned out. Time to go home and commence a lifetime of boring Gisele and the kids with stories of the glory days.

The Patriots were cooked, too. Their season was a disaster. Their run of excellence was over.

And the biggest deal of all, it was time for New England to take a close look at rookie quarterback Jimmy Garoppolo. Because the aging Brady clearly was in a steep and inescapable decline.

It had to be true. The sports media all said so.

The Patriots had just suffered their second loss of the season, a humiliating 41–14 manhandling by the Chiefs in Kansas City. And it happened in front of a national audience on *Monday Night Football*.

Brady had easily his worst outing of an early season that had been uneven at best. He'd completed just 14 of 23 passes for a scant 159 yards. He'd been intercepted twice while throwing just a single touchdown. And, after his second interception of the night was returned for a Kansas City touchdown, he'd been pulled in favor of Garoppolo. And the rookie QB had gone 6 of 7 for 70 yards and a TD (albeit all in garbage time).

Stacking that on top of the results from the previous three games, over the course of which Brady had thrown for just three TDs and 632 yards, the media was not impressed. Not with Brady. Not with the reconstituted offensive line that had struggled to protect the 37-year-old QB. Not with Rob Gronkowski, who'd looked rusty and tentative as he worked his way back from the torn ACL and MCL that had ended his 2013 season (not to mention the time missed over the previous two seasons due to a twice-broken forearm). Not with Bill Belichick's coaching. Not with anything about 2014 team.

ESPN's Trent Dilfer sounded off right after the game from the field at Arrowhead: "We saw a weak team," Dilfer said. "The New England Patriots, let's face it, they're just *not good* anymore."

New York Daily News columnist Mike Lupica, during a spot on ESPN radio's *Mike & Mike Show* the following day, said he believed Brady had reached the end of the road.

"I had been asking this question coming into the season: Will Peyton Manning or Tom Brady ever win another Super Bowl?" Lupica offered. "I think it's a fair question.... Young offensive line, aging quarterback. You know, Brady's at the point in his career where he's not buying green bananas. So, you know, it seems like an odd mix. And there aren't enough weapons. And it's funny that the same things were being said after last night's game that Jets fans have been saying about Geno [Smith]. You know, does he have enough guys? Does he have enough help? Except, it's Brady. So that's a long way of saying, yes, I don't believe this group is ever going to play in another Super Bowl."

On Boston.com, columnist Eric Wilbur, who has never been afraid to go off the deep end in reaction to a big Patriots loss, posited that the team should consider trading Brady.

"Brady's future in New England was on a tight leash to begin with, even before his decline in play became one of the primary reasons why the 2–2 Patriots are in the midst of an identity crisis," Wilbur wrote in column titled "Trading Tom Brady May Make More Sense Than the Patriots Are Willing to Admit."

"Trade Tom Brady? Has it really come to *this?*" *Wilbur continued.* "It's not likely that this is to be Brady's final month in a Patriots uniform, but don't brush off the possibility, however slight it may be, that he could be gone either."

Ben Volin of the *Boston Globe* was more reserved, pointing out that there was little chance a Brady trade was imminent. Volin did think, though, that the transition to Garoppolo at QB might not be terribly far away.

"But it's time to start wondering if the clock is running out on Brady's Patriots tenure a lot more quickly than we thought," Volin wrote. "He says he wants to play well into his forties, but the way he has opened the 2014 season, the Patriots look smarter each day for drafting Garoppolo in the second round this past May."

"Everything should be on the table now with Brady and the Patriots, if Belichick truly wants to do what's best for the team, as he constantly stresses."

Boston sports talk station WEEI's Kirk Minihane chimed in with his typical mix of reactionary negativity and foolish overconfidence.

"Brady will never win another MVP," Minihane wrote in his column on the station's web site. "He's never going to play in another Super Bowl in New England. His best days are gone, and the days at a level right below his best days are gone. There will be flashes of the old form, but those will be outnumbered by what we've seen the last year and a half. It's only going to get worse for Brady and the Patriots over the next couple of years."

It went on and on.

And then, six days later, as the Patriots prepared to host the Cincinnati Bengals, who were 3–0 and coming off a bye, ESPN's Chris Mortensen dialed it up a couple of notches. Claiming to have sources inside the Patriots organization, Mortensen took time on *Sunday NFL Countdown*, to describe an alleged atmosphere of growing mutual discontent between the quarterback and the team.

"Several players, coaches and former players have rendered an unsettling picture that all does not look well with Tom Brady and the Patriots and there's a reason for it," Mortensen said. "Even though Bill Belichick chuckled when asked Monday night about Brady's status, others close to the team now believe that when the Patriots used that second-round pick on Jimmy Garropolo that they were, in fact, choosing Brady's successor.... Sources say Brady is uncomfortable with the personnel and coaching changes. The consequences have led to tensions between Brady and the coaching staff, with Brady's input into game plans, personnel packages, formations, pre-snap adjustments being significantly diminished."

Those aware of the extent to which Mortensen's reputation as a reporter had always been a product of the ESPN hype machine knew enough to question the reliability of his unnamed "sources." In New England, many were reminded of another *Sunday Countdown* Patriots slam from a decade earlier: Tom Jackson's "They hate their coach," moment.

Still, many in Patriots Nation gave in to a panic that was exacerbated by the constant national buzz about the certain doom facing the team at the hands of the surging Bengals. And there was only so much comfort fans could take from the frequently aired clip of Bill Belichick dismissing a reporter who had asked whether the team was thinking about a change at quarterback with the most wilting look ever delivered by the artistically sardonic head coach.

★ ★ ★

The Patriots, meanwhile, insisted they weren't interested in the noise. In the frequently repeated words of their coach, the team was "on to Cincinnati."

And, boy, were they ever.

Not only did the Patriots fail to collapse as predicted in the face of the NFL's last unbeaten team and its crushing defense, they made it look like they had been onto the Bengals in a major way, dominating the game from start to finish.

The Bengals went into Foxborough having allowed just 33 total points over the first three games of their season—an average of 11 points per game. After giving up a single-game high of 16 points in their season opening visit to their division rivals the Baltimore Ravens, the Bengals had allowed just 17 total points in their next two games.

The Patriots put up 14 points on their first two drives, 20 in the first half.

New England's broken-down old quarterback opened the game with a 20-yard strike up the middle to Brandon LaFell, whom the Patriots had signed away from Carolina in the offseason. Brady's second completion of the game, on his second pass attempt, also went to a newcomer to the squad, tight end Tim Wright, who had come to the Patriots on the eve of the regular season in a widely criticized trade that sent veteran guard Logan Mankins to the Buccaneers.

On a first down play from the Cincinnati 44-yard line, with defensive tackle Geno Atkins bearing down on him from his right side, Brady threw a dart that found Wright between the hashmarks and the numbers on the left side of the field at the Bengals' 27. Wright turned toward the end zone and, had he been able to maintain his footing, might have made it all the way—or at least advanced the ball inside the Cincinnati 5. As it was, with a few strides and a good roll, Wright took the ball to the 14.

On fourth-and-one at the Bengals' 5, old-man Brady set his walker aside long enough to run up the middle for four yards. And the Patriots completed the drive with a one-yard Stevan Ridley rushing TD.

Following a Bengals drive that ended in a missed field goal, the Patriots took over at their own 42 and advanced to the Cincinnati 44 before briefly stalling.

On third-and-eight, Brady took the

By the Numbers — 2014

Total Yards	4,109
Yards Per Game	256.8
Attempts	582
Completions	373
Completion Percentage	64.1
Yards Per Attempt	7.1
Touchdowns	33
Interceptions	9
Passer Rating	97.4
Games Rated Higher Than 100 *(Includes Two Postseasons)*	8
Best Single-Game Rating	148.4

snap out of the shotgun and took advantage of outstanding protection to deliver a pass to Gronkowski in double coverage on the left side of the field. Gronk made the grab at the sticks and powered his way to the 17. With that play, Brady became the sixth quarterback in NFL history to amass more than 50,000 career passing yards.

On the next play, Brady threaded a pass through heavy traffic to Wright, who made the catch at the 2 and tumbled into the end zone.

Media experts might not have believed in Brady and the Patriots, but the crowd in Foxborough certainly did. The roar in celebration of the TD quickly turned to a chant of, "Brady! Brady! Brady!" as the suddenly rejuvenated quarterback celebrated with Julian Edelman on the Patriots sideline.

Brady had completed just five passes (on six attempts) in the game, but he had 98 yards and a TD to show for it. And New England had big, bad Cincinnati on the ropes before the end of the first quarter.

With the D keeping Cincy's offense in check through the half, and big offseason free agent acquisition Darrelle Revis providing a strip that set up a field goal right before halftime, the Patriots took a commanding 20–3 lead into the break.

The Bengals tightened things up a bit with a TD early in the third quarter, but Brady and Vereen alternated heroics on the ensuing Patriots' drive to build the lead back to 17. The 16-yard touchdown pass that capped the drive was the 45th Brady-to-Gronkowski hookup, tying Drew Bledsoe and Ben Coates for most between a quarterback and tight end in Patriots history, second most in league history (behind Philip Rivers and Antonio Gates, who at the time had connected for 65 TDs).

The TD catch also put Gronkowski right at 100 yards on the day for the first time in the season, the 13th time in his career. It was starting to look like Gronk might have a chance at returning to his pre-injury form after all.

When the game ended, the Patriots had beaten Cincinnai 43–17, scoring 10 more points than the Bengals' first three opponents combined. Brady finished the day with 23 completions on 35 attempts for 292 yards and a pair of touchdowns. If Brady truly was approaching the end of his playing career, he clearly was determined to stretch out his big death scene as long as possible.

★ ★ ★

The day after the Bengals game, Belichick made his weekly paid appearance on WEEI's *Dale & Holley Show*. Asked about Mortensen's report from the previous day, the coach threw shade as only he can.

Belichick: "A bunch of anonymous reports? I mean, who are we talking about here?"

Michael Holley: "Chris Mortensen."

Belichick: "But I mean, who said it?"

Holley: "Multiple sources."

Belichick: "So it's an anonymous report?"

Holley: "Anonymous report."

Belichick, audibly scoffing: "Yeah, I'm not really in the anonymous report responding mode. I mean, it's ridiculous."

Over their next six games, the Patriots repeatedly punctuated Belichick's final statement.

Brady had his first 300-plus-yard passing day when the Patriots visited Buffalo in week six, completing 27 of 37 passes (73 percent) for 361 yards and four touchdowns and earning a passer rating of 139.6.

With their 37 points in the victory, the Patriots had scored as many points in their fifth and sixth games of the season, 80, as they had in their first four.

The Bills game did come with a downside, though, as the Patriots lost both Ridley and Jerod Mayo to season-ending injuries. It was the second time in as many years that Mayo's season had come to an early end.

The Patriots had a tougher time when they hosted the Jets in a Thursday night matchup just four days after the Buffalo game. But New England came out ahead just the same, with all three of their touchdowns coming by way of Brady's arm.

The first TD of the night was particularly pretty. On the game's opening possession, Brady quickly moved the Patriots from their own 20-yard to just past midfield with a pair of completions to LaFell. On second-and-seven from the Jets' 49, Brady took the snap out of the gun, rolled right, and lofted a pass to Vereen who'd got behind coverage and was streaking all alone down the sideline. Vereen made a diving catch at the goal line and rolled untouched into the end zone for the score.

The Jets battled back behind a strong ground attack, but couldn't keep up with Brady and the New England offense.

In his 200th career regular season start, Brady had earned his 153rd win.

More important by far, in 18 days following the embarrassment at Kansas City, the Patriots had won three straight, improving their record to 5–2. Brady had thrown for 914 yards and nine touchdowns against zero interceptions (as compared to his 791 yards, four TDs and two picks in the season's first four games). Gronkowski was getting it done. Edelman was getting it done. Vereen was getting it done.

Brady once again found himself watching Garoppolo play quarterback in the fourth quarter of a blowout when the Patriots journeyed to Chicago to wrap up the first half of their season. But this time it was the Patriots who had put the game away early.

Brady's output during a workday that ended five minutes into the final period of play included 354 passing yards and five touchdowns. Brady completed 30 of 35 pass attempts (85.7 percent, the second best regular season single-game completion percentage of his career) and earned his best passer rating of the season, 148.4. His three touchdown passes to Gronkowski brought the pair's career total to 48, breaking their tie with Bledsoe and Coates and giving them sole possession of second most of any QB-TE combo in NFL history.

★ ★ ★

Over their next three games, the Patriots faced, and defeated, a trio of division leading teams, the Broncos, Colts and Lions.

The run started with a home game against 6–1 Denver, a match that was close through the first quarter but over by halftime. Brady ended the game 33 of 53 for 333 yards and four touchdowns. Brady saw a pass glance off the fingers of Danny Amendola and fall to the Broncos for his first pick since the Kansas City game, bringing his passer rating for the day down to 97.4. But each of his TD passes was a product of pinpoint accuracy as he hit Edelman, Vereen, LaFell, and Gronkowski, each in heavy traffic either in the end zone or at the goal line.

The game's most memorable play didn't put points on the board. At the start of the fourth quarter, on first down at the Denver 21-yard line, Brady fired a deep pass to Gronk that appeared to be just too high even for the big tight end. But Gronkowski with a trio of defenders closing in on him, made a backward leap, reached up, and pulled the ball in with one hand, landing on his back just shy of the goal line.

The play set up the one-yard TD pass to Gronk that closed out scoring for the day. It also put Brady over 300 passing yards in a regular season game for the 62nd time in his career, tying him with Brett Favre for fourth most all time.

The Patriots' 43–21 victory gave them an edge over Denver for postseason seeding, which meant they'd transitioned from falling apart to tracking home field advantage throughout the AFC playoffs. But there was still a lot of football to play.

New England enjoyed the luxury of a late-season bye week in advance of their trip to face the 6–3 Colts in Indianapolis.

The Patriots didn't ask much of Brady in the Indy game, instead opting once again to exploit a horrifically weak Colts run defense—this time for 256 yards and four touchdowns en route to a 42–20 win. Brady did put up 257 yards and a pair of TDs, including a 50th career connection with Gronk, but he also threw two interceptions.

Brady had a more productive day the following week when the Patriots hosted the 7–3 Lions. With LeGarrette Blount newly returned to the Pats after a mid-season release by Pittsburgh, where he'd signed as a free agent in the offseason, New England once again sought to emphasize the ground game. But the Lions were tougher than the Colts against the rush. And Brady made up the difference, throwing for 349 yards and two touchdowns while completing 38 of 53 passes.

Brady's 63rd career game passing for more than 300 yards moved him past Favre and in to a tie with John Elway for third most all time. And the Patriots logged another decisive win over a dangerous opponent, this one by a score of 34–9.

The Patriots couldn't upend a fourth straight division-leading foe, however.

In their week 13 visit to Lambeau Field, the Pats looked worn down as they failed to generate a run offense and consistently failed to make plays on D. Brady performed fairly well, finishing with 245 yards and two TDs, but it wasn't enough.

During a trip to San Diego the following week, the Pats struggled early but got it back together in time to make it count. The Pats won 23–14 behind a 317-yard, two-touchdown effort from Brady. The game gave Brady sole possession of third all time in 300-plus-yard games, 64.

New England leaned on the run game and defense again in a 41–13 home victory over the Dolphins that gave them a sixth straight AFC East Championship (and 12th in 13 seasons with Brady at quarterback). They dodged a bullet with a lackluster effort in a 17–16 win over the Jets in New Jersey. And, having clinched the AFC one seed, they treated their closing game against the Bills in Foxborough like the fourth game of the preseason, taking a loss as a result.

The Pats finished their fifth straight season with at least 12 wins, their 14th straight with a winning record.

Brady wrapped up the regular season with 4,109 passing yards, his seventh season throwing for 4,000 yards or more; 33 touchdowns, his fifth season with 30 or more; and a passer rating of 97.4. It seemed fair to say that reports of his decline had been greatly exaggerated.

★ ★ ★

That just left the hard part.

For Brady and the Patriots, a 12-win season was nice, but it wasn't enough. Same with home field in the playoffs and the first-round bye that went with it. Not having to travel in January perhaps gave the players more time to enjoy their new caps and T-shirts. But it didn't accord them the ability to pretend they'd accomplished their goal. An AFC Championship wasn't going to be enough, either. It was Lombardi Trophy or bust and everybody knew it.

For the Books 2014

League Records

Most Super Bowls Won by a Quarteraback (Tied with Joe Montana and Terry Bradshaw)	4
Most Super Bowl Starts by a Quarterback	6
Most Times Named Super Bowl MVP (Tied with Joe Montana)	3
Most Career Super Bowl Touchdown Passes	13
Most Career Super Bowl Passing Yards	1,605
Most Career Super Bowl Pass Attempts	247
Most Career Super Bowl Completions	164
Most Completions in a Super Bowl	37
Most Passing First Downs in a Super Bowl	21
Most Conference Championship Appearances	9
Most Division Titles by a Quarterback	12
Most Career Postseason Wins by a Quarterback	21
Most Career Postseason Appearances by a Quarterback	29
Most Career Postseason Touchdown Passes	53
Most Career Postseason Passing Yards	7,345
Most Career Postseason Pass Attempts	1,085
Most Career Postseason Completions	683

Team Records

Most Career Touchdown Passes	392
Most Passing Yards in a Postseason Game	367
Most 3,000-Yard Seasons	12

Honors and Career Milestones

Pro Bowl, 10th Career Selection
Super Bowl MVP, 3rd Career Selection

It wasn't the Baltimore Ravens' job to make it easy. And the Ravens most decidedly were not a team that was intimidated by a postseason trip to Gillette Stadium. They'd beaten the Patriots in Foxborough in the 2009 wild card round and the 2012 AFC Championship.

Baltimore had been an uneven team through the season, and had entered the playoffs as the conference six seed as a result. But they'd traveled to Pittsburgh in the wild-card round and knocked the heads off of the 11–5 division-champion Steelers in a typically brutal AFC North battle. The Ravens were tough, confident and ready.

And the Ravens got off to a great start. They took the opening kickoff and proceeded to mount a five-play, 71-yard touchdown drive to take an early lead. Then, after holding the Patriots to 16 yards on their first possession, the Ravens conducted a second scoring drive that put them ahead 14–0 with five minutes remaining in the first quarter.

It looked like the Ravens were going to succeed where both the regular season schedule and the pundits had failed: They were on their way to burying the Patriots.

But just as they'd done after the Kansas City game, the Pats pulled a Lazarus act.

In a drive that started at the New England 22-yard line, Brady drove his team quickly into Ravens territory with a pair of critical completions to Gronkowski. The first, on third and eight from the Patriots' 24, came on a play that looked at first like a potential disaster as Brady had to jump for a high snap. By the time he gained his footing, Brady had Ravens pass rushers coming at him from all sides. Still he stood firm and delivered the ball to Gronk at the marker, and Gronk picked up eight more yards to the New England 40 before he was brought down.

On the next play, Brady took the snap from under center, dropped back seven steps, slid back up into the pocket with good protection and fired deep down the left seam, finding Gronk at the Baltimore 30. Gronkowski dragged a defender to the 16 before he was tackled (and very nearly pantsed).

Brady capped the drive with a four-yard scramble for a touchdown that cut the Ravens' lead in half.

The teams traded punts—with Brady taking more than his fair share of big hits from Ravens pass rushers along the way—until halfway through the second quarter, when the Patriots staged a drive that took them from their own 33 to the Ravens end zone to knot the score at 14. The drive included a 23-yard pass from Brady to Gronk that made Brady the all-time leader in postseason passing yards. It ended with a nice catch-and-run by Amendola, who scooped up a low throw at the Baltimore 12-yard line, broke a tackle, broke down the left sideline, and dove from the 5-yard line to the end zone with defenders charging hard at him.

The Amendola score brought Brady's postseason touchdown pass total to 44, pulling him even with Favre for second most all time, just one behind Joe Montana.

Brady had a chance to catch up with Montana, and to put his Patriots ahead, in the final 75 seconds of the half, but he attempted to force a pass to Gronkowski and was intercepted by linebacker Daryl Smith at the Baltimore 43. And the Ravens made the most of the opportunity with a quick touchdown drive that put them ahead 21–14 at halftime.

When the Baltimore D forced the Patriots to go three and out on the opening possession of the second half, and the Ravens O responded with yet another touchdown drive, it became hard to believe that the Patriots could climb out of a 14-point hole for a second time.

But Brady wasn't in the habit of giving up. And the Patriots still had a few tricks up their sleeves.

After opening the Pats' next possession with an incompletion, Brady hit on five straight passes to move New England from their own 20-yard line to the Baltimore 24. On the seventh play of the drive, with the Patriots looking at second and six from the Baltimore 24, Vereen reported to the officials as ineligible, then lined up wide, creating the appearance that tight end Michael Hoomanawanui was serving as New England's fifth offensive lineman on the play even though Hooman was, in fact, an eligible receiver. Unsure of who to cover, the Ravens defense allowed Hooman to dash into the flat, where he caught a pass from Brady at the 18, then charged ahead to the 10.

Ravens coach John Harbaugh, infuriated by what he believed was an illegal act of deception by the Patriots (it was, in fact, a legal play) ran onto the field to get the officials' attention and drew an unsportsmanlike conduct penalty that moved the Pats to the 5.

Two plays later, Brady spotted a blitz package that was going to leave Gronkowski in single coverage, seized the opportunity, and delivered his second touchdown pass of the day. The TD was Brady's 45th in the postseason, which tied Montana's record.

After the D forced Baltimore to punt on their next possession, Brady threw a pair of completions to bring the Patriots to midfield. And then New England rolled out a real trick play. On first down at the Patriots' 49, Brady took the snap and tossed the ball backward to Edelman near the left sideline in what looked like a standard screen pass. As Ravens defenders swarmed toward him, Edelman, the one-time college quarterback, took a step forward then threw deep to Amendola, who had been left uncovered when Baltimore defenders broke off pursuit with Brady's toss to Edelman. Amendola took the pass at the 17 and raced into the end zone for his second TD of the day. The score was tied.

The Ravens took the lead again early in the fourth quarter, but this time only by three.

And when Brady got the ball back, he engineered a drive that turned out to be the game-winner. Brady completed eight of nine passes for 72 yards on the Patriots' final meaningful possession. He opened with a seven-yard throw to LaFell that pushed him over 300 yards passing for the seventh time in his postseason career, second most all time behind Manning's nine. He closed the drive with a beauty of a 23-yard touchdown pass that dropped over LaFell's right shoulder and into the receiver's hands right at the goal line.

With the TD, his third of the game, Brady set a new NFL record for post-season touchdown passes, 46. He also became the first quarterback in history to attempt 1,000 passes in the postseason. And he set new franchise single-game postseason records for passing yards, 367, surpassing his own previous mark of 363 from 2011, and completions, 33, breaking the record of 32 he'd set 13 years earlier in the Snow Bowl and tied in Super Bowl XXXVIII.

The Patriots held on for the win, extending Brady's record for playoff wins by a quarterback to 19 and propelling the Patriots on to a fourth straight appearance in the AFC Championship.

But they still needed two more wins to make the postseason really matter.

★ ★ ★

They got the first of those in the AFC Championship against the Colts.

Indianapolis didn't pose much of a challenge. The Patriots jumped out to a 7–0 lead on their first possession, led 17–7 at halftime, put the game away with a trio of touchdowns in the third quarter, and finished the scoring with one last touchdown early in the fourth quarter. With the 45–7 win, the Patriots earned their sixth trip to the Super Bowl in the Belichick-Brady era, the eighth overall for the franchise, tying the Cowboys and Steelers for most all time. Brady became the first quarterback in NFL history to lead a team to six Super Bowls and extended his record for postseason wins to 20.

Brady finished the game with 23 completions on 35 attempts for 226 yards and three touchdowns. He extended his record for postseason touchdown passes to 49. It was the seventh time in Brady's career that he had thrown for three or more touchdowns in postseason game, second most all time behind Montana's nine. Brady finished the day with a passer rating of 100.4.

If it hadn't been for the absurd media circus surrounding the phony Deflategate "scandal," it would have been as perfect an entrée to the Super Bowl as one could have imagined.

But Deflategate did take over, dominating the conversation nationally and providing an ongoing distraction for the Patriots as they tried to focus on preparing for the biggest game of the year. (It was almost as if that had been at least part of the idea.)

Even if the subject of ball inflation had never been raised, though, the Patriots still would have had to grapple with the fact that getting to the Super Bowl and winning the Super Bowl were entirely different things. It was something the Pats and their fans had come to understand all too well over the previous seven years. Earning a trip to the NFL championship game always means that your season ends either in unparalleled glory or unbearable heartache. But with this sixth trip of the Belichick-Brady era, it seemed there was even more on the line than usual. Brady and the Patriots had secured a third chance to win their fourth title. The road they'd traveled had been longer, steeper, and more difficult than they'd faced in any of their previous Super Bowl seasons. They needed to finish strong, to finish not *near* the top but *at* the top for the first time in a decade, to prove that they still had the capacity to win it all. Brady had made it clear to everyone that he wasn't breaking down. But age catches up with everyone sooner or later. This might be his last chance to hold the Lombardi for the fourth time and to catch up with Montana and Terry Bradshaw.

And the NFC team the Patriots would meet in Glendale, Arizona, on February 1 was undeniably scary. The defending champion Seattle Seahawks, the team that humiliated Manning's Broncos in Super Bowl XLVIII, was looking to become the first team to repeat as champs since the Patriots of 2003 and 2004. Once again, the Seahawks boasted the stingiest defense in the league, a unit that gave up only 15.9 points per game. Their power running game was stronger than it had been a year before. And their quarterback, Russell Wilson, had a third season of NFL experience to draw on.

The Seahawks didn't play football like the Colts. They played like the Ravens. Only their coach, former Patriots coach Pete Carroll, was a good bit smarter than Harbaugh. There was no doubt whatsoever that Carroll would have his team ready for anything the Patriots might pull out of their bag of tricks.

★ ★ ★

Sure enough, the Seahawks went into Super Bowl XLIX amped up and ready to rock and roll.

Seattle didn't enjoy the same early success that they'd achieved against Manning and the Broncos a year earlier, but they kept the Patriots off the board through the first quarter. The Seahawks did a great job of preventing the New England run game, which had been such a critical aspect of the win over Indianapolis, from getting started, rendering the New England offense largely one dimensional. And, in a reflection of the Baltimore game, Brady found himself frequently under pressure and too often taking big hits from the Seahawks' athletic pass rushers.

When the Patriots threatened to put up the game's first points late in the opening period, the Seattle D clamped down. With the Patriots facing third-and-six at the Seahawks' 10-yard line, the Seattle defense found a way to bring heavy pressure on Brady despite rushing only three men. With a pair of pass rushers closing in, Brady made a bad decision to try to connect with Edelman in the back of the end zone, underthrew his receiver, and was picked off by cornerback Jeremy Lane at the goal line.

The Patriots D was doing its job, too, however. They held Seattle to just 12 yards on the possession following the pick, forcing a punt that gave the New England offense possession at their own 35 early in the second quarter.

Brady led the Pats offense on a nine-play scoring drive during which New England picked up just two yards on as many run plays.

On the first play of the drive, Brady connected with Amendola on a swing pass that the receiver caught four yards in the backfield an advanced all the way to the Seattle 48.

Six plays later, with the drive threatening to stall as the Patriots faced third-and-a-very-long-nine at the Seattle 35, Brady took the snap out of the shotgun, got outstanding protection, and found Edelman on a crossing route at the 32. Edelman found space and wove his way into the Seattle secondary before being stopped at the 12.

And, after an unproductive Blount run up the middle, the offense huddled up and headed to the line for second-and-nine at the 11. Brady took the snap out of the gun, faked the handoff to Blount, and fired a bullet to LaFell on an inside slant. LaFell made the catch at the 1 and stepped into the end zone. The Patriots had drawn first blood. And Brady had become the first quarterback in NFL history to throw 50 touchdown passes in the postseason. It was also Brady's 10th career touchdown pass in the Super Bowl, bringing him within one of Montana's record.

He would pull even with Montana before halftime. After the Seahawks scored a tying touchdown just before the two-minute warning, Brady and the New England offense did their part to get the Patriots into the locker room with a lead.

With the ground game coming on a bit, but still not consistently productive, Brady moved the Patriots from their own 20 to the Seattle 22 with a series of short passes. Amendola and Vereen took turns picking up chunks of yards after the catch while Gronkowski served mainly to occupy multiple defenders in the middle of the field.

Then, on second and five from the Seahawks' 22, Gronk finally got in on the action. Gronkowski lined up wide right for a second straight play. The Seahawks walked linebacker K.J. Wright out in man coverage. And Brady saw his opportunity. Gronkowski, running a go route, made a nice move to get around Wright at the first down marker then outran coverage into the end zone where Brady delivered a ball that only the tight end had a chance to catch.

Gronk's score put the Patriots ahead 14–7. It brought Brady up even with Montana in Super Bowl TD passes at 11.

It also looked like it would allow the Patriots to head into the break with a lead. Only the Patriots defense, which had played so well to that point, folded in the final 30 seconds before halftime, allowing Wilson to work his patented end-of-the-half magic and drive the Seahawks 80 yards for the tying score.

★　★　★

The first half had ended on a bad note for the Patriots. Katy Perry and her pal Left Shark kept the vibe going through halftime. Then the Seahawks picked up where they left off.

Seattle victimized the New England defense for 70 fairly easy yards on the opening drive of the second half before the Pats finally dug in and held the Seahawks to a field goal.

The Patriots did not respond well. They moved the ball just 12 yards on their first possession of the half before Brady threw his second interception of the game. Although he'd faced fierce pressure on the drive to that point, Brady couldn't attribute the pick to the Seattle pass rush. Brady had good protection on the play and simply made a bad decision to try to thread a pass to Gronkowski who was in tight coverage in the middle of the field. The ball ended up in the hands of linebacker Bobby Wagner. Not only had Brady never thrown two interceptions in a Super Bowl before, he'd thrown a total of two picks in his previous five trips.

Wilson and the Seattle offense took over at the 50. And six plays later, Seattle had a 10-point lead. It was starting to look as if another Seahawks Super Bowl blowout might be in the cards after all. And even if things didn't go completely south for the Pats, there was this: No team had ever won a Super Bowl after trailing by 10 points in the second half.

Seahawks cornerback Richard Sherman, for one, felt pretty good about the state of the game. As NBC TV headed to commercial following the Seattle TD, Sherman found a network camera and directed a taunt to Revis, who had been beaten by receiver Doug Baldwin on the scoring play. (Sherman probably wasn't terribly bothered by the fact that Baldwin had used an official to set a pick.)

With the Seahawks holding a big lead and their defense turning up the pressure accordingly, the Patriots sputtered on their next two drives. But the New England D held strong and kept the game from getting out of hand.

Three minutes into the fourth quarter, the Patriots took possession at their own 32, knowing they were running out of time and chances.

"We're getting a little bit closer to serious crunch time," Al Michaels observed from the NBC broadcast booth.

"No doubt about it," Cris Collinsworth said. "And for Tom Brady, it has been a week of distractions. He's had good moments in this game. He's made big mistakes. I'm sure it's been tough to focus this week."

Brady's focus kicked in soon enough.

The possession started badly, as Brady couldn't find an open receiver and ended up taking an eight-yard sack. The Patriots got four yards back on a swing pass to LaFell on second down, but that still brought up third-and-14 from the New England 28.

A three-and-out might have been a back breaker. There's only so much you can ask a defense to accomplish when you give it short rest with fruitless drive after fruitless drive. And beating the Seattle D on third and long didn't seem likely.

With the crowd in a roar worthy of a Seahawks home game—and as Michaels and Collinsworth jawed about ball inflation—Brady broke the huddle, walked the New England offense to the line, settled into the gun and signaled for the snap. Brady took the ball at the 23, slid up into the pocket, shuffled toward the line, and fired a rocket 21 yards to Edelman who was in double coverage in the middle of the field.

The completion gave the Patriots offense new life. They moved the ball quickly into Seattle territory, where they once again found themselves up against a third and long, this time needing to pick up eight yards from the Seattle 25.

And once again, Brady-to-Edelman got it done, and in much the same fashion. Brady delivered the ball to Edelman at the Seahawks' 15 and the receiver picked up the next 11 yards.

Brady looked for Edelman again on the next play, on the goal line, but missed on a back-shoulder throw to his wide-open receiver. The quarterback made up for it a moment later, though, as he drilled a touchdown pass to Amendola at the back of the end zone.

Brady had taken sole possession of the record for Super Bowl touchdown passes, 12. And with the successful point after, the Patriots pulled to within three points of the Seahawks.

The New England D came up big yet again on the ensuing Seattle possession, holding the Seahawks to just five yards on three plays, and forcing a punt that gave the Patriots the ball at their own 36 with just under seven minutes remaining.

Over the following 4:46, the Pats progressed 61 yards in nine plays with Brady throwing seven completions on seven attempts, for 52 yards while Vereen and Blount combined for an additional nine yards on the ground. The drive included two huge passes to Gronkowski, a 20-yard hookup on second-and-11 from the Patriots' 48-yard line and a 13-yard gainer on second-and-10 from the Seattle 32.

Finally, on second-and-goal from the 3-yard line, Brady made up for missing Edelman at the goal line earlier, connecting with his favorite target with the exact same back-shoulder throw that had missed on the previous drive.

The crowd changed loyalties as only a Super Bowl crowd can, chanting, "Brady! Brady! Brady!" as Stephen Gostkowski added the extra point that made the Patriots' lead a field goal proof 28–24.

Brady had thrown 37 completions in the game, a record not just for the Super Bowl but for all NFL postseason games. He had led the Patriots to a Super Bowl–record 21 passing first downs. His 328 passing yards made it his eighth career postseason game with 300 or more, one shy of Manning's record. He'd extended his records for touchdown passes in the Super Bowl, 13, and the postseason, 53. He'd also extended his Super Bowl and postseason records for attempts (247/1,085), completions (164/683), and passing yards (1,605/7,345). And he'd set a new team record for passing yards in a single postseason, 921.

Brady had led his team back from a 10-point deficit in the fourth quarter of the Super Bowl. And he'd done it against the best defense in football. If the Patriots could just hold on for the win this time, Brady would extend his record for game-winning drives in the postseason to nine. More important, he would finally join Montana and Bradshaw as the only quarterbacks to win four Super Bowls.

That was the nerve-racking part of it all, though. Because once again, the Patriots had put the go-ahead touchdown on the board with a fair amount of time left on the clock. Wilson would have a chance to play the role of Eli Manning, taking away a win that Brady and the Patriots had appeared to earn.

And once again, all Brady could do was stand on the sideline and watch the opposing team march, aided again by an incredibly unlikely circus catch, toward the game-winning touchdown.

The fact that victory wasn't ripped away from Brady once again is the reason that Super Bowl XLIX will never be wholly the quarterback's game. The play that undrafted rookie cornerback Malcolm Butler made to save the game, intercepting Wilson at the goal line, was the single greatest play in Super Bowl history. And fittingly, the Patriots' victory will always be associated with Butler more than any other player.

Brady knows that as well as anyone else. Although he was named the game's MVP, tying Montana for the Super Bowl record at three each, Brady turned around in the days following the game and gave the new truck that came with the honor to Butler.

But the fact that the game turned on Butler's last-second heroics was strangely perfect. Brady had long since made the transition from unlikely hero of Super Bowl XXXVI to all-time great. Still, Brady's undying quest for excellence has always been driven in part by the afterthought of a 199th overall draft pick who still lives within him. And there he was, finally equaling his boyhood hero, Montana, in Super Bowl wins and MVP nods, besting Montana in Super Bowl TD passes, besting everyone in virtually every conceivable category tied to the championship game—and knowing that it wouldn't have come to pass without the unlikely heroics of a young afterthought of an undrafted rookie free agent.

Brady had spent four months making it clear that his career was far from over. But there, in Glendale, Arizona, it had strangely come full circle.

CHAPTER 32

★ ★ ★

Tom Brady vs. Bart Starr

Five championships. That's probably the most important thing to consider when you talk about Bart Starr. Well, that and a .900 career winning percentage in the postseason. Stats don't get a whole lot more impressive than that.

In fact, those numbers are the biggest reasons why Starr was generally considered the greatest quarterback in NFL history from the time he retired following the 1971 season until somewhere around Joe Montana's fourth Super Bowl victory in January 1990. They're the primary reasons why there are those—fans and experts alike—who still hew to the belief that Starr was the best who ever played.

Starr is the only quarterback in NFL history to lead a team to five titles. (And Tom Brady is the only current NFL player who can be viewed as a threat to equal that achievement.) He's also the only QB ever to win three consecutive league championships. Starr's Green Bay Packers were NFL champions three times in the pre–Super Bowl era, winning the title games in 1961, 1962, and 1965. And in 1966 and 1967 Starr and the Packers not only won the NFL Championship Game, but went on to defeat the AFL champion Kansas City Chiefs and Oakland Raiders in Super Bowls I and II (known at the time as AFL-NFL World Championship Games).

There's a lingering perception that the AFL teams in those early interleague championships were simply overmatched by the representative from the much better NFL. But that idea was borne less of fact than of a preference among sportswriters of the era for the older league. That it persists is substantially a result of what the Packers did to the Chiefs and Raiders, both of which were very good football teams.

The Packers were more than a good football team. They were a dynasty. Coached by Vince Lombardi, who's still widely regarded as the greatest coach in the history of the pro game (though it's increasingly easy to make a case for Bill Belichick), and led on the field by Starr, Green Bay's 1960s teams included many of the best players of the era. The Packers rosters included future Hall of Famers Jim Taylor, Paul Hornung, Forrest Gregg, Ray Nitschke, Willie Davis, Willie Wood, Henry Jordan, and Herb Adderley, as well as a host of other great talents.

The Packers may have made shredding the AFL's best teams look easy, but that shouldn't be read to mean that the Chiefs and Raiders were pushovers.

In Super Bowl I, Starr went 16-for-23 for 250 yards and two touchdowns with a single interception. That adds up to a 70 percent completion rate, 10.9 yards per attempt, and a passer rating of 116.2. With an equally dominant performance from their defense, the Packers came out on top 35–10.

The 1966 Chiefs were a team that should have been more competitive in the Super Bowl. The 1967 Raiders, on the other hand, were a squad that had a solid chance of upending the Packers in Lombardi's final game.

Though they lost Super Bowl II by a score of 33–14, the Raiders were among the best teams ever fielded during the 10-year pre-merger history of the AFL. The Raiders went 13–1 during the regular season, scoring 468 points (33.4 per game) and allowing only 233 (16.6 per game). Oakland's quarterback, Daryle Lamonica, threw for 3,228 yards and 30 touchdowns during the '67 campaign. And in the AFL Championship Game, the Raiders dismantled the Houston Oilers 40–7.

The 1967 Packers were a 9–4–1 team that averaged just 23.7 points per game, fewer than half the teams in the NFL. They won with defense, allowing only 14.9 points per game.

The Packers limped into the postseason weary from their back-to-back championship seasons, battered from a brutal season, and reeling from the NFL Championship Game two weeks earlier.

You Can't Argue with Figures

	Tom Brady	Bart Starr
Regular-Season Record	172–51	94–57–6
Winning Percentage	.771	.614
Postseason Record	22–9	9–1
Winning Percentage	.710	.900
Overall Record	194–60	103–58–6
Winning Percentage	.764	.635
Passer Rating	96.4	80.5
Touchdown Percentage	5.5	4.8
Interception Percentage	1.9	4.4
TD/INT	2.9/1	1.1/1
Completion Percentage	63.6	57.4
Yards Per Attempt	7.4	7.8
First-Team All-Pro	2	2
League MVP	2	1
Super Bowl MVP	3	2
League Championship Record	4–2	5–0*

*3 NFL championships plus Super Bowls I and II

To reach the Super Bowl, the Packers had to defeat the Dallas Cowboys in one of the toughest football games ever played, the Ice Bowl. Starr's brilliance in that game is the stuff of legend. Operating on an ice-covered field in game-time temperatures that opened at minus-13 degrees Fahrenheit and dipped to minus-18 by the fourth quarter, Starr led his team to a 14–0 lead before the Cowboys fought their way back into the game and held a 17–14 lead with just under five minutes remaining. With frostbitten fingers, Starr led the Packers on a 62-yard drive to the Dallas goal line, at which point Green Bay's offense stalled. Then on third-and-goal with 16 seconds remaining and no timeouts, Starr called his own number. Instead of rolling out and looking for a pass as everyone expected, Starr plunged forward into the end zone for the win.

The Packers were exhausted both physically and emotionally by the victory. The prospect of facing the powerhouse Raiders two weeks later certainly wasn't something they cherished. Still, when game day came around, the Packers prevailed. And although their triumph over Oakland was substantially defensive, Starr was a solid 13-for-24 for 202 yards and a touchdown before he was knocked out of the game with a thumb injury early in the fourth quarter. Starr's passer rating for the game was 96.2. His overall passer rating in his two Super Bowl appearances was a stellar 105.9.

Starr was named MVP of both those first two Super Bowls, cementing his place as the most successful postseason quarterback in league history.

Starr wasn't just a big-game quarterback, though. Through nearly the entire decade of the 1960s, and particularly in his championship seasons, he not only was the best QB in the NFL but in all of professional football. He brought to the position a combination of leadership, football intelligence, and athletic ability well beyond what anyone else would exhibit until more than a decade after he retired.

And even 45 years after he took his last snap—and in the middle of an age of football that will be remembered for putting spectacular passers on the field—Starr remains part of any serious conversation about the NFL's greatest QBs ever.

Does he still have a legitimate claim on the title? Probably not.

★ ★ ★

Starr's career statistics are undeniably impressive for a quarterback of his day. In an era in which the passing game, long regarded as a necessary evil, was truly only beginning the long process of becoming the focal point of football, Starr amassed 24,718 yards passing over his 196 career games. He was a 57.4 percent passer, threw for a still-incredible 7.8 yards per attempt, and finished his career with a passer rating of 80.5.

That those numbers don't stack up with modern-day quarterbacks is understandable. Starr played in a different league with a different set of rules. He didn't benefit from the efforts the NFL has made since the late 1970s to open up the passing game. Then again, neither did he face the kind of sophisticated defenses that have evolved in response to the emergence of the passing game. Starr was a unique talent who paired off during his career against Ds that weren't designed to stop a player like him. If he had fewer opportunities to shine as a passer, he also faced less resistance on those plays in which he put the ball in the air.

Starr also had his share of on-field failures. Though his Packers were dominant in all but one of their championship seasons, they were, in other years, a team that sputtered a bit in spite of their roster and their coach. The Packers finished second in the NFL's Western Conference in both 1963 and 1964. And while Starr's performance in '63 didn't cost his team the conference title, his 54 percent completion rate and 10 interceptions, for an interception percentage of 4.1, certainly didn't help. Oddly enough, while Starr fared far better in '64, the team fared worse, finishing with a record of 8–5–1 in spite of Starr's league-leading 59.9 percent completion rate, 2,144 passing yards, and 97.1 passer rating.

Starr's performance before Lombardi's arrival in Green Bay in 1959 and after the great coach stepped down following Super Bowl II are something else again.

In 1957 and 1958, during which he split time with Babe Parilli, Starr's record as a starter was 3–14–1 (.194). He completed just 195 of 372 passes (52.4 percent) during that time and threw 11 touchdowns and 22 interceptions. That adds up to a passer rating of just 57.5. Starr never posted a winning record as a starter in the post-Lombardi years. From 1968 through 1971, he went 14–19–1 (.426), threw 32 touchdowns and 30 interceptions, and completed 365 of 619 passes (59 percent) for 4,709 yards. That works out to a passer rating of 80.0 Not terrible for a quarterback in the waning years of his career but not on par with a late-career Montana or even a late-career Brett Favre. (Whether and to what extent Tom Brady's performance will dip over the final seasons of his career, of course, has yet to be seen. But it's worth noting that Brady as of 2015 was a year older than Starr was at retirement, and was playing at a considerably higher level than Starr reached in any of his last three seasons.)

None of that undoes the fact that when Starr was at his best, he was downright unstoppable. But it does leave one to wonder how much of Starr's success was Starr and how much was Lombardi.

One also has to wonder whether Starr's Packers would have been able to capture five championships if there hadn't been so few postseason opponents for them to overcome. Through the 1966 season, the NFL playoff system was this: the team with the best record in the East played the team with the best record in the West in the NFL Championship Game. The Packers thus took the 1961 and '62 championships by winning a total of two postseason games.

Green Bay needed to win two games to take the 1965 championship, because the Packers and the Baltimore Colts both finished 10–3–1 and, with no established tiebreaker system in place, a one-game divisional playoff was needed. The Packers played two postseason games again in 1966, the NFL Championship Game and Super Bowl I. With realignment in 1967, the NFL moved to a four-team postseason tournament, which meant the Packers needed to win three games—a divisional match, the league championship, and Super Bowl II.

That's nine wins to produce five championships. And because neutral-site games were only introduced with the advent of the Super Bowl, in three of their NFL title games (1961, 1965, and 1967) the Packers were at home.

Starr and the Packers won those championships—and they did it under the rules that existed at the time. No one can fault them for that. But no one can argue that it isn't significantly easier to win a single game, let alone a single home game, than it is to battle through a series of at least three postseason matches, the last of them a neutral-site championship game.

The championship teams that have come after the Packers had a more difficult road to travel. The championship dynasties that have emerged in the years since Super Bowl II have faced challenges that are simply far beyond anything Lombardi's teams ever encountered. The single dynasty that has emerged to date in the salary-cap era—in which maintaining the kind of roster the Packers enjoyed under Lombardi would be entirely impossible—has won under the most deliberately challenging conditions in league history.

Brady won't retire with a postseason winning percentage that comes anywhere close to Starr's .900. Neither did Montana (.696). Unless someone downright godlike comes along, no one ever will. But Brady's already won more than twice as many playoff games as Starr. Brady's also on track to finish his career with a better regular-season record, a significantly better passer rating, and better stats virtually across the board. And although his career isn't over yet and anything can happen, Brady's yet to have a season that anyone would describe as *bad*.

Bart Starr was a great NFL quarterback, one of the best ever. But his accomplishments were eclipsed by Montana's 25 years ago—and they've since been eclipsed by Brady's.

CHAPTER 33

★ ★ ★

On Fire and On Ice: 2015

The thing about "next man up" is that it has a tipping point. That point might not be the same for every team, but it's there. And if you're around any team for long enough, you're eventually going to find out just where it lies.

In a league like the NFL, the tipping point is a function of parity. Or at least of the desire to create parity.

Every NFL team has to grapple with the difficult realities of a hard salary cap. The ability to achieve meaningful roster depth is tied in part to the ability to set a firm value on every player and to be willing to walk away when any player's price exceeds his value. The New England Patriots, during the Bill Belichick years, have been as good at making those tough choices as any team in the league—and better than most. (Really, other than the Pittsburgh Steelers, it's hard to name a team that has been as good as the Patriots at cap management. The Baltimore Ravens think they are, but they've got a grotesquely overpaid quarterback putting the lie to that notion.)

So the Patriots routinely anger fans by being "too cheap" to hold on to a favorite like Wes Welker, or unwilling to empty their bank account to retain a talented mercenary like Darrelle Revis. They part ways with players like Logan Mankins and Lawyer Milloy when they won't take pay cuts. They pass on big-name free agents in favor of lesser-known players who bring better value. They stack their preseason roster with players who potentially can be coached up and earn a spot on the team—or who can be released without killing cap space if they don't fit. They position themselves better than most to withstand the vicious attrition of an NFL season.

Every NFL team also has to grapple with the realities of roster limits, the injuries that are part and parcel of a violent game, and strict rules regarding the management of injured players.

A team can carry 53 players on its active roster. On a given game day, a team can dress 46. That's it.

As for dealing with injuries, teams can designate players to start the season on the physically unable to perform list, but then they have to do without them for more than a third of the season. During a season, they can place just one player on injured reserve with a "designated to return" tag, but then they have to be willing to do without him for eight weeks. Beyond that, there are few options available when a normally productive player is unable to get on the field: A team can place him on injured reserve, ending his season; or they can carry him the active roster, leaving one fewer spot for player who is healthy and able to contribute. In either case, the injured player's salary counts against that hard cap.

And good cap management only goes so far. No matter how deep a team's roster, no matter how good an organization may be at developing the players on its practice squad, when they hit one of those seasons where the injuries start piling up early and never stop, its going to derail them eventually. It's just a matter of when.

For the 2015 Patriots, that "when" was in the AFC Championship at Denver. Just as it had been two years earlier. But while in 2013, the end came by way of an erosion of talent at skill positions that started in the off-season and continued through the regular season, in 2015, it was the product of a brutal slog from September to January that hit hard in the trenches and left New England unable to protect Tom Brady when it mattered most.

By the time the end came, the Patriots had placed 16 players on season-ending injured reserve. Two players spent the entire season on the PUP list. And another 24 missed one or more games due to injury. That's 42 players in all who were absent for some or all of the season.

The list of those lost to injured reserve included starting left tackle Nate Solder and starting right guard Ryan Wendell. Other members of the offensive line who missed games during the season included starting center Bryan Stork (who began the season on injured reserve with a designation to return), starting right tackle Sebastian Vollmer, and Marcus Cannon, who opened the season as the Patriots' starting left guard. Adding in the off-season retirement of Dan Connolly, that meant that not one member of the Patriots starting offensive line from Super Bowl XLIX

2015

By the Numbers

Total Yards	4,770
Yards Per Game	298.1
Attempts	624
Completions	402
Completion Percentage	64.4
Yards Per Attempt	7.6
Touchdowns	36
Interceptions	7
Passer Rating	102.2
Games Rated Higher Than 100 *(Includes One Postseason)*	9
Best Single-Game Rating	143.8

played a full season in 2015. As for those next men up, O-linemen Tre' Jackson, Josh Kline, Shaq Mason, and LaAdrian Waddle all missed time with injuries during the season. The result: the Patriots employed 37 different offensive line combinations over the season. The unit never had anything close to an opportunity to jell.

Injuries (and an illness) hit the defense as well. Jerod Mayo finished a third straight campaign on IR. Dont'a Hightower missed four games with rib and knee injuries. Jamie Collins missed three games due to an illness. Dominique Easley was lost to IR late in the season. Chandler Jones missed time with an abdomen injury. Devin McCourty missed a pair of games with an ankle injury. Patrick Chung, Jabaal Sheard, Sealver Siliga, Jonathan Freeny, and Tavon Wilson all missed time. Dane Fletcher spent the entire season on the PUP list.

As always, though, most visible were the injuries that affected the availability and performance of offensive skill players.

Julian Edelman missed the final seven games of the regular season with a broken bone in his foot. Though it was worth it to get Edelman back for the playoffs, weathering the Edelman injury meant holding his roster spot, not an easy task for a team banged up as badly as the Patriots. Rob Gronkowski missed just a single game after sustaining a bone bruise in his right knee in week 12, but was hampered by the injury down the stretch. Aaron Dobson found his way to IR (as usual) with a high ankle sprain suffered in week 11. Brandon LaFell started the season on the PUP list while recovering from foot surgery, and never looked right even after he returned to the field. Danny Amendola missed a pair of games with a knee injury. Brian Tyms missed the entire season with a foot injury (not that much of anyone noticed). Free agent–pickup Brandon Gibson also missed the entire campaign due to a preseason knee injury. Dion Lewis, whose first season with the Patriots got off to an explosive start with 49 rushes for 234 yards (4.8 per carry), 36 receptions for 388 yards, and four total touchdowns over the first seven games of the season, landed on IR after tearing an ACL. LeGarrette Blount joined Lewis on IR after suffering a hip injury in week 14. Fullback James Develin missed the entire season with a broken tibia suffered in the preseason. And tight ends Scott Chandler and Michael Williams both missed time due to injury.

In short, 2015 was a mess for the New England Patriots.

★ ★ ★

What's astonishing and unfortunate is that for Tom Brady, 2015 was a very productive season. Indeed, until the pile of bodies around him grew too high to see over let alone throw over, Brady appeared to be headed for one of the most productive seasons of his career.

It's unclear whether the quarterback was extracting some form of revenge for an off-season consumed by Deflategate, was determined to continue making the point about his not-diminishing skills that he had pounded home in the previous season, was driven to seize an opportunity to win back-to-back championships (again), or simply was being Tom Brady. Perhaps it was that he'd settled in to his relationships with all of his top receivers. Or perhaps it was a combination of all those factors.

Whatever it was, Brady came roaring out of the gate. He opened the season with a four-touchdown outing against the visiting Pittsburgh Steelers, connecting with Gronk on three of his scoring passes, and leading the Patriots to a 28–21 victory. Brady earned what would hold as his best single-game passer rating of the season, 143.8. Brady also earned his 161st regular season win, breaking the record previously held by Brett Favre for wins with a single NFL team.

By the time the first four games of the season were behind him, Brady had completed 116 of 160 attempts, racking up 1,387 yards and throwing 11 touchdowns without a single interception. His passer rating for the season at that point was 121.5.

Along the way, during a week three home game against the Jacksonville Jaguars, Brady became the fourth quarterback in NFL history to throw 400 career touchdown passes with a bullet to Amendola in the back of the end zone on second-and-goal from the 1-yard line.

And even when Brady's first pick of the season ended up going for six points the other way, it didn't feel like anything to get worked up about. Early in the second quarter of a road game at Indianapolis, with the Patriots facing second-and-10 at their own 10-yard line, Brady looked for Edelman on the right sideline. Edelman, who was playing with a badly dislocated right pinky finger, bobbled and tipped the ball into the hands of safety Mike Adams, who had a short, clear path to the end zone. Brady still ended up with 312 passing yards, three touchdowns, and a passer rating of 104.8. And the Patriots still ended up with a 34–27 victory.

The injury rate had become noticeable by the time the Patriots got to the midpoint in the season. Solder and Wendell were gone. Cannon was out. Kline was nursing a shoulder. Lewis had missed a game with an abdomen injury, but had returned to the lineup.

Then, in their eighth game of the season, the Patriots lost Lewis for good. But Brady and the offense kept going. Brady came out of the Washington game with 299 passing yards and a pair of touchdowns. And the Patriots came away with a decisive 27–10 win.

The Patriots were 8–0. Brady was 225 of 328 (68.6 percent) for 2,709 yards (8.3 yards per attempt), 22 touchdowns, and two interceptions, for a passer rating of 113.4.

In their ninth game, a hard-fought 27–26 win over the Giants in New Jersey, the Patriots lost Edelman for the balance of the regular season. Edelman exited at the end of the first quarter en route to having hardware installed in his broken foot. To that point in the season, he'd caught 61 passes for 692 yards and seven touchdowns.

For the Books ★ 2015

League Records

Most Conference Championship Appearances	10
Most Division Titles by a Quarterback	13
Most Career Postseason Wins by a Quarterback	22
Most Career Postseason Appearances	31
Most Career Postseason Touchdown Passes	56
Most Career Postseason Passing Yards	7,957
Most Career Postseason Pass Attempts	1,183
Most Career Postseason Completions	738
Most 300-plus-yard Passing Games, Postseason	10
Most Wins With a Single Team	172

Team Records

Most Career Touchdown Passes	428
Most 3,000-Yard Seasons	13

Honors and Career Milestones

Pro Bowl, 11th Career Selection

Even still, the Pats got to 10–0 with a win over Buffalo. Then they traveled to Denver for a Sunday night meeting with the 8–2 Broncos.

At Mile High, the Pats opened strong with Brady and Gronkowski connecting for a 23-yard score on their first possession. The offense took advantage of Jones' interception of Brock Osweiler early in the second quarter to go ahead 14–0 with a nine-yard touchdown pass from Brady to Chandler.

New England gave up a touchdown toward the end of the first half that brought the Broncos to within seven. And the teams went scoreless through the third quarter. But on the opening play of the fourth, the Patriots opened up another 14-point lead in yet another historic moment for Brady.

With the Patriots facing third-and-eight at their own 37-yard line, Brady took the snap out of the shotgun formation, went through his reads, then unloaded just ahead of pass rusher coming up hard from behind. He connected with running back Brandon Bolden along the right sideline at the Denver 42. And Bolden proceeded to break tackles and power into the end zone.

The strike was Brady's 420th career passing touchdown, tying him with Dan Marino for third most all time. Better still, it felt like the score that would put the game away.

The Pats were still ahead, by a score of 21–17, and driving late in the fourth quarter, at the moment when Patriots fans, and Brady, saw the season flash before their eyes.

On first down from the Patriots 40-yard line, Brady threw to Gronkowski at the Denver 38. As Gronk went up for the pass, safety Darian Stewart crashed full force into his right knee. The pass fell incomplete. And Gronkowski fell to the turf, flailing about in what was clearly horrific pain. Gronkowski was carted off the field, and the Patriots went on to lose 30–24 in overtime.

The injury would turn out to be less severe than it looked at the time. Gronk hadn't planted his foot at the time of the hit, and as a result suffered a strain and a bone bruise rather than a ligament tear. He was back on the field two weeks later. But the hit had done its damage just the same. By taking Brady's most potent weapon off the field (Gronkowski had caught six passes for 88 yards and a TD in the game), Denver positioned itself for the win. And that win, in the end, would play a critical role in determining both teams' fates in the postseason.

★ ★ ★

In a home game against the Eagles the following week, Brady broke his career TD tie with Marino to move all alone (for the moment, at least) into third place all time. The score came simply enough with running back James White running a slant out of the backfield on second-and-goal from the Philadelphia 4-yard line. It was the first of three touchdowns Brady would throw that day.

The Philly game also included a Brady highlight that was unusual to say the least, his second career reception (also his longest, and his first since 2001). It came with three minutes remaining in the third quarter and New England trailing 28–14. Facing third-and-three at their own 25-yard line, the Patriots caught the Eagles off guard by snapping the ball to White while Brady moved along the right side of the offensive line, seemingly in the act of directing traffic. Brady stood still for a moment as the Eagles defense broke in pursuit of White, who was running left, parallel to the line of scrimmage. Then Brady broke downfield and White flipped the ball to Amendola, who darted to the right hashmarks and tossed to Brady at the 30. With no defenders immediately in front of him, Brady was able to trot down the sideline until he was finally chased out of bounds at the Philadelphia 39.

The play was wasted, however, as Brady threw his second interception of the day on the following snap. And the Patriots, had dropped from 10–0 to 10–2 in a matter of eight days.

Over the two weeks that followed, Brady and the Patriots took the opportunity presented by a pair of games against struggling AFC South teams, Houston and Tennessee, and appeared to get their legs back under them. Brady threw a pair of touchdown passes in each game and posted passer ratings of 116.8 and 107.7, his first 100-plus outings since week eight.

But the Patriots finished the season on a sour note, squandering two consecutive opportunities to sew up the AFC one seed, and home-field advantage through the playoffs, with road losses to the Jets and Dolphins.

New England had gone 2–4 over their final six games. With Edelman out of the lineup, Gronkowski limited by his knee and a sore back, and Blount on IR, the lack of production down the stretch was understandable. And at the very least, the Pats were due to get Edelman back for the playoffs.

But what was truly concerning was that Brady had been chased all over the backfield over the final weeks of the season. The offensive line appeared to be disintegrating, and the Patriots' chances at postseason success were crumbling with it.

★ ★ ★

Fans in New England got some hope when the Kansas City Chiefs reported to Foxborough for a divisional round game on the other side of the Patriots' first round bye. Brady got good protection for the first time in forever, didn't take a sack, and threw for 302 yards and a pair of touchdowns (both to Gronk) in a 27–20 win. He added another touchdown by way of one of his patented sneaks late in the second half, just one play after he was denied the end zone by a matter of inches on a scramble from the Kansas City 11-yard line. Edelman caught 10 passes for 100 yards, and Gronk another seven for 83.

There was a chance the Patriots were coming back together just in time to make it count.

With the win, the Patriots became just the second team to advance to five straight AFC Championships (after the 1973–77 Oakland Raiders). Brady had extended his record for postseason wins to 22. And he'd put up his ninth career postseason game with 300 or more yards passing, tying Peyton Manning's NFL record.

Brady broke that record a week later in the AFC Championship game at Denver, throwing for 310 yards (to Manning's 176).

But while Brady was breaking that record, the Patriots offensive line was breaking down. Brady was sacked four times by Denver's powerful pass rush, and hit a total of 23 times during the game. He put in a valiant effort just the same. But too much went wrong, including a failed attempt at a two-point conversion that could have tied the score with 12 seconds remaining.

Had the Patriots won at Denver in week 12, the championship would have been played in Foxborough and may well have turned out differently. (It's hard, at the very least to imagine that the usually spot-on Stephen Gostkowski would have missed an extra point at home, which is what made the two-point try at the end of the game necessary.) They also would have hosted had they been able to beat the foundering Eagles in week 13, or to hold off the 5–10 Dolphins in week 17.

And given the success the Broncos had in Super Bowl 50, in spite of a quarterback who achieved nothing in that game, it's tempting to think that the Patriots could have repeated as champions in spite of their injuries had they been able to overcome Denver.

But those things didn't happen. What did happen was that the Patriots posted double digit wins for the 13th straight season, and finished with at least 12 wins for the sixth straight. Brady led the league in passing touchdowns, 36, and interception percentage, 1.1. He finished third in passing yardage, 4,770, and fourth in passer rating, 102.2. He set a new record for postseason games played with his 31st (moving past Adam Vinatieri's 30). And he extended his records for postseason touchdowns, passing yards, attempts, and completions.

Brady did all of that at age 38, and he did it with teammates falling all around him. It's not the same as winning the Super Bowl. But it's absolutely something to admire.

CHAPTER 34

★ ★ ★

Tom Brady vs. Joe Montana

There are pro football fans who will never accept Tom Brady (or whoever the next contender to the title may be, or the one after that) as the greatest NFL quarterback of all time for one simple reason: he isn't Joe Montana.

Just as there were fans during Montana's playing career, and a handful of holdouts still, who wouldn't accept Montana as the greatest ever purely because he wasn't Bart Starr.

Prior to Super Bowl XLIX, the Montana loyalists always led their argument with this: Montana won four Super Bowls and was the MVP of three. That first feat had been accomplished by only one other quarterback in NFL history. And outside of western Pennsylvania, it would have been hard to find someone willing to argue a case for Terry Bradshaw. (Hell, even in western Pennsylvania, loyalties are divided between Bradshaw and local products Montana and Dan Marino.) The second, three Super Bowl MVPs, for 25 years was Montana's distinction alone.

It was a great argument while it lasted. In pro sports, championships count for more than anything else. So until someone else collected four rings and three MVPs, there was an undeniable standard by which Montana defeated all comers. Anything less came with a built-in "Yeah, but…"

Then Tom Brady held the Lombardi trophy for the fourth time and was named MVP for the third. And the Montana crowd's argument changed.

The reasonable ones (mostly reasonable)—which is to say, the ones who don't go into their defense against Brady with, "But, but, but Spygate" or "But, but, but Deflategate"—now lean on two key points: Montana never lost a Super Bowl, they proclaim; and Montana threw 11 Super Bowl touchdowns and zero interceptions.

That Montana never lost a Super Bowl is a solid place to start a case for continuing to view him as the greatest of all time. It is, after all, a fact…and a damned impressive one at that. Because it's not as if Montana advanced to the Super Bowl once or twice and came away with a spotless record. (Not that even that accomplishment would be anything to scoff at.) He was 4-for-4. Over the course of 46 seasons in the Super Bowl era, only six quarterbacks—Montana, Bradshaw, Tom Brady, John Elway, Roger Staubach, and Jim Kelly—have even appeared in the championship game four or more times. Only two of them are undefeated. And of those two, Montana and Bradshaw, only one also has Montana's overall career record.

That record, by the way, is one of the best in football history. Over his 15 seasons in the NFL—13 in San Francisco, two in Kansas City—Montana compiled a winning record of 117–47 (.713) in the regular season and 16–7 (.696) in the postseason. He threw 273 career touchdowns in the regular season. He also threw 45 touchdowns in the postseason, a record that held for 20 years before Brady broke it.

Montana's career passer rating, 92.3, was the best in league history when he stepped away from the game. (He's since fallen to 11th on the all-time list behind a group of players that includes Brady.) Montana continues to hold the best career passer rating in Super Bowl history (among players with 40 or more pass attempts), 127.8. It's unlikely any active player will top that mark. And the odds against any quarterback ever compiling a better passer rating over four Super Bowls are astronomical. That, of course, goes back to those 11 TDs and 0 picks.

Montana, who completed five touchdown passes in his final championship game, Super Bowl XXIV, held the record for career Super Bowl touchdowns, 11, until Brady broke it in Super Bowl XLIX, his sixth appearance.

★ ★ ★ ★ ★ ★ ★

Tom's had a great career, and the thing with him is, he's still got enough age on him that he can probably get back here another time or two. So it'll be fun to watch him. You've got guys who've done not anywhere near what he's accomplished and made it to the Hall of Fame. So obviously he's well past that.

—Joe Montana

Montana also held the record for most career Super Bowl completions, 83, from 1990 until Super Bowl XLII in 2008, which Brady finished with 100. (Brady has since pushed the mark to 164.) His 13 consecutive completions in Super Bowl XXIV was a league record for 22 years until Brady topped it with 16 straight in Super Bowl XLVI.

Montana also is credited with 31 career fourth-quarter comebacks. He isn't the all-time leader in that category. Brady, Dan Marino, John Elway, and Peyton Manning all have at least a few more comebacks to their credit. But he's one of just two QBs to have led his team from behind that frequently en route to four championships. The comebacks total is also the stat that points most directly to who Montana was as a player and what his leadership meant to his teams.

★ ★ ★

Montana gained fame in his first full season as a starter (his third year in the league) as a cool-headed field general who always found a way to inspire his offense to triumph under the most difficult of circumstances. In his first trip to the NFC Championship Game, following the 1981 season, Montana led a game-winning 79-yard touchdown drive in the final five minutes of play. The drive was capped by Montana's off-balance throw to Dwight Clark in the back of the Dallas Cowboys end zone on third-and-three from the Cowboys' 6-yard line. The play, known ever after simply as "the Catch," is one of the most memorable in league history.

Montana's defining moment came seven years later in Super Bowl XXIII, when he led his team on a 92-yard game-winning touchdown drive in the final 3:20. The drive began with Montana calming his teammates' nerves in the huddle by remarking that he'd spotted comedian John Candy in the stands and ended with a 10-yard pass from Montana to John Taylor that put the 49ers on top of the Cincinnati Bengals 20-16 with just 34 seconds remaining.

Montana was consistently spectacular to watch throughout his career. His fundamentals were virtually flawless. His knowledge of 49ers coach Bill Walsh's playbook was encyclopedic. And his ability to read defenses and exploit the weakness of any formation was astounding.

It's not surprising that Brady, whose family held 49ers season tickets, became a huge Montana fan at a young age. During the 1980s every football fan in Northern California, not to mention millions from across the country, were in awe of the great 49ers quarterback.

Montana earned his way to the starting job in San Francisco after being chosen in the third round of the 1979 NFL Draft. He earned every championship, every record, and every accolade. And he absolutely earned the enduring adoration of his fan base.

What Montana didn't earn, though his supporters can and surely will continue to assert otherwise, is the unquestioned title Greatest of All Time. In fact, though Montana's supporters (and Brady haters alike) don't accept it, and though they continue to be able to make arguments based on Super Bowl records and Super Bowl MVPs, in reality it's a title that Montana has lost.

★ ★ ★

Brady had a bead on the greatest-ever crown from the moment the Patriots beat the Philadelphia Eagles in Super Bowl XXXIX. Brady was 27 years old at the time and had just completed his fourth season as a starter. He was a three-time league champion and a two-time Super Bowl MVP.

Montana, by contrast, was 28 when he won his second Super Bowl. When he won his third, Montana was 32 and had been the 49ers' starting quarterback for eight and a half seasons.

One could argue in February 2005 that Brady hadn't been in the league long enough to have truly proven anything. One could argue then that he was still a title away not only from challenging Montana but even from truly standing on par with Bradshaw. Those arguments had fallen even before Brady pulled even with Montana in championships and Super Bowl MVP honors.

Montana won the Super Bowl four times in his 12 seasons as his teams' principal starter. That accomplishment will never cease to be astonishing. It will also always be true that it took Montana three fewer seasons than Brady to achieve four Super Bowl wins (10 seasons vs. 13). But it's just as true that Brady reached six Super Bowls in those 13 seasons. And while it's fine to assert that Montana never lost in a title game, the fact is we have no idea of how Montana might have fared in a fifth Super Bowl. Because he never reached one.

Not that he didn't have his chances. While Montana's winning percentage in the Super Bowl may be better than Brady's, the same can't be said of the postseason overall, or of conference championships. Montana reached seven conference championship games in his career, finishing 4–3. He came up on the losing side of the NFC championship twice in his time with the 49ers—in 1983 and 1990. He lost an AFC Championship Game with the Kansas City Chiefs in 1993, the penultimate season of his career.

In the 1983 NFC title game against Washington, the visiting 49ers lost 24–21 in spite of a strong performance by Montana. Though the game ended with Montana throwing an interception, that pick came only on a desperation pass thrown after Washington took a lead with 40 seconds remaining. Through the rest of the contest, Montana went 27-for-48 for 347 yards and three touchdowns.

In the 1990 NFC championship, the 49ers lost a defensive struggle to the visiting New York Giants. It bears noting that the Niners were ahead 12–9 when Montana was knocked out of the game with a concussion, an elbow injury, and a broken finger in the fourth quarter. It's also only fair to point out that the game was effectively lost by way of a Roger Craig fumble that set up the Giants to win the game with a field goal as the final seconds ticked off the clock. Montana's numbers in that game were entirely respectable: 18-for-26 for 190 yards and a touchdown. (The loss marked the de facto end of Montana's career in San Francisco, as he would miss the entire 1991 season and would see action in only one game in 1992.)

In his AFC championship start with Kansas City, Montana was able to complete just nine of 23 passes for 125 yards, with no touchdowns and an interception, before he was knocked out of the game with a concussion in the

You Can't Argue with Figures

	Tom Brady	Joe Montana
Regular-Season Record	172–51	117–47
Winning Percentage	.780	.713
Postseason Record	22–9	16–7
Winning Percentage	.710	.696
Overall Record	194–60	133–54
Winning Percentage	.764	.711
Passer Rating	96.4	92.3
Touchdown Percentage	5.5	5.1
Interception Percentage	1.9	2.6
TD/INT	2.9/1	2.0/1
Completion Percentage	63.6	63.2
Yards Per Attempt	7.4	7.5
First-Team All-Pro	2	4
NFL MVP	2	2
Super Bowl MVP	3	3
Super Bowl Record	4–2	4–0

third quarter. By that time, the Chiefs were behind 20–6 in a game they would ultimately lose 30–13 to Jim Kelly's Buffalo Bills.

Circumstances notwithstanding, that lands Montana at 4–3 (.571) as a starter in conference championships, which isn't quite Brady's 6–4 (.600). That Brady has reached three more conference championship games than Montana reflects his better overall postseason record. Brady is 22–9 (.710) in his playoffs career; Montana finished 16–7 (.696). In neither case is the distinction huge, but when viewed as part of the body of Brady's work, those numbers help paint a compelling picture.

★ ★ ★

In addition to getting to more Super Bowls than his boyhood idol, and winning as many, Brady has eclipsed others of Montana's career marks in both the regular season and the postseason.

Brady achieved his 100th overall career victory in 126 games, breaking Montana's record by 16. It took Brady only 131 games to get his 100th regular-season win; that's eight fewer than Montana, who had been the record holder at 139.

Brady's regular-season stats are almost universally better than Montana's. Brady's winning percentage, .771, is the best in league history. Brady's career passer rating, touchdown percentage, interception percentage, and touchdown-to-interception ratio all are better than Montana's. And while some of those measures could conceivably even out before Brady's career ends, Brady also has time to build on the regular and postseason stats in which he has Montana beat.

Brady sits ahead of Montana on the vast majority of regular season, postseason and Super Bowl leaderboards. In addition to overtaking Montana's records for postseason and Super Bowl touchdown passes, Brady has far outpaced Montana in passing yards and completions in the postseason and the Super Bowl alike. Brady's regular season completion, passing yards, and passing touchdown totals dwarf Montana's. While it's not yet a safe bet, it's entirely within the realm of possibility that Brady will end his career with 100 more combined regular season and postseason wins than Montana.

Montana finished five seasons with a passer rating of 90 or better and three with a passer rating of more than 100. Brady has passer ratings of 90 or more in nine seasons and 100 or better in four. Brady's high and low single-season passer ratings, 117.2 and 85.7, are better than Montana's high and low ratings, 112.4 and 80.7.

In 14 seasons as a starter, Brady has led the Patriots to a perfect 16–0 record once, 14–2 records three times, and a 13–3 record once. Brady has led the Patriots to double-digit win totals in 13 of his 14 seasons as their starting QB. Montana reached 14 wins only twice in his career. He won 13 or more games only three times. And his teams achieved double digit wins in just six of his 12 seasons as principal starter. Even if Brady never posts another 10-win season, he'll finish his career with many more dominant campaigns to his credit than Montana.

Montana won nine NFC West titles with the 49ers and one AFC West title with the Chiefs. Brady's Patriots have won the AFC East title 13 times. And it's also true that the Patriots have finished with the best record in their division in every season of Brady's career, missing out on the title in 2002 by virtue of a three-way tiebreaker. The 49ers, by contrast, finished the strike-shortened 1982 season a wretched 3–6 and qualified for the 1985 playoffs as a wild-card team after finishing 10–6.

Brady and Montana both are two-time league MVPs, but Brady is the only player ever to be accorded that honor by unanimous consent of the 50-member voting committee.

★ ★ ★

And then there's the matter of context. While critics have been quick to charge over the years that Brady has been carried by the Patriots defense, Montana typically has been spared the same criticism. This, despite the fact that during Montana's career, the 49ers consistently fielded one of the best *D*s in the NFL.

The 49ers defense during Montana's 10 seasons as San Francisco's starter allowed an average of just 16.6 points per game. The highest point total they surrendered in any season was 294. The lowest (excluding the nine-game 1982 season) was 227.

Patriots defenses over Brady's 14 seasons behind center have allowed an average of 18.8 points per game. Their fewest points allowed in a given season has been 237, their greatest 346. If one were to consider it even remotely true that Brady has succeeded thanks to great defense, then what does that say about Montana?

Brady obviously has been the beneficiary of great coaching. He's played his career under arguably the best coach in league history in Bill Belichick. But Belichick is greater than Montana's principal head coach, Bill Walsh, only by a matter of a scant few degrees. And while Belichick has brought new dimensions to the game and has consistently outthought the rest of the NFL's head coaches, he is not credited, as is Walsh, with the introduction of a radical new offensive system that changed the way the game is played.

Though the West Coast Offense is a common system in the NFL today, when Walsh unveiled it with the 49ers, it was unlike anything the league had ever seen. To defensive players and coaches who where accustomed to stopping offensive schemes that turned on power running and downfield passing, the West Coast's emphasis on short, horizontal passes was a shock to the system. It required a rethinking not only of defensive schemes and play calling, but of defensive personnel groupings and personnel types. Montana and the 49ers had a pair of Super Bowl championships to their credit before the league truly began to catch up. The coaching advantage Brady has enjoyed simply doesn't compare with that.

It's also important to consider that there's a good reason the Niners were able to field strong offenses and strong defenses for season upon season. The San Francisco teams Montana played for were stacked with talent and had consistent rosters year in and year out, because they didn't have to contend with a salary cap or free agency. With the exception of his final year in Kansas City, Montana played his entire career in the pre–salary cap era. Nor was there any real free agency in the NFL until 1993, well after Montana's last season as San Francisco's starter.

Montana played in a league in which good teams stayed good and bad teams stayed bad. He didn't have to contend with continually having to get in sync with different teammates as Brady has done. He didn't have his top targets depart in-season as a result of salary disputes.

Montana's accomplishments aren't diminished by that. Like every quarterback before and after him, Montana played the game that was there for him. But it doesn't make sense to ignore the fact that Brady has achieved greater success under circumstances that were designed specifically to make winning on a consistent basis more difficult.

The point of having a salary cap and free agency is to create competitive balance. The point of competitive balance is to open up the potential for every team in the league to succeed. That means eliminating dynasties like the 49ers of the 1980s.

And still, the Patriots behind Brady have achieved more in both the regular season and the postseason than Montana's 49ers. Unless, that is, you want to hang your hat on the facts that Montana and the Niners never lost a Super Bowl and Montana never threw an interception in the Super Bowl.

Those are both nice distinctions, but if you believe they make Montana a greater quarterback than Brady, you're running not on fact, but on emotion. That's OK. Emotion is part of what being a fan is about. But it doesn't change reality.

And the reality is that the greatest quarterback in NFL history is not Peyton Manning, not Bart Starr, not John Elway nor Dan Marino. It's not Sammy Baugh or Otto Graham. And no, it's no longer Joe Montana.

When you sit down and honestly and fairly review and compare the careers of the best who ever played, you can only reach one conclusion: The greatest quarterback in the history of the NFL is Tom Brady. Pure and simple.

APPENDIX

★ ★ ★

NFL Passer Rating

If you don't much care about NFL history and you don't much care about statistics, here's what you need to know about passer rating.

- It's determined using a complicated mathematical formula based on completion percentage (the number of passes completed divided by the number of passes attempted), total yardage, touchdowns, and interceptions. A quarterback who completes a lot of his passes, racks up a bunch of yards, throws touchdowns, and doesn't throw picks, is going to wind up with a pretty high number.

- It's meant to compare passers, not quarterbacks. It doesn't take into consideration rushing attempts, rushing yards, or any of a whole long list of intangibles (including intelligence, leadership, focus, or ability to perform under pressure) that make a QB good. (Nor does it offer bonus points for endorsement contracts, charisma, or winning smiles.)

- The highest rating is 158.3; that's considered perfect. The lowest is 0. Why the weird high number? Because the whole thing is set up so that a guy who has an excellent game comes in at around 100. (The same goes for great seasons. For a number of reasons, great careers always come out lower.) But to get to a round number for excellent, the formula for calculating passer rating got twisted in such a way that it produced a bizarre number for perfect. These are the sacrifices we make.

- Rule of thumb: If a guy has a bunch of games in which his passer rating is up higher than 100, it's a good indication that he's having a standout season. If he comes out of a game with a rating higher than 120, he's had a hell of a day. If he gets to 140 or above, he kicked butt. At 150 or better, he's had a game for the ages.

★ ★ ★

Want to understand a little more but don't want to sit around solving math problems? Here you go.

In 1971, after decades during which the NFL tried to determine who was the top passer in the league by looking at an ever-changing assortment of statistics—for a while they based the whole thing on total yards; then they went with completion percentage; then they started looking at touchdowns, interceptions and average yards per attempt, assigning points to each as if they were playing fantasy football—the powers that be decided it was time to create a consistent method for comparison.

At the direction of commissioner Pete Rozelle, the league asked Don Smith, who worked as director of public relations at the Pro Football Hall of Fame but was known as a statistics expert, to come up with a formula. Smith worked with Rozelle's trusted advisor Don Weiss and Seymour Siwoff of Elias Sports Bureau, the league's official stats keepers, to come up with a formula that would allow the league to compare passers based on a consistent set of criteria.

Smith took the four passing statistics the league was recording at the time—completion percentage, passing yardage, touchdowns, and interceptions—and came up with a formula that would facilitate easy comparison.

Since the point at the time was to look at seasons rather than single games, stretches of seasons, or even careers, Smith based his math on season averages and season records.

So in a league in which the average completion rate for a season was roughly 50 percent, Smith set his threshold for acceptable at exactly that. And since no one at the time had completed much more than 70 percent of his passes in any season, he set 70 percent as the mark of greatness. Smith's formula scaled performances between those two points and allowed for players to achieve higher scores for truly exceptional efforts and lower scores for everything from a bad day to a complete fiasco.

Smith took a similar approach to the other stats, though in the interest of evening things out between players in pass-oriented and run-oriented systems, he based his computations on yards per attempt, touchdown percentage (number of touchdowns divided by total number of pass attempts), and interception percentage (number of picks divided by the total number of attempts).

It's at this point that things start to get woogy.

Because Smith's primary purpose was to produce a set of numbers that would indicate at a glance whether a passer's season had been average, above average, or excellent, he worked his formula to produce straightforward numbers in that common area of the performance spectrum. If that meant the measurement of perfection came out uneven, it didn't matter. Because over a full season, it's possible for a passer to achieve excellence but impossible to achieve perfection.

Smith wanted to get to a point where a nice, round number (100) would tell you that a quarterback had a standout season. So he set that standard and worked backward from there.

What Smith came up with was a formula that establishes values for each of the four statistical categories, combines them, then twists itself in knots to get to the bit where 100 equals excellent.

- **Completion Percentage:** 50 percent is worth one point; 70 percent is worth two points; everything in between is calculated proportionally, and anything better than 70 percent earns additional fractions of a point up to .375—for a maximum total value of 2.375 (awarded for a completion percentage of 77.5 or above.)
- **Yards Per Attempt:** 7 (the average in 1970) is worth 1 point; 11 is worth two. Fractions up to .375 are awarded for anything up to 12.5.
- **Touchdown percentage:** 5 is worth a point. 10 is worth 2. Fractions of points up to .375 are awarded for everything up to 11.9.
- **Interception percentage:** 5.5 is worth a point. 1.5 is worth two. Fractions of points up to .375 are awarded for everything down to 0.

So a quarterback who achieves a perfect passer rating, 158.3 (we'll get to that in a second), has achieved a completion percentage of at least 77.5, thrown for at least 12.5 yards per pass, thrown a touchdown on at least 11.9 percent of his passes (which is to say one touchdown for every 8.4 times he throws the ball), and thrown no interceptions. That's a tough row to hoe, as well it should be.

To make those point values fit into the whole 100=excellent model, Smith set up his formula so that you calculate the individual points, divide by six and multiply by 100. (That's where most of the wooginess comes in.)

So you get to this: 2.375 x 4 = 9.5; 9.5/6 = 1.583; 1.583 x 100 = 158.3.

You also get a system that almost nobody understands and that everybody always complains about. But it's still true that a guy who breaks 100 has had an excellent season or an excellent game.

And at least now you know what the point of the whole thing is.

★ ★ ★

One last bit of business, for those who want to see how it works. Or in case you're the type who loves applying ridiculous formulas to sports statistics. Or maybe you're just bored and you don't have the internet and its many handy passer rating calculators at your disposal, but you do have a bucketful of No. 2 pencils and a pile of spiral-bound notebooks.

Here's the formula for calculating passer rating.

C (completion percentage): (Completions/Attempts − .3) x 5

Y (yards per attempt): (Yards/Pass Attempts − 3) x .25

T (touchdown percentage): (Touchdowns/Pass Attempts) x 20

I (interception percentage): 2.375 - (Interceptions/Pass Attempts x 25)

Adjust values below 0 to 0, and values above 2.375 to 2.375, and calculate:

(C+Y+T+I)/6 x 100 = Passer Rating.

So if on opening day of the 2011 season, Tom Brady completed 32 of 48 passes for 517 yards and four touchdowns while throwing one interception.

C: 32/48 = .6666 −.3 = .3666 x 5 = 1.833

Y: 517/48 = 10.77 − 3 = 7.77 x .25 = 1.942

T: 4/38 = 0.0833 x 20 = 1.667

I: 2.375 − (1/48 = 0.020 x 25 = 0.52) = 1.855

And

1.833 + 1.942 + 1.667 + 1.855 = 7.297/6 =

.1216 x 100 = 121.6

Brady's passing rating for the game: 121.6.

Fun, right?

★ ★ ★
Sources

Attner, Paul. "The Wonder of It All: It's No Longer So Hard to Figure Out How Tom Brady Keeps Winning." *The Sporting News*, October 11, 2004: 12.

Associated Press. "Salary Fight Ends with Shocking Cut." *The Register Guard,* September 3, 2003: B5.

———. "The Patriots Complete Their Perfect Regular Season, Beat Giants." http://www.nfl.com/news/story?id=09000d5d8058c525&template= without-video&confirm=true (accessed July 23, 2011).

———. "Brady, Patriots Keep Rolling, Advance to AFC Championship." http://scores.espn.go.com/nfl/recap?gameId=280112017 (accessed July 23, 2011).

———. "Chargers Stun Colts, Will Face Patriots in AFC Title Game." http://scores.espn.go.com/nfl/recap?gameId=280113011 (accessed July 23, 2011).

———. "Pats Put Away Chargers for Fourth Super Bowl in Seven Years." http://scores.espn.go.com/nfl/recap?gameId=280120017 (accessed July 23, 2011).

———. "Pats' Brady Says Recovery on Track." http://sportsillustrated.cnn.com/2009/football/nfl/02/18/brady.fine/index.html (accessed March 3, 2011).

———. "Welker Eases Injury Concerns, Lifts Pats Over Bengals With Two Touchdowns." http://www.nfl.com/news/story/09000d5d81a7735f/printable/welker-eases-injury-concerns-lifts-pats-over-bengals-with-two-tds (accessed September 15, 2011).

———. "Brady Continues Hot Start in Patriots' Victory Over Mistake-Prone Chargers." http://www.nfl.com/gamecenter/2011091811/2011/REG2/ chargers@patriots#menu=highlights&tab=recap&recap=fullstory (accessed September 19, 2011).

———. "Patriots Overcome 21-Point Deficit vs. Bills to Clinch Top Seed in AFC." http://www.nfl.com/gamecenter/2012010101/2011/REG17/ bills@patriots#menu=highlights&tab=recap&recap=fullstory (accessed January 2, 2012).

———. "Brady Ties Playoff Record With Six TD Passes as Patriots Silence Broncos." http://www.nfl.com/gamecenter/2012011400/2011/POST19/ broncos@patriots#menu=highlights &tab=recap&recap=fullstory (accessed January 15, 2012).

Banks, Don. "Litmus Test." http://sportsillustrated.cnn.com/2007/writers/ don_banks/10/12/dallas/index.html (accessed October 17, 2011).

Battista, Judy. "Vikings Gamble on Moss, Helping Patriots." *The New York Times*, October 7, 2010: B15.

Benbow, Julian. "More Questions Than Answers for Redskins." http://www.boston.com/sports/football/patriots/articles/2007/10/29/more_questions_than_answers_for_redskins/ (accessed July 23, 2011).

Breer, Albert R. "Brady Dealing With Broken Finger on Throwing Hand." http://www.boston.com/sports/football/patriots/articles/2010/01/04/patriots_brady_dealing_with_broken_finger_on_throwing_hand/ (accessed September 15, 2011).

Byrne, Kerry J. "The Definitive List: Top 10 NFL Quarterbacks." http://www.coldhardfootballfacts.com/Articles/11_2103_The_definitive_list:_Top_10_NFL_quarterbacks.html (accessed March 3, 2011).

Clayton, John. "Running It Up: Belichick, Pats Take No Prisoners." http://sports.espn.go.com/nfl/columns/story?columnist=clayton_john&id=3084539 (accessed October 17, 2011).

Corbett, Jim. "Determined Pats QB Tom Brady 'Playing on a Different Planet.'" *USA Today*, December 16, 2010: C1.

Curran, Tom E. "Brady Behind Schedule in Recovery from Surgery." http://nbcsports.msnbc.com/id/28399629/ (accessed March 3, 2011).

Garber, Greg. "Brady, Belichick Not Satisfied." http://espn.go.com/nfl/playoffs/2011/story/_/page/hotread-brady-belichick-super-bowl-2012-tom-brady-bill-belichick-eager-prove (accessed February 2, 2012).

Gasper, Christopher L. "Patriots decision not to pay Wes Welker could be costly." http://www.boston.com/sports/columnists/gasper/2012/07/patriots_decisi.html (accessed February 15, 2016).

Glennon, Sean. *The New England Patriots Playbook: Inside the Huddle for the Greatest Plays in Patriots History.* Chicago: Triumph Books, 2015.

———. *Game Changers: The Greatest Plays in New England Patriots History.* Chicago: Triumph Books, 2010.

———. *The Good, the Bad and the Ugly: Heart-Pounding, Jaw-Dropping, and Gut-Wrenching Moments from New England Patriots History.* Chicago: Triumph Books, 2008.

———. *This Pats Year: A Trek Through a Season as a Football Fan.* Lanham, Maryland: Taylor Trade Publishing, 2004.

Greenberg, Alan. "Brady Doesn't Let Pats Down." http://articles.courant.com/ 2001-10-15/sports/0110151480_1_patriots-brady-three-times-tom-brady (accessed October 17, 2011).

Hackenberg, Dave. "Moss Wants A Ring...and Brady Wants 10." http://www.toledoblade. com/DaveHackenberg/2008/02/01/ Moss-wants-a-ring-and-Brady-wants-10.html (accessed October 17, 2011).

Hyldburg, Bob. *Total Patriots*. Chicago: Triumph Books, 2009.

Easterbrook, Gregg. "Colts-Patriots Tilt Shaping as Battle of Good vs. Evil." http://sports.espn. go.com/espn/page2/story?page=easterbrook/071023 (accessed March 3, 2011).

Isidore, Chris. "StubHub's Winning Ticket." http://money.cnn.com/2007/12/28/ commentary/ sportsbiz/index.htm (accessed November 22, 2011).

King, Peter. "San Francisco Cheat: Niners Lose Two Draft Picks, $300,000 for Violating Cap." http://sportsillustrated.cnn.com/football/nfl/news/2000/12/01/king_salarycap/#more (accessed December 15, 2011).

———. "A Game for All Ages." http://sportsillustrated.cnn.com/2007/writers/ peter_king/10/14/ mmqb/index.html (accessed March 3, 2011).

———. "Why NFL Should Give Back Picks to Pats (But Won't)." http://mmqb.si.com/ mmqb/2016/02/21/roger-goodell-new-england-patriots-nfl-draft-picks-combine-preview (accessed February 22, 2016).

King, Richard J. *Meeting Tom Brady: One Man's Quest for Truth, Enlightenment, and a Simple Game of Catch with the Patriots Quarterback*. Lebanon, New Hampshire: ForeEdge, 2015.

MacCambridge, Michael. *America's Game: The Epic Story of How Pro Football Captured a Nation*. New York: Random House, 2004.

Meyers, Naila-Jean. "Week 8 in Preview; Redskins' Best Offense May Be the Defense." *The New York Times*, October 28, 2007: D3.

Minihane, Kirk. "The Uncomfortable Reality That Is a Fading Tom Brady." http://www.weei. com/sports/boston/football/patriots/kirk-minihane/2014/10/02/uncomfortable-reality-fad-ing-tom-brady (accessed March 1, 2016).

Nocera, Joe, "True Scandal of Deflategate Lies in the N.F.L.'s Behavior." *The New York Times*, January 22, 2016: D5.

Noverr, Douglas A. *The Games They Played: Sports in American History, 1865–1980*. Chicago: Nelson-Hall, Inc., 1983.

Pierce, Charles P. *Moving the Chains: Tom Brady and the Pursuit of Everything*. New York: Farrar, Straus and Giroux, 2006.

Politi, Steve. "Tom Brady, New England Patriots' Superstar, Is Caught in a Chase for Perfection." http://www.nj.com/giants/index.ssf/2012/02/politi_tom_brady_new_england_p.html (accessed February 1, 2012).

Powers, John. "The Great Chase." *Boston Globe*, February 5, 2012: C1.

Rapoport, Ian R. and Karen Guregian. "Vikings and Patriots in Talks: Randy Moss Asked for Trade." *Boston Herald*, October 6, 2010: 75.

Reiss, Mike. "Sources: Moss, Coach in Exchange." http://sports.espn.go.com/boston/nfl/news/ story?id=5655198 (accessed July 23, 2011).

———. "Patriots don't feel like celebrating." http://espn.go.com/boston/nfl/story/_/id/8776536/new-england-patriots-win-jacksonville-jaguars-bring-smiles (accessed February 21, 2016).

Rosenberg, Michael. "Tom Brady as You Forgot Him." http://sportsillustrated.cnn.com/vault/article/magazine/MAG1193473/5/index.htm (accessed February 5, 2012).

Sanneh, Kelefa. "Monday Night Lights." http://www.newyorker.com/reporting/2011/12/12/111212fa_fact_sanneh (accessed January 4, 2012).

Schorn, Daniel. "Tom Brady: The Winner." http://www.cbsnews.com/2100-18560_162-1008148.html (accessed March 3, 2011).

Volin, Ben. "For Tom Brady, the End Game Has Become Apparent." http://www.bostonglobe.com/sports/2014/09/30/for-tom-brady-end-game-has-become-apparent/HkkQMtH3T6hbJMEDlJioqI/story.html (accessed March 1, 2016).

Werder, Ed. "Vikings Owner Irate." http://sports.espn.go.com/nfl/news/story?id=5768760 (accessed July 23, 2011).

Wilbur, Eric. "Not So Safety Call: Blame Brady for This One." http://articles.boston.com/2012-02-05/sports/31027533_1_tom-brady-wes-welker-patriots (accessed February 5, 2012).

———. "Uncle." http://articles.boston.com/2012-02-07/sports/ 31034643_1_pats-fans-tom-brady-wes-welker (accessed February 7, 2012).

———. "Trading Tom Brady May Make More Sense Than the Patriots Are Willing to Admit." http://www.boston.com/sports/columnists/wilbur/2014/10/_if_forced_to_lay.html (accessed March 1, 2016).

Wilson, Ryan. "Report: Offensive Changes Have Led to Tensions With Tom Brady, Coaches." http://www.cbssports.com/nfl/eye-on-football/24738474/report-offensive-changes-have-led-to-tensions-with-tom-brady-coaches (accessed March 1, 2016).

Websites

www.ColdHardFootballFacts.com
www.ESPN.com
www.FootballOutsiders.com
www.NFL.com
www.ProfootballHOF.com
www.Pro-Football-Reference.com
www.ProFootballResearchers.org